TALKING ABOUT DISABILITY: THE EDUCATION AND WORK EXPERIENCES

OF GRADUATES AND UNDERGRADUATES WITH DISABILITIES

IN SCIENCE, MATHEMATICS, AND ENGINEERING MAJORS

A collaborative study, undertaken at the
University of Minnesota, Institute of Technology,
with financial support from the
National Science Foundation, and
the American Association for the Advancement of Science

ELAINE SEYMOUR & ANNE-BARRIE HUNTER

Ethnography & Evaluation Research
Bureau of Sociological Research
Campus Box 580
University of Colorado
Boulder, Colorado, 80309

(303) 492-0084
FAX: (303) 492-2154
E-mail: seymour@spot.colorado.edu

This study was supported by a grant from the National Science Foundation, Directorate for Engineering, "Recruitment, Retention of Students and Faculty with Disabilities in Colleges of Engineering," (NSF grant EEC-9101122). The opinions, findings, and conclusions or recommendations expressed in this material do not necessarily reflect the views of the National Science Foundation or the American Association for the Advancement of Science.

Printed in the United States of America.

International Standard Book Number: 0-87168-617-1

AAAS Publication Number: 98-02S

CONTENTS

LIST OF FIGURES

LIST OF TABLES

EXECUTIVE SUMMARY

Edited by

Virginia W. Stern

and

Shirley M. Malcom

Based on the study *Talking about Disability: The Education and Work Experience of Graduates and Undergraduates with Disabilities in Science, Mathematics and Engineering Majors*

by Elaine Seymour & Anne-Barrie Hunter

American Association for the Advancement of Science

Washington, DC

Talking about Disability: The Education and Work Experiences of Graduates and Undergraduates with Disabilities, in Science, Mathematics, and Engineering Majors

EXECUTIVE SUMMARY

Introduction

Students with disabilities, although often acknowledged as "the largest minority," are still significantly underrepresented in undergraduate and graduate majors in science, mathematics, and engineering (SME) curricula.

At first glance, the causes of this are not unlike those of other underrepresented groups: the reasons lie in the structure and culture of SME teaching, not in the inherent difficulty of these disciplines. What distinguishes the persisters from those who leave, regardless of their gender, ethnicity or disability, is the development of particular attitudes and strategies.

A strong interest in their discipline and focused career aspirations are characteristics common to successful graduates within SME. Equally significant is receipt of appropriate forms of support and accommodation at critical periods in the early stages of their studies.

On the other hand, there are many unique issues and barriers faced by students with disabilities. The formal and informal systems that govern progress in their discipline do not usually have the flexibility to accommodate the individual requirements of students with disabilities, which often vary even within one disability group. There is frequent tension between the personal characteristics favoring persistence and the cultural and structural barriers to academic progress. The realities of financial survival only exacerbate the issue. Students with disabilities simultaneously demonstrate a high potential for success and a high risk of being lost.

The Study and the Participants

The University of Minnesota was selected for this study because of its strong reputation in science and engineering, and a record of enrolling a significant number of students with disabilities. Within the University of Minnesota, the Institute of Technology (IT) offers degrees in several engineering disciplines, as well as physics, astronomy, chemistry, geology, mathematics, and computer science.

University of Minnesota Institute of Technology students who had registered with the Disabled Services (DS) office of the university were invited to participate in this confidential study. They included full-time undergraduates registered at the Institute of Technology in the fall of 1993 (n=93), and a small random sample of recent graduates (i.e. 2-5 years since graduation) who were working in the Twin Cities area. The total number of participants was 65, 60 of whom were Institute of Technology undergraduates or graduates, and 5 of whom were undergraduates with disabilities majoring in disciplines other than SME.

The University of Minnesota has a national reputation for excellence in serving students with disabilities. All students who register themselves as having a disability gain access through the university's Disability Services (DS) office to a well-established and expanding system of services. These services were developed first in compliance with the federally-mandated 504 Regulations (1977) which required postsecondary institutions to make all programs accessible to qualified students with disabilities. This office continues to provide reasonable accommodations, in accordance with the Americans with Disabilities Act (1990).

The students participated in interviews and focus groups, varying in length from forty-five to ninety minutes. Interviews were conducted in the style of a focused conversation.

Choice of an SME Major

The predominant motivation mentioned by every IT undergraduate with a disability was a strong liking for science, mathematics, computer science, or engineering and/or a strong preference for a career base in these fields. Motivation by intrinsic interest was much stronger amongst the IT undergraduates with disabilities than among SME majors in general in a previous study (Seymour & Hewitt, 1994). Undergraduate students with disabilities were clearer about their educational and career objectives than the general sample of SME majors.

As shown in the 1994 study, entering an SME major largely for reasons of intrinsic interest was the best predictor of persistence. This helps explain why SME undergraduates with disabilities may be more likely to persist despite barriers which students without disabilities do not have to overcome.

The Study Findings

Despite the greater degree of barriers they face, students with disabilities can be regarded as more likely to persist in SME majors than some others. Students with disabilities demonstrate a high level of commitment to their majors; a high degree of intrinsic interest in the disciplines and careers they have chosen; and a high degree of clarity about what they want to accomplish and why.

These students do, however, have significant obstacles to overcome to complete a university SME education. The three major barriers common to SME undergraduates with disabilities are:

- Faculty attitudes regarding certain accommodations
- Some aspects of the financial aid system
- The disability itself and its limitations

Students who are most successful have communicated their needs regarding these issues and /or identified appropriate accommodation and support. These students have developed a combination of persistence, excellent organizational skills, knowledge of assistive technology, and the ability to invoke the necessary support systems or agencies when dealing with barriers. **The most successful scenarios have been when the students, faculty, and support organizations have teamed to address the problems together. It is important to understand that all three members of this team have significant roles and responsibilities in addressing the unique issues faced by students with disabilities.**

Faculty Attitudes Regarding Certain Accommodations

None of the study participants recommended changes in the accommodation system administered by Disability Services (DS). They did suggest that, in many cases, faculty attitudes undermined the system and needed to be addressed.

IT faculty responses to formal accommodation requests from students with disabilities included:

- Discounting the need for accommodation
- Refusing the accommodation as a way to "prepare" the student for "real world" competition
- Encouraging students to drop the class or change majors
- Placing the students in inappropriate testing places (subject to noise or periodic interruptions)
- If the student arranged testing under DS administration, forgetting to send the test, or not communicating changes or errors
- Lowering grades for work done under accommodated conditions

x

- Insistence on knowing personal details about the disability
- Embarrassing student by talking about the disability or accommodations in front of peers

Study participants perceived, based on faculty responses to requests for accommodations, that some SME faculty "approved" certain conditions as "genuine disabilities" and exercised various degrees of skepticism about all others. The conclusion made by many students is that the rigors of the process imposed on them have little to do with academic issues, but are regarded by faculty as an appropriate way of testing for fitness to belong to the academic and professional communities based on SME disciplines. The essential question raised by many requests for accommodations is, whether in granting it, a student with a disability would be given an unfair advantage over other students.

The Financial Aid System

The main difficulties of students who sought financial aid through the university's financial aid office were the rules, required of all financial aid recipients, that make no allowances for carrying less than a full class load. The nature of the disability, its variability or unpredictability, the effects of particular medications, problems of fatigue, and unexpected crises of mobility and transportation are issues which can make a full complement of classes very difficult or impossible for many students with disabilities. Taking a full load, to qualify for financial aid, very commonly creates a pattern of "incompletes," failures, and temporary withdrawals.

Some   students in this study believed they would have spent less time, energy, and money repeating classes, had they been allowed to work at a pace commensurate with the constraints of their disability.

The Disability and its Limitations

People who have little regular contact with disability issues may assume that mobility problems are the dominant type of difficulty experiences by persons with disabilities. Although mobility issues certainly exist, particularly in terms of access to lecture halls, laboratories, field stations, and public accommodations, there are other common situations which cut across the range of disabilities. These common circumstances are less visible and often less acknowledged and addressed, but can be characterized by the following one or more descriptions:

- Disabilities vary over time, in severity and effect, and in ways which are unpredictable
- Unpredictable interruptions can include periods of hospitalization or therapy, which do not necessarily fit into academic calender breaks
- Disruptions can occur as a result of medication or medication changes
- The need to be "pushy" to obtain accommodations can be stressful in itself

The interaction between the disability and its management can produce quite dramatic peaks and troughs in academic performance. Students find they are often unable to take classes which have early morning starts when either the requirements or the effects of medication make it difficult to be fully functional for early morning appointments. Students with spinal cord injuries have regimes which may limit their class schedule. Deaf and hard-of-hearing students, who rely on lipreading or interpreters, often experience eye fatigue in the afternoons.

To avoid a poor attendance record or grades which underrepresent actual knowledge and ability levels, some students with disabilities try to schedule classes in the time slots when they will be have the most energy. However, when a required class or lab is only offered at one particular time, this may be impossible.

Students with disabilities cope with the variability of their circumstances and the need to pace themselves by pre-planning and a high degree of organization. Those incidents which were harder to cope with were close deadlines, unscheduled tests or assignments, and sudden changes of syllabus or venue. **What the students found to be the most successful strategies was when they were able to clearly communicate their individual needs to faculty members and have those needs respected and met. This included cooperation with accommodations, classes which were well structured, and the ability to get class materials ahead of time.**

Other Disability-related Issues

•Many students had problems with the physical lay-out of the classrooms. Sitting for long periods and seeing the board clearly enough were issues for some. For hearing-impaired students, room acoustics, seating in class, and the teacher's delivery and accent all affected how much of the lesson could be heard.

•Some aspects of lab work presented challenges for students with dexterity limitations or pros-thetic hands

•Although campus buildings were wheel-chair accessible, the long distances between buildings and the occasional locked elevator posed barriers to students with mobility impairments.

•For those who could not drive, the public transportation system dictated the class schedule. Where possible, students with disabilities organized a complex system or rides and emergency back-up arrange-ments.

Attrition and the Stop-Go Phenomenon

Although the attrition rate of students with disabilities appears comparable with those of students of color, there are major differences. The "attrition" of students with disabilities is often temporary, more of a stop-go pattern to their progress rather than an abandonment of their education or their field.

Approximately one-third of the IT undergraduates with disabilities reported feeling sufficiently discouraged to consider leaving either their major or the institution. The issues which prompted these projected moves out of the Institute of Technology were not the same as those which prompted switching to non-SME majors among undergraduates without disabilities in the 1994 study. Four related issues re-curred in the explanations of undergraduates with disabilities who were considering leaving or who had left:

- Financial problems
- Intermittent troubles due to disability
- Accumulation of "incompletes" in record, related both to the disability and financial difficulties
- Accommodation difficulties

Most students with disabilities resumed their studies once a specific disability set-back and or their financial situation had improved, or they were able to address problems with their academic record. This is not, however, a pattern indicated in the SME attrition rates of students of color, women, or white males. Because time out of school was reported by the undergraduates with disabilities themselves to be, typically, one semester, **the overall time taken to complete IT majors (i.e. a little over 5 years) is similar to IT majors without disabilities.**

Disability as a "Disadvantage of Time"

Coping with time-related problems was a universal feature of the experience of all study participants. It distinguishes their circumstances from those of other SME majors, is a facet of every type of barrier they encounter, and transcends differences of students with disabilities of different types. One way to understand the commonality of students with disabilities in SME is to see them as students who are "time-disadvantaged."

The time issues which participants raised were of five broad types:

- problems of pace
- speed of learning, comprehension, and recall
- temporal disruptions in physical and mental functioning
- time-related educational needs
- time expended in coping with difficulties raised by their disabilities

Because SME faculty have traditionally made the execution of particular learning tasks to particular standards in particular time-frames the criteria for academic success (as opposed to demonstrations of knowledge and comprehension in other forms), the **slower pace** at which students with many types of disabilities must work becomes a critical disadvantage.

Students with learning and other neurological disabilities usually do not learn in the same way as other students and must find **alternative way to absorb and apply class materials**, all of which takes longer than working by so-called standard learning methods.

Students who have a **temporary set-back in physical or mental functioning** due to the fluctuations of their disability or the side effects of necessary medication may lose a morning, a day, or a week of productive study and have to exert double effort to catch up and stay level.

Basic educational requirements and activities of daily living take more time. Students with mobility and visual impairments need extra time to get to and from campus or from class to class. Students with learning disabilities can require more than double the time to complete a reading assignment. Students with hearing impairments must find a TDD pay phone to make a telephone call from campus, or use the TDD relay, which takes more time. Low-vision students read assignments with magnification devices; this takes longer to read each page. Students with asthma must adjust their schedule to demands of medication and energy. Students with diabetes cannot work overtime in a lab if that causes them to miss medication and/or meals.

Coping with difficulties raised specifically by the disability can be frustrating and take valuable time away from studies. Prostheses need adjustment; wheelchair batteries need re-charging; new editions of textbooks cannot be recorded in time; interpreters are not available for *ad hoc* meetings; assistive technology of all sorts requires maintenance and the wear-and-tear cycle of technology does not always match the cycle of core classes.

Thus, to be a student with any form of disability almost certainly means needing more time than is normally allowed to do almost anything that the university expects of its students. **The strength of faculty resistance—especially of time-related accommodations—which students of all disabilities and especially invisible disabilities routinely encounter, supports the findings of the earlier, more comprehensive study (Seymour and Hewitt, 1994). Whether SME majors switch or persist, they experience problems with SME pedagogy, curriculum, and student assessment practices shaped by long-standing traditions about appropriate ways to teach. Because particular requests for accommodations are determined by the nature of disabilities themselves, students are, inadvertently, obliged to challenge some of the pedagogical rules which SME faculty see as necessary for the protection of high academic standards.**

Disability Services

To meet the needs of students with all types of disabilities, the University of Minnesota has established a set of policies, processes and services, administered by the Disability Services offices. The system is intended to accommodate whatever disability-related limitations on educational progress which students bring to this office. The assistance of the DS staff is available to all students who register as disabled. Students with learning disabilities and other invisible disabilities may not wish to disclose their disabilities because of real or assumed stigma. However, only students who register with Disability Services can take advantage of the services. It is also true that some students with learning disabilities are not diagnosed until they are undergraduate or graduate students. Typically they have developed their own coping strategies which served them in precollege and college coursework but were not adequate when they enrolled in a more rigorous curriculum.

Services and accommodations arranged by DS which students with disabilities identified as having special value were:

- Pre-registration
- Arranging priority access to particular classes
- Changing inaccessible or remote classrooms
- Arranging services of note-takers, readers, and interpreters as necessary
- Getting text books recorded prior to start of classes
- Arranging special test accommodations involving extended time, quiet location, assistive technology, or readers or scribes
- Helping students withdraw from class if necessary
- Assistance in locating and trying out assistive technology
- Workshops on resume writing and interview techniques
- On-line job search facility
- A regular supportive relationship with specific DS staff members

Of all services listed above, the supportive counseling and the test accommodations were most frequently cited by all students.

The DS office plays a significant role when the students themselves are unable to negotiate a satisfactory solution between themselves, faculty, administration, or outside agencies such as state vocational rehab, and insurance companies.

STUDY IMPLICATIONS BASED UPON THE AAAS EXPERIENCE

Based upon the recommendations of the participants in the study, as well as the accumulated experience of AAAS working with deans and faculty of colleges of engineering, and students with disabilities in all technical fields, the following issues need to be recognized in order to attract and retain students with disabilities in science, mathematics, and engineering:

Individuality of Students with Disabilities

Scientists and engineers with disabilities are a microcosm of society as a whole. Students with disabilities represent all the diversity of the student population — and more, because students with the same disability each have their particularistic functional strengths and limitations. The sample used in this study is not random distribution, so the distribution of disabilities in this sample might not be the same on every campus, nor every school of engineering. The comments made here cannot be assumed to be the point of view of every student with a disability, or even every student of that disability group.

Similarly, students with disabilities, like all students, have different personalities. Although even a minor disability will present barriers and cause frustration, some students have developed such resilience and determination that they plan and persist after every set-back. Some people are optimistic and have a sense of humor; others internalize every hurt and disappointment.

Most students with disabilities, no matter how high achieving, do not want to be looked upon as heroes. They want to succeed like people without disabilities, in professional and in personal life.

Changes in Faculty Attitudes

Misconceptions, fear, and negative societal attitudes about disabilities are reflected in the higher education community just as everywhere else. Faculty need specific assistance in responding. Training and exposure to positive role models would remind them of the need to focus on the ability rather than the apparent limitation of a student. Renowned scientists and engineers like Thomas Edison, Charles Steinmetz, Albert Einstein, Steven Hawking, and Geerart Vermeij are celebrated for their accomplishments, not for their different way of thinking, inability to see, lack of intelligible speech, or crooked posture.

Faculty, however, often focus first on the disability of the student, and this remains dominant in their interactions with the student. They cannot make the conceptional leap to recognize that talent is present and can be developed in a student who is different (Thomas, 1993).

Changes in the Classroom Environment

Some of the problems that students with disabilities experience are related to poor teaching and classroom management. Addressing these must be a shared responsibility, since now the accommodation seems to be often one-sided — all on the students, who must accommodate to meet the traditional expectations. If faculty were more accepting, the development of classroom accommodations could be a mutual challenge to professor and student, and would benefit from joint problem-solving.

Impact of Technology

In the past two decades, nothing has had greater influence on science, mathematics, and engineering (SME) education and career options for students with disabilities than developments in assistive technology. So much of science, mathematics, and engineering is now computer connected, students with any disability have access to virtually any field. Alternative input to use computers — voice recognition systems, headpointers and switches that work with special scanning software give those with limited mobility keyboard access. Alternative mice, trackballs, and keyboards allow more controlled input with hands or other parts of the body. Alternative output includes voice sythesis systems with screen readers that convert words on the screen into synthesized speech, refreshable tactile displays of braille or graphics, and braille embossers that produce hard copy braille. Recorded texts are now available more quickly through e-text and digitized speech. The ubiquitous use of e-mail has opened communication to all students and faculty, and has become a special boon to students who are deaf. Real-time captioning can make available every word of a professor's lecture Specialized software such as word prediction packages and spell-check assist all students, including those who have learning disabilities.

Some students with disabilities are accommodated with a one-time low technology solution, e.g., raising a table with some wooden blocks under the legs, or adding a piece of non-slip tape to a glass laboratory instrument. Other students, who may be wheelchair riders, and have the arm strength to use a manual wheelchair, are able to preserve significant energy resources for studies by using an electric wheelchair to go distances on campus. For others, many of the hurdles of research are surmounted through the use of the same technology used by all students, which gives them access to the resources of the libraries from a distance, or permits quick and satisfactory appointments with faculty advisors via e-mail.

Faculty, especially faculty in engineering and science, have an opportunity to understand the impact of the technology and encourage its use.

Students with Disabilities are Enrolled in Higher Education

More than 9 percent of college freshmen report having a disability. The percentage of full-time, first time freshmen reporting disabilities has increased significantly since the late 1970s. In 1994, 9.2 percent of all freshmen reported having some type of disability, compared with 2.6 percent in 1978. With such a large and growing population, colleges and universities need to accommodate this cohort in ways not envisioned before (Henderson, 1995).

Post-secondary institutions are also enrolling increasing numbers of non-traditional students, e.g., women returning to the workforce and students of both sexes who seek new skills when their original careers become obsolete. Some of these students became people with disabilities mid-career and need to be accepted and served.

Existence Proofs of Successful Scientists and Engineers with Disabilities

The American Association for the Advancement of Science has worked for two decades with its Resource Group of Scientists and Engineers with Disabilities. Records of the hundreds of individuals in this group are evidence that people with any disability are able to meet the most rigid criteria in every field of science and engineering and hold professional positions in academia, government, and the private sector (Stern and Summers, 1995).

Some faculty will need to readjust their concepts of the academic potential and professional capabilities of students with physical, sensory, or learning differences, and realize that one can have a full professional life using different approaches. The AAAS database of this Resource Group is available for faculty who wish to interact with peers in their discipline who are also individuals with disabilities.

"Hidden" or Invisible Disabilities Predominate

Students with hidden disabilities —learning, health, and other— account for more than half of all freshmen with disabilities. The largest growth, both in numbers and proportions, has occurred among students with learning disabilities (National Science Foundation, 1996).

SME faculty may be particularly resistent to students with learning disabilities because of the perception that the department would have to lower its standards in order to accommodate anyone with a "learning disability." The term itself, unfortunately, seems to contradict academic and professional achievement.

When faculty recognize that many students learn in many different ways, this negative bias will fade.

Financial Aid

The financial aid restrictions that impact so severely on students with disabilities who cannot carry a full class load, in every discipline, every semester, are generally established by federal guidelines. Postsecondary institutions are beginning to collaborate to address this issue, so that students with disabilities, who are registered with the disability service office on campus, can be considered qualified for financial aid with a modified schedule of course units.

Changes in Higher Education for Everyone

Institutions of higher education are undergoing profound adjustments in all areas. Many are revisiting the structure of their introductory courses. Others are exploring greater incorporation of technology into their teaching. The role of inquiry and undergraduate research are being reviewed. All are being challenged to connect the disciplines to employment opportunities in the "real world."

As the higher education community goes about its own reform it needs to consider how it responds to the needs of individual students and makes the knowledge and excitement of learning available to all. In that re-invention of teaching and curriculum design, the inclusion of students with disabilities can indeed be seen as an opportunity for creativity and flexibility. Typically, these students have brought innovations to their own environment long before they entered a postsecondary program. Their personal resilience has necessitated alternative approaches to many apparent barriers. Their innovations involve the inclusion of both high and low technology in studies and everyday life, and the use of different styles of learning. The range of life experiences that students with disabilities bring to the classroom and laboratory contribute not only to the education of peers, but potentially to the advancement of the engineering and science professions.

Not all students with disabilities who need science, mathematics and computing courses will seek degrees in these fields. Education in these areas is a significant part of a liberal education for the new millennium. In addition, these courses form a critical gateway to medicine, allied health professions, business, education, law and the social and economic sciences. Lack of access to these courses closes off most of the professional opportunities a students might seek.

The recent experiences of AAAS with an internship program for students with disabilities with business and government reinforce the importance of the perspectives that diverse groups contribute to the workforce. In addition to the talent, skills and creativity that the interns bring they also provide a critical window into the experiences of the customers with disabilities (Hoffert,1998). In a company seeking a competitive edge, "different" can mean "value added."

Meeting the learning needs of individual students does not mean that they are being coddled, just as accommodating their differences does not mean that expectations for them are lower. Including students with disabilities is not charity but rather enabling them to support themselves while contributing to the human resource pool of the Nation.

As these students enter the workforce with invaluable skills we have an opportunity to learn from their successes and build a foundation for utilizing this talent on the basis of case examples rather than case law.

References

Henderson, Cathy. 1995. "Postsecondary Students with Disabilities: Where Are They Enrolled?" *Research Briefs*, 6. Washington, DC: American Council on Education.

Hoffert, Stephen, P. 1998. (16 March). "Associations' Programs Aid Aspiring Disabled Scientists," *The Scientist*, Vol 12. No 6. p.3.

National Science Foundation. *Women, Minorities, and Persons with Disabilities in Science and Engineering: 1996.* Arlington, VA, 1996. (NSF 96-311)

Stern, Virginia, W., and Summers, Laureen. 1995. *Resource Directory of Scientists and Engineers with Disabilities (3rd edition).* Washington, DC: American Association for the Advancement of Science.

Thomas, Charlotte. 1993. (December) "Gatekeepers vs. Gate Crashers." *Graduating Engineer.* pp.60-62.

In affectionate memory of

Irving Kenneth Zola,

friend and mentor.

ACKNOWLEDGMENTS

This work was jointly funded by:

      The American Association for the Advancement of Science, Project on Science,
      Technology & Disability
      (Director: Virginia W. Stern)

      The National Science Foundation, Programs for Persons with Disabilities
      (Directors: Lawrence A. Scadden & Mary M. Kohlerman)

      The University of Colorado

On-site assistance was given by the University of Minnesota:

      Disability Services
      (Director, Sue Kroeger, & Executive Assistant Lisa Kreuger)

      The Institute of Technology, Office of Student Affairs
      (Associate Dean Russell K. Hobbie)

The authors warmly acknowledge the support of the project's funders, and thank staff of
the University of Minnesota, Disability Services, and Institute of Technology, for their
practical help. They especially thank Virginia Stern and Sue Kroeger for their editorial
commentary.

Finally, they thank the undergraduate and graduate students, working graduates, and
members of the Disabled Students Cultural Center at the University of Minnesota, all of
whom gave the investigators their time and their trust. Without their willingness to tell
their stories, and discuss issues of concern to them, this work would not have been
possible.

CHAPTER ONE: THE STUDY AND THE PARTICIPANTS

Background to the Study

This study offers a contribution to the ongoing debate about the causes of under-representation of students with disabilities in science, mathematics, engineering and technology (SMET) undergraduate and graduate majors, and in careers based upon them. At a national level, the debate has been marked by a selective dis-attention to what the Final Report of the Task Force on Women, Minorities, and the Handicapped (NSF, 1990b) acknowledged as "the largest minority."[1] Neither this nor a number of other NSF reports which address under-representation in SMET education (NSF, 1986; 1989a; 1989b) focus on students with disabilities to any significant extent. Similarly, "although it was clear at the time of passage of the Science and Engineering Equal Opportunities Act that persons with disabilities were included in the language of the act, people with disabilities were not specifically named, as were women and minorities" (NSF, 1990b, p.1).

An effort to remedy this lack of attention is now under way, beginning with basic questions about the size and composition of the "largest minority." McNeil's (1993) Bureau of the Census Report for 1991-1992 estimates the number of Americans with disabilities at 49 million. Drawing on other recent sources (NCES, 1987; NHIS, 1985), the NSF Task Force (1990b) estimated the proportion of young people with disabilities in the college-aged population as between 4% and 11%. The only sources of national data on undergraduates with disabilities are the Cooperative Institutional Research Project (CIRP) studies of college freshmen, which, since 1978, have included questions on disability (Astin et al., 1987, 1988). The HEATH Resource Center collects data on disability issues in post-secondary education from available sources, and issues periodic summary reports (Henderson, 1992; Hippolitus, 1987).

---

[1]An important exception to this generalization is the work of the American Association for the Advancement of Science, Project on Science, Technology, and Disability, some of which has been funded by the National Science Foundation. This contribution is briefly discussed over-leaf.

Henderson's (1992) statistical profile of college freshmen with disabilities (drawn from a special run of CIRP data) concludes that one in 11 (i.e., 8.8%) of all first-time, full-time freshmen enrolled in two- and four-year institutions in 1991 reported a disability. This represents a three-fold increase from the 2.6% of freshmen so reporting in 1978. From both the Henderson (1992) and the NCES study (1989), we also learn that most students with disabilities are disproportionately white and male, and are older than their cohorts. To this, Henderson (1992) adds that students with learning disabilities are the fastest-growing group among freshmen declaring a disability—from 15% in 1985 to 25% in 1991. This information applies only to college freshmen. We do not, as Hippolitus (1987) notes, "have any data about the participation of students with disabilities during their later undergraduate and/or graduate years" (p.10). We also know little about the potential or actual pool of students, or working graduates, with disabilities in science, mathematics, or engineering.

An important, early, and continuing source of information about the contribution of scholars with disabilities are the three editions (1978, 1986, and 1995) of the AAAS *Resource Directory of Scientists and Engineers with Disabilities*. This work, supported by the NSF, was followed by the 1991, *Barrier-Free in Brief* booklet series which comprehensively reviews the sources of adaptation and accommodation available to NSF grant recipients. Identification of the constituency of science, mathematics, and engineering scholars with disabilities led to a series of AAAS studies at four-year institutions (the "Access to Engineering Project"), conducted with the support from the NSF Engineering Directorate. The overall purpose of the endeavor is to increase our understanding of the size and composition of the pool of potential science and technology students with disabilities, and what helps or hinders persistence and career success among students with disabilities who choose SMET fields. This report is the fifth in this series of studies. The work has been co-sponsored by the Division of Human Resource Development, Persons with Disabilities Program, of the National Science Foundation.

This study also arises in response to the NSF Task Force's (1990b) solicitation of research intended to discover "what is actually happening on campus;" why there are "low numbers of persons with disabilities in science and technology careers;" and what works best in seeking "to overcome some of the barriers" (pp. v & vi). It is the view of the principal investigator and her collaborators in the study that the best people to answer such questions are the undergraduates and working graduates concerned.

We made no prior assumptions about what might, or might not, improve the recruitment or retention of students with disabilities; nor did we set out to evaluate particular programs. Rather, we have sought to understand, from the perspective of the graduates and undergraduates themselves, what experiences during college, and in their working, family, and social worlds beyond academe, support or discourage entry to, and persistence within, this group of educational and career fields.

Choice of the University of Minnesota as a research site

Although little data on the numbers of students and faculty with disabilities in science, mathematics and computer science are yet available, in a collaborative venture, the AAAS (Access Project) and the Engineering Work Force Commission (formerly, the Engineering Manpower Commission) have begun to construct a national profile of engineering students, graduates, and faculty with disabilities. The project began in 1991 with a pilot survey of 50 engineering schools of different size, who, together, account for approximately one-third of all U.S. engineering enrollments in 15% of all engineering schools.

The study allowed its author, Richard Ellis, to test approaches to the collection of data in a field bedeviled by unresolved problems: in defining and categorizing 'disabilities'; in reconciling wide variations in the data collection practices of institutions; and in the under-counting of disabilities—whether by institutions or by student self-reporting. The findings from 36 schools were reported in October, 1992. Almost 300 engineering schools were asked to provide data for the nationwide survey. From the pilot study data, Ellis offered 0.7% as a conservative estimate of the proportion of students with

4

disabilities in engineering undergraduate programs (with a range of 0.0% to 2.2%). The Institute of Technology at the University of Minnesota, who reported 78 students with one or more disability from a total of 3,527 full-time engineering undergraduates, enrolled the highest proportion (2.2%) of students documenting a disability.[2]

Ellis observes that, across his data set, the proportion of people identified as having a disability tends to increase during the college years—whether by enhanced risk of accident or impairment in this life period, or an increased willingness, over time, to identify themselves as students with disabilities.[3] From enrollment and graduation data for 1990-1992 made available by the Institute of Technology, it was clear that, in Fall 1991, the percent of those documenting a disability rose steadily from 0.4% in the first year, 1.2% in the second, 2.0% in the third to 3.5% in years four and five combined (i.e., 3.0% among upper-classmen overall).

Ellis found that the proportion of students with disabilities who graduated in engineering in 1991 (0.3%) was less than the number participating in engineering classes (0.7%). This was also discernable at the University of Minnesota, which shows graduation rates for students with disabilities for the years 1990-91, and 1991-92 as 0.8% and 1.1% of all engineering graduates, compared with 2.2% of all those enrolled in classes for 1991. Comparable national data on the participation and graduation rates of students with disabilities in science, mathematics, and computer science, to those offered by the Engineering Work-force Commission for engineering, are not yet available.

The University of Minnesota has a strong, national reputation for its education in the sciences and applied sciences, and a record of graduation for SMET students with disabilities which is well above the national average. The Institute of Technology (I.T.) offers majors in several engineering disciplines, as

---

[2]At the time of our interviews for this study, the number of full-time undergraduates with disabilities enrolled in the Institute of Technology in all S.M.E. majors was 93. This number does not include the 10 graduate students also included in this study.

[3] In the course of the study, we found additional reasons for this phenomenon, which are discussed later.

well as physics, astronomy, chemistry, geology, mathematics, and computer science: I.T. undergraduates with disabilities in these majors were, at the time of the interviews, 55.3% (N=57) of all SMET undergraduates with disabilities at the University of Minnesota (N=93). The remaining 46.7% (N=46), were enrolled in the Colleges of Liberal Arts, Biological Sciences, Agriculture, Pharmacy, Human Ecology, Natural Resources, Public Health, Medicine, or Veterinary Medicine—as such, they are thinly scattered across several campuses. The coherence of the Institute of Technology as an academic entity—by location, administration, student selection, academic structure, and traditions—made it a particularly useful site at which to study the effects of institutional structure and culture on recruitment, retention, and career placement.

This university is also somewhat in advance of other institutions in its provisions: students who document their disability have access to an established and expanding system of services, including provision of reasonable accommodation, in accordance with the Americans with Disabilities Act (1990).[4] Access to these services is through the university's Disability Services office. It was, therefore, possible to use the university's records to locate SMET undergraduates and graduates who were both self-reported and officially identified as having one or more disability in a sample which was large enough for generalization. We also had the opportunity to learn what contribution to the persistence of students with disabilities in SMET majors, and in careers based upon them, was made by the policies, services, practices or attitudes which they encountered in SMET majors or elsewhere on campus. We also wished to know what contribution to success or difficulty was made by institutional factors, compared with other aspects of their lives. We assumed non-institutional factors might include personal attitudes, choices and behaviors, and the level of support received from family, friends or peers, official agencies and schools. We set out to identify sources of discouragement or difficulty, as well as of support.

---

[4]These provisions are based upon, but reinforce and expand, those made for all post-secondary institutions under Section 504 of the Rehabilitation Act, 1973.

6

Institute of Technology records of the location of its graduates also made it possible to ask some recent SMET graduates with disabilities what factors had shaped the direction of their careers. The main issues which we proposed to explore with a sample of recent I.T. graduates with disabilities were: what factors had most helped or hindered their educational access and achievement, their career entry and progress, and their attainment of job satisfaction; what had shaped their career aspirations; which aspects of their educational experiences at the Institute of Technology were most and least supportive of their educational and career aspirations; and what (if any) compromise of these they had felt constrained to make.

The local culture was also expected to have some bearing on these issues in that the Institute of Technology is located in a state which has a good record of provision for its citizens with disabilities. Minnesota is one of five states reporting the lowest rates of 'work disability' among adults aged 16 to 64, and one of 10 states reporting the smallest proportions of adults in need of financial assistance due to disability, or with unmet needs with mobility or self-care (LaPlante, 1993).

Issues raised in a pilot study of students with disabilities at the University of Minnesota

We were offered some indications of the kinds of issues which might be raised by students with disabilities by an M.A. dissertation study done at the University of Minnesota by Mary Litsheim (1993). The author conducted focus group interviews with a sample of 25 undergraduates with disabilities who were randomly drawn from all majors on the Minneapolis and St. Paul campuses. Her informants expressed a number of needs and concerns:

1. A strongly expressed, and largely unmet, need for positive personal encouragement and support by faculty

2. Feelings of low self-esteem, which had a depressing effect on academic performance

3. The belief that the faculty's apparent emphasis on competition over learning is counter-productive, and that the faculty's assumption of a level playing field for all students is unrealistic and unfair

4. An appreciation of the value of study group learning

These issues and recommendations are very similar to those raised by students in other groups who are under-represented in SMET majors, namely, women, and students of color of both sexes, in a recent, seven-campus study co-authored by the principal investigator (Seymour & Hewitt, 1997; 1994). Litsheim also highlights several concerns with more exclusive relevance for students with disabilities:

1. Frustration at the faculty's refusal of requests to accommodate particular needs dictated by the student's disability

2. The perception that faculty often do not believe that a non-visible disability is 'real'

3. The need to make existing assistive technologies more readily available

4. Ambivalence about forming support groups and networks. (Concerns about increased negative labeling, and costs in time and energy, were balanced with the desire to share experiences and information.)

5. The need for financial help and retention services comparable to those available to other minority groups

6. Pessimism about employment opportunities, fears about the difficulties they would face as employees with disabilities, and an expressed need for assistance with transition into the work place

The issues identified by Litsheim were incorporated into the list of topics which we explored in interviews with the undergraduates and graduates.

Defining 'disability'

As two recent reports (NSF, 1990b; Davies, 1992) have observed, while federal legislation defines 'disability', it has no universally-accepted social definition. Discrepancies between legal, cultural, and personal understandings of who should, and should not, be included within the group of persons with disabilities are apt to be a source of difficulty in and of themselves. We sought to accommodate some of these differences in constructing our sample, and anticipated that some definitional problems would be reflected in the experience of our informants. Only the individual who experiences them knows the real height of the barriers they encounter, and whether they possess the inner- and outer-resources to surmount them. In defining our sample, we began by using the University of Minnesota's system of disability classification, which is based on legislative categories. Where official classifications were different from those used by the participants to describe themselves, we reassigned students to the categories of disability to which they felt they belonged. The nature of these adjustments are explained later.

Students at the University of Minnesota may opt to identify themselves as persons with disabilities post-admission, or at any other time. A disability which was documented in high school, in another educational institution, or with the state Vocational Rehabilitation service, may be transferred direct. Alternatively, students may document their disability with Disability Services on a confidential basis, and not disclose a disability on the university's central computer system. However their documentation is made, in order to receive the services and accommodations offered by the university through Disability Services, each student's claim to disability status must be legitimated by documentation from an appropriate professional. Students are then placed on a confidential register kept by Disability Services, whose services to all students with disabilities on their register include: information, referral, support, determination and provision of reasonable accommodations, consultation with faculty, career development, and help in identifying job openings (including summer jobs). As we shall later discuss, the services of the Disability Services staff extend well beyond these formal roles. Some auxiliary services include provision of sign language interpreters, alternative print formats, readers, and test modifications. The identity, and personal details, of students with documented disabilities are not available to faculty or administrators.

Method of Inquiry

Full-time undergraduates who were registered at the Institute of Technology in Fall, 1993 (N=93), and a small random sample of recent graduates (i.e., 2 to 5 years since graduation), all of whom had documented disabilities, received letters from the director of Disability Services explaining the nature of the study, and inviting their participation. The confidential nature of the data-gathering, analysis and reporting processes was stressed. Prior to each interview, the investigator knew nothing more than the first name of each interviewee. All other information was provided by the participants during interview, or was drawn from their records with their written consent. Two staff members of the Disability Services office made initial telephone contact with those people who agreed to take part, and arranged interview times with them. Forty-one (i.e., 44.1%) of the undergraduates with documented disabilities who had enrolled with the Institute of Technology in Fall, 1993, were interviewed at the University of Minnesota by the principal investigator during the month of April, 1994. Nineteen recent graduates (i.e., 1-5 years since graduation) were also interviewed: working graduates were interviewed at their place of employment; graduate students, and unemployed graduates were interviewed on campus; and six graduate students who had moved from the area, were interviewed by telephone.

In addition, two focus groups were held on campus at the Disabled Students' Cultural Center (DSCC). These groups were arranged by a DSCC committee member and the DSCC co-ordinator (both of whom were students with disabilities who also took part in the discussions). Seven students (five undergraduate and two graduate), who were active members of the DSCC, and who had not previously been interviewed, joined these groups. Of these seven, two were undergraduates in the Institute of

Technology, and five were not. These five offered perspectives based on their experiences in business education, social work, sociology, theater arts, and women's studies at the University of Minnesota, and at neighboring institutions. The focus group discussions centered on campus-wide issues, and on the role of the DSCC in addressing them.

The total number of participants was, thus, 65, of whom 60 were Institute of Technology graduates or undergraduates.

From policy documents based on consultation (NSF, 1989, 1990b; Matyas and Malcolm, 1991), and on the small body of empirical work available (Litsheim, 1993; Davies, 1992; Lucky, 1989), we constructed a tentative list of issues thought to bear upon the research questions.[5] Additional items were derived from our recent (1991, 1994) study of factors contributing to attrition among SMET undergraduates without disabilities. As some undergraduates were expected to be mature students with work experience, and all interviewees were likely to be able to discuss undergraduate and career issues, separate check lists of topics were not developed for each group.

At the beginning of each interview or focus group, the purpose and nature of the inquiry was again described by the principal investigator, and written consent to tape-record the discussion was secured. The confidential and anonymous nature of participants' contributions was stressed. Interviews and focus groups varied in length, from 45 to 90 minutes—depending on how much time participants wished to spend on particular issues, and how many new issues they raised. Interviews were conducted in the style of a focused conversation, in which topics were raised as appropriate opportunities arose. The central issue explored in discussion of each topic was: its significance (relative to other issues) for the participant's access to and progress in undergraduate or graduate SMET education, and for their work experiences beyond graduation. Women and students of color were also asked to comment on factors which they saw as distinguishing their experiences as students or workers with disabilities from those of

---

[5] See Appendix.

their white, male peers. Issues on the topics list which were not spontaneously mentioned were raised at natural breaks in the conversation. Topics which did not seem important to particular participants were not pursued; those which they raised were explored. The relative importance of particular issues gradually emerged across the whole sample.

This method of semi-structured interviewing, in which the informants shape much of the content and structure of their own interview, and the direction and scope of future interviews, lies squarely within the traditions of ethnographic research (Spradley, 1979). It is particularly useful where, as in this case, there is limited prior research. It has the advantages of bringing to light issues which have gone unnoticed. The relative importance of issues is suggested by the frequency with which they are raised, and the emphasis placed on them. Ultimately, this method provides the means to develop well-grounded, testable theory (Cicourel, 1970).

Each tape-recorded interview or focus group discussion was transcribed *verbatim* into a word processing program, then submitted to 'The Ethnograph' (Seidel, Kjolseth & Seymour, 1988)—a set of computer programs designed to assist with the mechanical aspects of qualitative data analysis (line-numbering, coding, sorting, retrieval, code frequency counts, and code book development).

The line-numbered transcriptions were searched for patterns of common experience: lines or segments of text which referenced issues of different type and levels of importance (as perceived and expressed by the informants) were indexed by code names. There were no preconceived codes: each new code name indexed a discreet idea which had not previously been raised. Codes were developed from responses to questions, as well as from observations, narratives, arguments, and illustrations that were spontaneously offered. Answers to the same question were not necessarily of the same character; nor did they necessarily cover the same set of issues. Because speakers may make several points in the same statement, segments of text were often coded in several ways, each with a different code name. Each instance of any code was separately entered, and could be retrieved and counted along with others with

12

the same code name. Groups of codes which clustered around analytic themes were given a domain name, and the whole collection of codes and domains was gradually built into a code book containing the definition and scope of each code and domain. A project code book, which was updated with the coding of each new transcript, represented the state of analysis at any point in time. This report is based on the completed code book, frequency counts of codes and domains, and illustrative material from the text data.

Characteristics of the Participants

The degree status and gender of all 65 participants is summarized in Figure 1, the degree status, gender, and discipline of the 60 Institute of Technology participants in Figure 2, and the current career status and gender of the 19 Institute of Technology graduates in Figure 3. For the I.T. sample overall, of all current and former SMET majors, 59% were in engineering, and 41% were in physics, chemistry, mathematics, computer science, or geology. However, among graduates, the balance was 42% in engineering, and 58% for all other I.T. disciplines.[6]

As already noted, Henderson (1992), and the NCES study (1989), describe students with disabilities as disproportionately white, male, and older than their cohorts. This generalization partly fits our sample: of the 41 Institute of Technology undergraduates, 24 (i.e., 59%) were older than their cohorts, and only four were students of color (i.e., one Hispanic, and three Blacks). Disability Services indicated that there were several more students of color in the Institute of Technology who had documented disabilities, including some Asian-American students, however, only the above four students responded to the invitation to participate.

---

[6]The sample of students with disabilities was more evenly balanced between engineering on the one hand, and mathematics and science on the other, than are I.T. students overall: 74% of all I.T. degrees are granted in engineering.

Figure 1: Profile of all participants by degree status and gender.

Status	Men		Women		Total	
	N.	%	N.	%	N.	%
Undergraduate	30	68	14	32	44	100.0
Graduate	17	81	4	19	21	100.0
TOTALS	**47**	**72**	**18**	**28**	**65**	**100.0**

Figure 2: Profile of I.T. participants by degree status, gender, and discipline as undergraduates.

Status & Discipline	Men		Women		Total	
	N.	%	N.	%	N.	%
Undergraduate:						
Engineering	19		8		27	
Physics/Chemistry	3		4		7	
Math	3		0		3	
Computer Science	4		0		4	
Sub-total	*(29)*	*(71)*	*(12)*	*(29)*	*(41)*	*(100.0)*
Graduate:						
Engineering	7		1		8	
Physics/Chemistry	5		1		6	
Math	1		0		1	
Computer Science	3		0		3	
Geology	1		0		1	
Sub-total	*(17)*	*(89)*	*(2)*	*(11)*	*(19)*	*(100.0)*
TOTALS	**46**	**77**	**14**	**23**	**60**	**100.0**

Figure 3: Profile of I.T. graduates with disabilities by career status and gender.

Career Status	Men		Women		Total	
	N.	*%*	*N.*	*%*	*N.*	*%*
Employed	7		2		9	
Unemployed	2		0		2	
Self-employed	1		0		1	
Contracted worker	2		0		2	
Graduate/professional degree student	4		0		4	
Post-doctoral research	1		0		1	
TOTALS	**17**	**89.5**	**2**	**10.5**	**19**	**100.0**

Gender balance

Our sample has one distinctive feature: undergraduate women with disabilities ($N = 12$) were, at 29%, a higher proportion of the I.T. sample with disabilities than were all undergraduate women (with or without disabilities) at the Institute of Technology at the time of the interviews (i.e., 21%).

A partial explanation for the greater representation of women in this, than in some earlier, samples of undergraduates with disabilities is that, although all I.T. students with documented disabilities were invited (by letter) to participate, women responded proportionately more positively to the invitation than did men. The women in our sample also proved to be more socially and politically active than their male peers with disabilities, both in seeking improved access for students with disabilities on campus, and in organizing mutual support systems (including the Disabled Students' Cultural Center). On a campus that reflects the liberal traditions of the surrounding community, the general level of consciousness of disability issues is, arguably, greater than that on other campuses. Also, that the participating women drew parallels between gender and disability issues became very clear in the focus group discussions. It was notable that those women who described themselves as disabled rights activists drew upon the concepts and rhetoric of the civil rights and women's movements in describing the DSCC's objectives and strategies. It is notable that the sample of women graduates was very small (i.e., two out of 21). This may reflect a change in the relatively short time period (approximately three years) during which the university has been restructuring its pre-existing provision for students with disabilities in response to the Americans with Disabilities Act. Indeed, a number of the participants whose time at this university had been split into two periods, commented on the improvements for students with disabilities which they noted since their earlier campus experience. Students across the sample also commented on the personal importance of knowing that what they requested via Disability Services was underwritten by effective civil rights legislation. It is possible that the proportions of female-to-male students with disabilities will become more balanced at other institutions which become pro-active in promoting a policy of increased diversity in the student population.

Mature undergraduates

The I.T. undergraduate sample also contained, as expected, a high proportion of mature students (i.e., eight women, and 16 men). In a general undergraduate I.T. population where the mean age (at the time of the interviews) was 21, and 90% of all I.T. undergraduates were aged 22 or less, 59% (i.e., 24 out of 41) of the I.T. sample of students with disabilities were aged 25 or more (the range being 25 to 47). This was, in part, for reasons offered by Ellis (1992), namely, serious accidental injuries, or adult onset of the condition. Almost one-third of the participants (i.e., 19) had experienced an accident, injury or disabling illness as adults, and nine of this group reported a career interruption directly caused by the onset of their disability. However, this explanation misses a second, more disturbing, explanation for mature college entry. We found that a further 16 of all the mature students (i.e., 37% of the I.T. sample) had, prior to university entry, experienced lay-offs from their regular employment which were not caused by the disability *per se*. This group felt that, regardless of the quality of their work, and of official company policies supporting the employment of workers with disabilities, they were more vulnerable than were workers without disabilities to lay-off, especially during economic recession. They had chosen to enter higher education at this later stage in their lives largely as a way to off-set this vulnerability. By gaining particular SMET degrees, they hoped to improve their competitive edge and their chances of secure future employment. Mature students were likely to have entered the university after one or two years in a community college. As Ellis also found, the growth of numbers of students with disabilities in later college years is partly to be explained by the transfer of students with disabilities from community and junior colleges. These mature transfer students included both those with an adult-onset condition and economically-displaced students with longer-standing disabilities. Community colleges were favored because their focus on teaching was seen as especially helpful to returning, mature learners, and because they were considerably less expensive than the university.

Ability

Four of the science graduates were taking, or had recently completed, graduate or professional degrees, including, one in law, one in computer science, and two in physics.[7] One of the latter recently completed a Ph.D. in physics at Princeton and is now doing post-doctoral work. Three other members of the graduate group were planning to return to graduate school, and two of the focus group participants (i.e., non-I.T.) were taking master's programs (in social work and public health). The high proportion of current (or intending) graduate students in the sample challenges the stereotype of students with disabilities as being less able than others.[8] The stereotype is further contradicted by the participants' record of performance scores. The mean GPA of the undergradutes with disabilities at the time of

---

[7]A fifth graduate student was attending medical school. He was not included in our sample because, due to school examinations at the time of the interviews, we were only able to interview him briefly by telephone.

[8]Henderson (1992) also found that college freshmen with disabilities were more likely than were their non-disabled peers to expect to complete a Ph.D. or Ed.D. (i.e., 14%, compared with 12%).

interview (April, 1994) was 2.88 (range = 2.00 to 3.80),[9] compared with a mean GPA of 2.92 for all I.T undergraduates in spring, 1994. The mean GPA of the graduates (at graduation) was 3.15 (range = 2.50 to 3.96). This compares favorably with a mean GPA of 3.0 for all I.T. majors graduating in the same period as the graduate sample (i.e., 1987-1993). Almost half (N=9) of the 19 I.T. graduates graduated with GPAs of more than 3.2, which places them in the top 25% of their graduating classes. Most of the participants expressed pride in their achievements:

> Despite all the problems I've had, I'm doing pretty well. I'm almost done here, and I have a 3.4, and should finish with a 3.5 or more in mechanical engineering. And since this is one of the top five programs in the country, I figure that's a pretty good accomplishment.

We also checked how long it had taken the graduates to complete their undergraduate degrees: their average of 5.2 years is exactly the same as the average for all graduating seniors in the Institute of Technology over the last five years. We asked the I.T. undergraduates who were in junior or senior year for their estimates of how long it would take to complete their degree programs. Their mean estimates of 5.1 years may reflect a little optimism, but promises to keep them close to the average for all I.T. graduates. Some of the undergraduates will, however, take longer than five years because of periods out of school directly related to their disability: three were temporarily out of school at the time of interview.[10]

From the interview narratives, we drew other kinds of information which illustrate the high overall ability of the sample members: two of the graduate students had presented conference papers and published journal articles; four of the undergraduates already had an undergraduate degree (psychology, microbiology, computer science, and art); two had received achievement scholarships; four were in honors societies; another was in an undergraduate research program; two had received honors awards

---

[9]This excludes the scores of three undergraduates who were temporarily out of school.

[10]Henderson (1992) reports that more college freshmen with disabilities (12%) than without disabilities (8%) predicted that they would need extra time to complete their overall educational goals.

18

from their high school; and one had switched into science from liberal arts—which is relatively rare for any undergraduate. One of the graduates, and five of the undergraduates were supporting themselves by businesses they had begun themselves. Two had established computer companies—one of which was six years old—one had a telecommunications business, two made custom-designed structures or machinery, and one had developed a home-based "mastering" service for companies producing music CDs. Two of the mature undergraduates had held high-level company positions prior to their accidents; one had developed a computer network for the banking industry. Seven undergraduates described other skills—flying (with a private pilot's license), rebuilding engines, sculpture, and specialized computer skills. As a group which included a high proportion of mature students, the combined pre-graduation experience of the engineering majors especially, reflects a higher level of hands-on experience in the fields they intended to enter (or re-enter) than we found among engineering undergraduates in the 1994 study.

Both the institutional and self-reported data portray a group of people who may be somewhat more talented, experienced and persistent than both their university peers without disabilities,[11] and other students with disabilities who either do not enter, or do not complete, a university degree. In discussions of community college experiences with the mature undergraduates, we were also made aware of other students with disabilities who did not persist as far as degree program entry.

Choice and Persistence in SMET Majors

Table 1 shows the reasons given by I.T. undergraduates for their choice of an SMET major, for a particular type of institution, and for their career field choices. The predominant motivation, mentioned

---

[11]Henderson (1992) reports that, across all disciplines, and all types of disability, a smaller proportion of college freshmen with disabilities than of freshmen without disabilities had earned As in high school, or were members of scholastic honors societies. However, there was considerable variation by type of disability in this regard. Freshmen with sight impairments (whom she reports are one-quarter of all freshmen with disabilities) were more likely to have high school As, and to be honors society members than were their non-disabled peers. Those with health-related disabilities (more of whom were women) were more likely to project an average B grade in college. No information on actual college performance grades is available from national data sources.

Table 1. Reasons offered for the choice of S.M.E. majors, careers, and types of institutions: by number and percent of all motivations offered by disabled undergraduates in the University of Minnesota, I.T. sample (N=41).

Reasons Offered	N. Of Times Offered	% of All Times Offered
STRONG INTRINSIC INTEREST	(43)	(46.7)
Very strong interest in the discipline and/or its career applications	35	38.0
Conventional success less important than enjoyment in the subject/career	6	6.5
Enjoyment of particular work field prompted return to higher education	2	2.2
UNEMPLOYMENT (not disability related)	(16)	(17.4)
Laid off: qualifications increase competitive edge/chance of job security	12	13.1
Laid off: prompts rethinking of career direction	4	4.3
ONSET OF DISABILITY INTERRUPTED CAREER	(9)	(9.8)
Forced reconsideration of work options	6	6.5
Seen as an education opportunity not otherwise available	3	3.3
SMET MAJORS ADVANTAGEOUS FOR SOME DISABLED STUDENTS	(15)	(16.3)
Math-based work presents fewer problems for learning disabled	13	14.1
Physically disabled find physics/math tradition of "eccentricity" congenial	2	2.2
ENCOURAGEMENT BY MENTOR	(1)	(1.1)
TYPE OF INSTITUTION CONGENIAL TO DISABLED STUDENTS	(8)	(8.7)
Looking for disabled community in larger institution	3	3.3
Established disability services/good accommodations record	2	2.2
Community colleges cheaper, create fewer financial problems	2	2.2
Institutions in this state have liberal policy toward disabled	1	1.1
TOTALS	**92**	**100.0**

by every I.T. undergraduate with disabilities, was a strong liking for science, mathematics, computer science, or engineering, and/or a strong preference for a career based in these fields. Motivation by intrinsic interest was much stronger among the I.T. undergraduates with disabilities than among SMET majors in general in our study of seven campuses (Seymour & Hewitt, 1997;1994). In that study, only 17% of all those who entered SMET majors, and 28% of those who persisted to senior year, cited intrinsic interest among the reasons for their choice of major. One explanation for the high level of interest in these fields among undergraduates with disabilities is that their struggles to get as far as university entry were much greater than for most students without disabilities. They were, as a group, clearer about their educational and career objectives than were our general sample of SMET majors.[12] As Table 1 indicates, some students with particular types of disability saw mathematics and the sciences as offering them some advantages over non-science fields. Students with learning disabilities reported fewer problems with mathematics or with the kinds of conceptual thought required for the sciences than with academic disciplines which are based on language and require good writing skills, rapid comprehension of reading materials and large amounts of both written work and reading. In default of published data on the choice of majors or career paths by students with learning disabilities, it is important to learn whether students with learning disabilities (at this, or other, levels of education and ability) prefer or experience less difficulty with mathematics and the sciences compared with language-based disciplines.

Given the high proportion of SMET entrants who had experienced disrupted careers, whether or not these were directly related to their disability, concern to become re-established in a career which seemed to promise security as well as intrinsic interest was a strong motivational factor: over a quarter (27%) of our I.T. informants reported these as important facets of their choice. Some mature students

---

[12]For a discussion of influences on the disciplinary choices of students with disabilities, and of factors in their persistence, see also Weisgerber, 1991.

ho had been working at a level which was lower than their abilities prior to the accident or illness which interrupted their career, reported that the "time-out" caused by their disability offered an educational opportunity not previously available to them. Though we also found pragmatic reasons for the choice of an SMET field among students who both did, and did not, have disabilities, we found no trace among either the graduates or undergraduates with disabilities of the materialist motivations which, in our 1994 study, we found to be common among undergraduates aiming at careers in medicine and engineering, and to be a poor foundation for SMET persistence. Nor (as in that study), did we find that students with disabilities had chosen their majors in order to please significant adults in their lives (i.e., family members, high school teachers, mentors).[13] The undergraduates with disabilities had made strong, personal choices for largely academic and career interest reasons, and were very clear about why they were in particular SMET majors. As we found in the 1994 study, entering an SMET major largely for reasons of intrinsic interest was the best predictor of persistence; this finding helps to explain why SMET undergraduates with disabilities may be more likely to persist despite having to deal with problems which do not arise for students without disabilities.

Also mentioned as significant to their choices were, the reputation of the university—both for the quality of its education in these fields, and for its system of support for students with disabilities—and the size and diversity of its student body. Smaller institutions were thought to be less-well-organized in terms of services and accommodations for students with disabilities, and less likely to offer opportunities for social contact—whether with others who shared a particular disability—or with peers without disabilities. This opinion was supported by those who had attended smaller institutions before transferring to the University of Minnesota.

---

[13] For all S.M.E. entrants in the 1994 study, 23% of all women, and 11% of all men, had chosen an S.M.E. major partly because of the active influence of significant adults. This reason for entering the major also tended to be a poor predictor of survival.

Other motivations offered by our general (1994) SMET sample which we did not find among the students with disabilities were: choosing a major because of high school success in that discipline; making uninformed or poorly-informed choices; wanting a particular career, and choosing the subject as a means to enter it; following a family tradition; making a compromise choice; recruitment into the major; and the promise of scholarship money. We did find an element of altruism or idealism in both samples, though among students with disabilities thoughts of how to use their qualifications to further social causes which they valued were not an initial source of motivation, but came at a later stage when considering how to make the best use of their SMET degree. The motivations which we did not find among undergraduates with disabilities are important because, in our larger study, we found persistence to be strongly associated with intrinsic interest in the discipline and/or the careers to which it might lead. With the exception of altruistic motivations (which were much more rarely cited), all of the types of motivation which were not related to interest were apt to break down under the rigors of completing an SMET major. Those who switched out of SMET majors were far less guided by intrinsic interest than those who persisted. This comparison points to the high potential of students with disabilities for persistence.

Notwithstanding these characteristics favoring persistence, approximately one-third (31.7%; N=13), of the I.T. undergraduates with disabilities were either not enrolled at the time of the interviews, or reported feeling sufficiently discouraged to consider leaving either their major or the institution. This group included three undergraduates who were not enrolled in the Institute of Technology at the time of the interviews. All three intended to return to the university to complete their degrees at a later stage. Two of these three students had, meantime, transferred to vocational colleges—partly because this was less expensive and partly because they assessed their post-graduate chances of employment as greater with a technical qualification than with an engineering degree. (This issue is further discussed in Chapter Four.) Ten more undergraduates portrayed themselves as at risk of switching out of SMET majors or of leaving the university. Thus, the loss rate from our I.T. sample was 7.3%, with another 24.4% describing themselves as "at risk" of switching, leaving or changing institutions.

The issues which prompted these actual or projected moves out of the Institute of Technology were not the same as those which prompted switching to non-SMET majors among undergraduates without disabilities in our 1994 study. Four related issues recurred in the explanations of undergraduates with disabilities who were considering leaving or who had left the Institute of Technology. The same set of issues were raised by other undergraduates with disabilities, some of whom also reported periods out of school. Prominent among these were financial problems. Undergraduates across the sample reported a stop-go/in-out pattern of university education, which was largely dictated by insufficient funds. Intermittent problems with health also caused periods out of college, and as we discuss in Chapter Two, were closely related to financial difficulties. The accumulation of "incompletes" in their academic record (which was also related to their health and financial problems) was a further cause of periods of non-enrollment among the undergraduates. Finally, difficulties in getting the accommodations from I.T. faculty that they deemed reasonable were a serious source of frustration and prompted some undergraduates to consider changing their majors or their career plans. (We discuss the nature of accommodation difficulties also in Chapter Two.)

Thus, although their high degree of intrinsic interest increases their chances of persistence to graduation, undergraduates with disabilities manifest a set of problems which can undermine their determination to persist, but which are somewhat different from the causes of SMET attrition among undergradutes without disabilities.

We compared the actual and potential attrition rates of our I.T. sample with that of all 93 undergraduates with documented disabilities who were enrolled in the Institute of Technology at the beginning of Fall, 1993. By the time of our interviews (the following April), 65 of these students were still enrolled in the Institute of Technology; one (only) had transferred to the College of Liberal Arts, and

27 showed no day school enrollment for Spring, 1994. Thus, the attrition rate for the whole population of I.T. undergraduates with disabilities from which our sample was drawn was 30.1%. As was also clear from our interview data, for students with disabilities, the definition of "attrition" has to be amended to include periods of time out of school, as well as leaving SMET majors or abandoning the intention to enter SMET-based careers altogether.

For comparative purposes, we asked the Institute of Technology to provide us with attrition rates for women, and for students of color of both sexes, for the same period. For all women entering the Institute of Technology as freshmen in the fall of 1993, 21.0% either switched into other colleges within the university or did not enroll in Spring, 1994. The comparable loss rate for undergraduates of color (other than Asian-Americans) was 30.0%.

Although the loss rates of I.T. undergraduates with disabilities appear comparable with those of students of color, there is an important qualitative difference between the two. As already indicated, many of the currently-enrolled students with disabilities whom we interviewed described a stop-go pattern to their progress through higher education. Although they left for periods of time (largely for the four main reasons outlined above), they resumed their studies once their health and financial situation had improved, or they were able to address problems with their academic record. The Office of Institutional Research confirmed that, over time, they too had noted this in-and-out pattern of temporary attrition among undergraduates with disabilities. This is not, however, a pattern indicated in the SMET attrition rates of students of color, women, or indeed, white males. Both our qualitative data, and that from institutional records, suggest that although approximately one-third of undergraduates with documented disabilities may not be enrolled at any particular point in time, the trend is for them, nevertheless, to complete their degrees. Because time out of school was reported by the undergraduates themselves to be, typically, one semester, the overall time taken to complete I.T. majors (i.e., just over 5 years) appears, as already indicated, to be very similar to that of I.T. majors without disabilities.

Taken together, their good level of ability, the appropriateness of their reasons for choosing SMET majors and careers, and their tendency to persist despite the extra difficulties they encounter, suggest that students with disabilities should be regarded as interested, able, highly-motivated and very persistent students, with a high chance of success in SMET majors.

Post-Graduate Work Experience of the Graduates

Notwithstanding their level of ability, the work experiences of the graduates somewhat reflect the job insecurity reported by the mature undergraduates. Of the 14 graduates in the working world, five described their work situation as "insecure." Two were unemployed at the time of the interviews, two were working on short-term contracts, and one had chosen self-employment (a small, specialized engineering company) following difficulties in finding a congenial work setting. Six of the graduates had experienced difficulties in getting positions appropriate to their qualifications following graduation: they had accepted lower-level positions in order to get started; had several less-satisfactory jobs before finding their present position; had been laid-off or placed on contract. A seventh graduate—now at law school—had returned to higher education partly because of his concerns about job insecurity in the longer term. One of the unemployed graduates had left his employment following a dispute over under-payment. Not all these difficulties were seen as disability-related: at the time of the interviews, the local economy was just beginning to emerge from a period of economic recession, and other recent graduates without disabilities were reported as experiencing difficulty in finding initial job placements appropriate to their qualifications and interests.

Three of the working graduates were in smaller companies; these were the only graduates with hidden disabilities who had disclosed their disability to the employer or colleagues. The five who worked in larger companies had hidden disabilities which they had not disclosed.

Profile of Disabilities

As indicated earlier, we modified the University of Minnesota's official designation of disability type for each participant so as to reflect the participants' view of their primary disability. As Figure 4 indicates, 20 of the 65 participants had more than one disabling condition. Some multiple conditions had been acquired as the result of injuries in adolescence or adult life; others were of long-standing. Those with multiple disabilities tended to define one condition as dominant. Either they cited the condition which created most problems for them on campus or at work, or in the case of hidden disabilities, they chose the least stigmatized condition for public presentation, preferring not to disclose the other. For example, one student presented the problems caused by an automobile accident as her "official" disability, rather than her longer-standing condition, epilepsy. The profile of disabilities shown in Figure 5 reflects the choice of a dominant condition by each of these 20 participants.

Almost one-third (N=20) of the participants had acquired at least one of their disabilities in adult life. Ten of these conditions were the result of automobile or work accidents; two were acquired by victims of violent crimes; three involved drug or alcohol dependency; and five were the result of illness (e.g., stroke, cancer, and infections). Most of those with accidental injuries had residual mobility impairments; some also suffered from visual or hearing impairment, depression or post-traumatic stress syndrome.

Participants with learning disabilities were the largest single group (i.e., six graduates and 12 undergradutes). The proportion of undergraduates with learning disabilities (i.e., 27.3% of the undergraduate sample) is slightly larger than that reported by Henderson (1992) for freshmen in all majors in Fall, 1991 (i.e., 25%). The proportion may prove to be higher in SMET majors. As already reported, the participants with learning disabilities indicated that they had chosen their major in preference to an arts or social science major partly because they saw SMET majors as having fewer disadvantages for people with learning disabilities.

Figure 4: Profile of participants with multiple disabilities by degree status and gender.

Participants	Graduates		Undergraduates		Total	
	Men	Women	Men	Women	N.	%
Students with multiple disabilities	3	2	7	8	20	100

Figure 5: Profile of all participants by types of disabilities, degree status, and gender.

Disability Groups	Graduates		Undergraduates		Total	
	Men	Women	Men	Women	N.	%
Learning disabilities	5	1	11	1	18	28
Mobility: systemic condition or injury	1	1	7	4	13	20
Systemic conditions	5	1	2	3	11	17
Emotional/Psychological	1	0	3	4	8	12
Sight: Legally blind, visual impairment	2	0	2	1	5	8
Hearing impairment	2	0	1	1	4	6
Chemical dependency	1	1	2	0	4	6
Speech impairment	0	0	2	0	2	3
TOTALS	**17**	**4**	**30**	**14**	**65**	**100**

All but one of those with learning disabilities had experienced educational problems since childhood—the exception had sustained a head injury in a car accident. Two of the group had more than one type of learning disability, and three had a second disability of a different type. The term "learning disability" glosses a range of neurological abnormalities which may appear early and be an issue throughout pre-college education. However, as several of our participants reported, the extent of their difficulties only become apparent once they encounter undergraduate, or even graduate, level work. These conditions are more common among men than among women.[14] (In this sample, there were 14 men and two women reporting specific types of learning disabilities.) All of those with learning disabilities reported that some teachers or faculty had mistaken their neurological problems for low intelligence. Notwithstanding their difficulties, the mean GPA of the undergraduates with learning disabilities was, at 2.80 (range = 2.0 - 3.34), the same as the I.T. undergraduate sample with disabilities overall, and only slightly less than the mean GPA (2.92) for all I.T. majors in spring, 1994. The mean GPA of the graduates with learning disabilities was 3.19, which is higher than the mean of 3.0 for all I.T. graduates. Two of the five graduate students were learning-disabled, including the post-doctoral fellow.

Participants with mobility impairments were the second largest group (N = 13). They reported a wide range of physical difficulties: four used a wheel chair; two used a walker; one had an artificial limb. Six had acquired their mobility impairments through accidents; six had non-visible mobility impairments (e.g., spondylitis); and eight had other disabilities, some of which were unrelated to mobility. Mobility impairments varied in severity; they included pain caused by both action and in-action; and conditions some of which were stable, some improving and some deteriorating.

Ten of the participants had conditions which were labeled "systemic" in the university's disability classification system. These are sometimes also referred to as "health-related" disabilities (e.g.,

---

[14]See Henderson, 1992.

Henderson, 1992). In our sample, they included epilepsy, diabetes, cancers, tumors, immune deficiencies (of which none were AIDS-related), asthma, the effects of stroke, and nerve damage (by accident). Four people in this group also had a second type of disability.

Six participants had psychological and/or emotional disabilities, including clinical depression, bi-polar disorder, post-traumatic stress syndrome, and anxiety disorder. Three had acquired their condition through accident or trauma as adults; four had a second disability.

Three undergraduates and two graduate students cited impaired vision as their primary disability; a third graduate student was visually-impaired and also depended on a wheel-chair for mobility. Five of these six participants described themselves as "legally blind";[15] two had a second disability.

Of the four hearing-impaired participants, three reported that with the use of hearing aids they could "pass" as "non-disabled"; the forth needed the assistance of a sign language interpreter for classes, meetings and discussions.

The four participants recovering from chemical or alcohol dependency were among those who expressed least need for accommodation and used off-campus therapeutic resources. However, two of this group had other conditions which required some accommodation through Disability Services.

Two participants had speech disabilities—one severe enough to require a communication device by which he could print out messages for help with conversations. The other participant described his condition as "manageable" most of the time. One of this group also had problems with mobility and used a walker.

Across the whole sample, 75.4% (N=49) of the participants (i.e., 35 undergraduates and 14 graduates) had one or more disabling condition that was either entirely hidden or not immediately apparent. On the one hand, this allowed people to choose whether or not to disclose their disability(ies);

---

[15]Although this term is no longer in legal use, students who were blind or who had low vision commonly used it to gloss all degrees of serious vision loss.

on the other, it created an extra layer of difficulty in getting the help they required. The wide range of types and causes of disabilities, and the high proportion of non-visible disabilities, may seem the most surprising features of the sample for those with limited direct experience of disability. Taken together, they flout the stereotypical expectation that most people with disabilities will have rather obvious problems with mobility, sight or hearing. The difficulties which the inaccuracy of these common expectations create for students and employees with disabilities will be discussed throughout this report.

Direct quotations from the interview transcripts are used in the balance of the report to illustrate and support the points being made. In the interests of preserving the anonymity of our informants, the speaker's gender, academic status or type(s) of disability are only cited where they are needed to clarify their remark.

CHAPTER TWO: SOURCES OF DIFFICULTY AND OF
SUPPORT IN COMPLETING SMET UNDERGRADUATE DEGREES

Broadly, undergraduates and graduates with disabilities have to deal with three types of difficulties in order to complete a university SMET education: problems caused by aspects of disabilities or their treatment; incompleteness, inadequacies or operational flaws in institutional systems (both those of the university and of other agencies); and attitudes which undermine the efficacy of the university's system of accommodation and support for students with disabilities. However, in their everyday experience, problems with different origins interact: for example, mobility problems arise for both medical and institutional reasons and may be exacerbated by unhelpful administrative responses to requests for help. Table 2 summarizes the main categories of problems reported by current and former undergraduates.

Problems Arising from the Nature of Disabilities and Their Treatment

As Table 2 indicates, the third most commonly reported type of problem experienced by undergraduates in the sciences (11% of all specific problems raised) occurs because some aspect of a student's medical condition, or of its treatment (especially medication), makes it difficult to meet the normal demands made on all students by faculty and the university administration. It is this group of problems which people with little contact with students with disabilities are likely to assume to be the main source of difficulties for students with disabilities. It was precisely to anticipate and respond to the problems which students with disabilities inevitably encounter in contexts primarily designed for people without disabilities, that universities have developed policies of accommodation and support in compliance with the Americans with Disabilities Act and with the prior provisions (1977) of Section 504 of the Rehabilitation Act. Because some attempt to anticipate and meet these difficulties has been made for students with particular types of mobility impairments, students reported problems created by mobility impairments in the context of these institutional adjustments. Mobility problems have been separately

Table 2. Sources of problems in completing S.M.E. majors: by number and percent of all problems reported by current and former disabled undergraduates at the Institute of Technology, University of Minnesota (N=60).

Sources of Problems	N. of Problems Reported	% of All Problems Reported
SMET FACULTY	**(282)**	**(20.3)**
"Gate-keeping" attitudes	148	10.7
Refusal, resistance, sabotage of accommodation, giving-in under pressure	121	8.7
Unintentional discrimination or problem-creation	13	0.9
FINANCIAL	**(156)**	**(11.2)**
Specific financial difficulties	83	6.0
System of financial aid incoherent, cumbersome, unfair, over-discretionary	42	3.0
Working full or part time; poor job availability/pay	31	2.2
EFFECTS OF DISABILITIES & THEIR TREATMENT	**(153)**	**(11.0)**
NATURE OF SMET MAJORS	**(130)**	**(9.3)**
Experience same problems as other SMET majors	88	6.3
Problems exacerbated, or negative consequences greater, because of disability	42	3.0
POOR ACCESS TO SOURCES OF HELP	**(114)**	**(8.2)**
Difficulty in knowing what services/help are available, or finding it	54	3.9
Difficulties in registering as "disabled"	30	2.2
Disclosure as the price for help	30	2.2
STUDENTS' OWN "CONTRIBUTIONS"	**(104)**	**(7.5)**
Not using available services	93	6.7
Difficulties in asking for help	11	0.8
ISSUES RELATED TO TIME	**(91)**	**(6.6)**
Academic pace set by aspects/consequences of disability	63	4.5
Time-related needs	24	1.7
Coping strategies require time	4	0.3
UNIVERSITY SYSTEM (other than mobility or financial issues)	**(71)**	**(5.1)**
Inflexibility, incoherence, obscurity	51	3.7
Limited/no access to facilities (i.e., classrooms, labs, computers, tutors)	16	1.2
Attitudes of university administrative staff limiting educational access	4	0.3

Sources of Problems (continued)	*N. of Problems Reported*	*% of All Problems Reported*
MOBILITY ISSUES	**(69)**	**(5.0)**
Getting around campus/getting to classes, labs, etc., on time	46	3.3
Physical difficulties in classrooms and labs	10	0.7
Physical stress of coping with mobility problems (e.g., class registration)	7	0.5
Getting to campus	6	0.4
MEDICAL/THERAPEUTIC ISSUES	**(60)**	**(4.3)**
Late recognition/diagnosis and consequences	24	1.7
Difficulty getting appropriate help	21	1.5
Lack/loss/cost of medical help	15	1.1
ELEMENTARY & HIGH SCHOOL EXPERIENCES	**(52)**	**(3.8)**
Poorer educational preparation in science/math than non-disabled	33	2.4
Ignorance, misperception, lack of help from teachers/advisors	19	1.4
DISABILITY SERVICES & COUNSELORS	**(27)**	**(2.0)**
Services	18	1.3
Counselors	9	0.7
FAMILY ISSUES	**(26)**	**(1.9)**
Family-of-origin discouraging/over-protective	19	1.4
Family responsibilities (mature students, single parents)	7	0.5
COMMON NEGATIVE ATTITUDES	**(24)**	**(1.7)**
Stigma	10	0.7
Impatience, unintended discrimination, intolerance of accommodations	10	0.7
Lower expectations of disabled students (teachers/advisors)	4	0.3
GENDER & ETHNICITY: DOUBLE BURDEN	**(15)**	**(1.1)**
OTHER (NON-DISABLED) STUDENTS	**(14)**	**(1.0)**
TOTALS	**1,388**	**100.0**

34

listed in Table 1. The main issues around mobility now are: how well do these adjustments work in meeting different kinds of mobility needs, and what more is needed?

People who have little regular contact with disability issues may assume that mobility impairment is the dominant type of problem experienced by people with disabilities. In this section, while we address some mobility issues, we draw attention to problems which are unrelated to mobility but which are common in other conditions, or which cut across the whole spectrum of disabilities. These common difficulties are less acknowledged and addressed.

One common problem which affects students with all types of disabilities is that their condition varies over time in its severity and effects and in ways that are unpredictable:

> Mostly, I have one day a week that, when I get up, I will not feel good—and the only thing I can do is go back to bed...I will be sleeping and waking all day. When that happens, I know I should not come to the U or drive. It would be dangerous. So if that is the day with the exam, that's really bad.

> The disorder stems from an over-production of this steroid hormone...It causes a sensation not unlike that of standing in a roadway with trucks speeding past you at close range...And to feel it continuously through the day and even through the night...At those times, I would get out of bed and start getting ready to leave for class, but just not be able to get out the door...It was a hopeless feeling.

> Tests are only a problem on the days when the hand hurts...I mean, the rest of the time, I've gotten 90s on tests...Sometimes it will hurt for a couple of days, then stop. There are times when I can tell the teacher the day before—it's already gotten puffy because it's cold and rainy.

With some conditions, these unpredictable interruptions include periods of hospitalization:

> My disabilities are very random in terms of how they manifest themselves. I have an immune deficiency, which means that sometimes I'm fatigued and get severe headaches...Sometimes, I'm in the hospital...My other disability is a variable mobility impairment. That's different almost every day...Sometimes, if I am limping or walking differently, you would know when it's flaring up. I guess it's really hard for any institution to deal with someone who's not the same all the time.

> I had a tumor in my head which was removed. And then I had radiation for that...I still went through school the whole time.

Other disruptions were described as the result of particular medication regimens, or changes in the medications prescribed:

They kept piling on the medications—I was at toxic levels of phenobarb and dilantin—and of course I was having seizures. I kept falling asleep in class. After a seizure—if it's a bad one—for up to five days, I can't do physics at all. I can barely multiply. Then, once it comes back, I'm back up there. If that happened before a test and they forced me to take it, I was sunk.

I went to see my TA, and he went to the professor and explained that I had a big headache that day and couldn't read. He insisted I try the test. So, more or less, I was trying to get the letters. But I couldn't see the questions, and I couldn't process the information...They had given me medication for the breast tumor—it's that which was making me sick—not the condition.

I was having a lot of side effects from my lithium—I'd have cramping and diarrhea a lot in the morning so it was really hard to get going early in the morning...So I missed his class all but two days in the first three weeks. However, I kept getting 10 out of 10 on the quizzes...And he said, 'Maybe you should drop the class.'...And I explained it wasn't usually a problem—just with this new medication. But he tried to talk me into switching into another section.

As these last three accounts indicate, the interaction between the condition and its treatment can produce quite dramatic peaks and troughs in academic performance. The timing of assignments is, thus, often a critical matter for students with disabilities. Some variations in the effects of conditions are seasonal, and students with disabilities who have learned these patterns, plan around them:

When I get severe migraines, I can be gone for a week. It's usually during the winter that it's that bad.

It's cyclical throughout the season—like November through January are my worst periods. I choose not to sign up for school then...I can do okay at the beginning, but by the end I get worse. I'd be wasting my money to go to school then.

A common problem which arises with many different conditions is inability to take classes which have early morning starts: either the condition itself or the effects of over-night medication make it difficult, or impossible, to be fully functional in time for early morning appointments. Having to take such a class, because it only meets early in the day, or being given tests, exams, labs or appointments with faculty advisors at such times, creates a 'poor attendance' record and grades which under-represent actual knowledge and ability levels:

And the problem, mainly, was entirely due to my disability, or the medication. It's a chemical imbalance—a physical disability in the brain. When you aren't getting the proper chemistry, you aren't getting what you need to perform. They don't understand what it's like to feel totally physically paralyzed.

I don't feel that my transcripts reflect what I've done because of the attendance problem—I often missed a pop quiz first thing in the morning. I get As for my homework, and that's supposed to help your grade—but often it's not counted...I feel like I've gotten a lot of punishment in the grading area: I was told by Disability Services that absenteeism isn't really protected.

A very common consequence of condition-related problems is that all students with disabilities are at risk of acquiring "incompletes" on their academic record—and need ways to deal with these:

I only managed to complete one of the three classes, and then I'd sign up again, and not complete those...The faculty know I know the material. When I cleared up the incompletes, I had a 3.5 GPA. They just can't understand why I can't just do it.

They were surprised at my high score. In fact, they were surprised that I was having any difficulty at all in I.T. But then they discovered that I often didn't get a chance to finish the class—so I never got through to the final. I tried getting an extension on it, but I'd been in bad shape all winter, and I didn't get a chance to do much.

My GPA is about a 2.7, but it got hit when I went in for heart surgery, and I had to drop three classes and take incompletes. The incompletes turn to failures after two or three months, so I'm making them up right now.

A different, but equally common, type of problem is the need to go at a slower pace to complete any particular task:

For me to work in a math class is twice as hard as for someone with normal sight. Because of my narrow field of vision, and my astigma, my eyes kind of wiggle out of focus. I can't look at an equation all at once. So it takes a bit more time and effort to marshal my thoughts...It really slows me down in class, even working with a monocular, because I can only see two feet of board at a time.

All I ever needed was extra test time to compensate for the time it took me to read the test paper...you know, with an extra 20 minutes, it seemed to work out okay...but many times I didn't have enough time to compensate for the amount of reading—but I didn't worry about it, so long as I was doing well.

Needing extra time for tests and examinations was one of the commonest forms of request for accommodation, although the impairments which created this need were very variable and spanned the whole range of disabilities:

I have a slow ability to recall information, so a test based mostly on memorization is a real trial. If I can't bring something I've worked on to recall accurately and fast enough, I can fail—not because I don't know it or understand it—but because I just can't get it out of my head fast enough. Some of the people I used to help with their homework have now graduated.

I have one hand that can't feel, and the other doesn't work very well. I was originally right-handed, but after the stroke I learned to write with my left. But I'm a bit slow. A three-hour test, especially in essay form, is a real trial and the anxiety makes it worse—wondering if I can hold out.

Students with impairments which affected the ways in which they read, learned, recalled, organized or processed information were especially likely to need extra time to produce work commensurate with their knowledge and abilities:

I learn in steps. I'll be lost for a while, then, all of a sudden, it hits me like a big Mack truck. Bam! Everything comes together. I'm not a fast learner, but when I get it, I get the whole picture....I read slower than the average person and it takes me longer just to read the test questions, let alone be able to work on them...I have an audio dyslexia—I don't mix up letters like people with visual dyslexia. Having a learning disability doesn't mean that I can't learn, but that I learn things in a different way. I have to bring all the pieces together, and part of that is taking more time...My fourth quarter of calculus, all of a sudden, I realized what the symbols meant and I went from Cs to being the best in the class in just a few months.

I have an innate, natural understanding of math—there's no way I could put together some of the things I do without that. I find I know things that I haven't learned yet. I take in the math that someone describes very easily, but sometimes I have experiences where I look at a piece of paper with English written on it and I can't understand a word. It all turns into marks—like alien hieroglyphics or cuneiform writing. It's like a blackout—all the information has gone. A complete hole—almost a zen thing. It would be almost hard to write my name at that point. And you can't explain that to someone who's never experienced it—especially not to a physicist...Some days it's there, and some days it isn't. On those days, it helps me to shift to a little chalk board—maybe just a confidence thing that nudges me back...It takes longer to do a test on lapse days... I don't know when it will happen, so I'm safer writing papers than taking tests.

I understood everything in class, and for the homework, where I had plenty of time, I would get 100 percent. Then, I would come to an exam and fail it. The professors knew I understood, so they couldn't figure out why I couldn't show it on paper...After one test that I almost failed, I persuaded the professor to give extra time on a remake test, and, bingo, I got 100 again. A bit more time—that's all I really need.

I have both a visual learning disability and an attention deficit disorder—and that's a disability that affects the whole quality of your life—I can't learn to play any type of game; I can't ride a bike or drive a standard transmission car, because the second-nature that most people develop in driving can never happen for me. I have to think through the process of everything I do all the time—and that's not the safest thing when you're driving...I get some of my text books recorded and listen to the tape while I'm reading. I can't do one without the other—I need both the verbal and the visual input...So I plan out my time very carefully. I can't deal with close deadlines. I may need longer for an assignment than is given because of all the time it takes me to do the ground work.

With a visual kind of dyslexia, you are apt to write words or groups of symbols backwards, or in some scrambled order. When you are taking a math test, that can be nasty. So you've got to take your time to check everything you do. Some of my exams last quarter, I wasn't capable of finishing them—even though I knew all the material on the test—because I have to read the problem two or three times before I realize what I'm looking at...And I need a quiet environment: if I get distracted, I may have to start the question over again. If I can get just a bit more time and a quiet place to work, I'm fine.

It's tremendously frustrating, because I have to keep going back over what I've written, and I will still leave out whole blocks of thought that I thought I had put down...I can sit down to write one page and it takes four hours...With some help from a tutor, I am now learning to just get my thoughts out as best I can and go back and edit. But editing probably takes up 90 percent of the time.

People in this group had an array of specific difficulties which were eased when classes were well-structured:

I can't organize information that comes at me orally, although I have very high reading comprehension. I just take in everything as it comes at me; I can't distinguish big points from minor ones, so I often misunderstand or miss things. I focus on how other people structure the material—the teacher, the other students. I did well in a class where the teacher put the structure of her lecture on the board.

It just means that you don't learn like the majority of people...The classes I did best in were when the teacher took the time to explain something in more than one way.

They also coped by being highly structured themselves in the way that they studied and in the way they lived:

I make the things around me very orderly. I need to know exactly where things are—even silly things, like putting a jar back in the cupboard exactly where I took it from—not two inches off—otherwise it seems to throw the whole pattern and I can't find it again. I need to see everything in its context.

Tests allowing reference to books and notes were also helpful for students with particular kinds of learning impairments:

My understanding of math and science is fine, but because of the way that I integrate and process information, I can't memorize formulas or concepts. I can't do a problem 50 times and remember it. I remember it once I see it, and when I see it I remember how to use it...So all my math tests are open book. The math department understands that it doesn't matter how many books you have, if you don't understand how to put that information together, it's going to do you absolutely no good.

An interesting facet of some learning disabilities is that the neurological abnormalities which create them, also sometimes create special mental abilities. Three of the graduates, and four of the undergraduates, with learning disabilities described unusual mental abilities, which that they had learned to trust and draw upon:

> I always score 99.5 or 100 on spatial tests because I can just take something and move it around in my head. It's part of the disability in that the sound of words like 'how' and 'who' will often switch in my head...But it's a curious, profound advantage in visual things: I always got very high grades in visual courses, and it's now a very useful skill in my work.
>
> I think pictorially and geometrically, and I can picture things in my head that other people can't seem to imagine. It's often hard to translate for them—I'm way ahead...And I look at things in meticulous detail and notice things that 'just don't look right.' It's been an enormous advantage in my research. (Post-doctoral science fellow)
>
> I've got a lot of physics up here, but I sometimes have a hard time pulling it out. It's exceedingly frustrating when I can't write about it. It's a bit of a roller-coaster, because on good days I get very lucid and know just how the math works long before others do. Something innate back there is working just fine. And I can't always tell you how I know it.

We have spent some time illustrating the different kinds of problems faced by students with learning disabilities because they are less-easily understood than visual, aural or mobility-impairment, and are often seen as one, rather than an array, of different information-processing disorders. Learning disabilities are often mistaken for poor intellectual ability, whereas they may equally affect people who are intelligent and gifted. They are more likely to be encountered among students in SMET majors than among those in the liberal arts, and as the performance scores and high incidence among graduate students attest, can be ignored or discounted only at the risk of losing good students. Students with learning disabilities usually ask for little more than extra time, or a quiet place to do tests (although, like many students without disabilities, they benefit greatly from a well-structured pedagogy that takes into account different learning styles.) Accommodations of time and place involve little or no cost, other than the time it takes to set them up on a formal basis.

We found that, as a group, students with disabilities coped with the variability of their conditions and the need to pace themselves by pre-planning and a high degree of organization. What they could not easily accommodate were close deadlines, unscheduled tests or assignments, and sudden changes of syllabus or venue:

> Planning ahead is the key. If I had no transportation problems and had the class seating problem solved, most days would be pretty good...When I have really bad days, I have to work around the deadlines. If they are spaced out, and don't get shifted around, I can cope with set-backs in my health. It's last minute changes that throw me.

> My school schedule, my approach to classes and tests, it all has to be very disciplined: I can manage just fine if I can keep going at a very steady, organized pace. But sometimes faculty throw you a curve ball—just throw in something extra—that's hard.

Although, as we have documented in the previous section, many students with disabilities were, by dint of hard work and good planning, able to complete their degrees in a time-frame similar to that of students without disabilities, for others, this was not possible. Their condition did not allow them to tackle the class loads required of full-time students, and attempts to manage this (often in order to qualify for financial aid) had counter-productive consequences:

> Under pressure from financial aid, I tried a full load, but I'm not the same person I was before all of this happened...So it was just too much, and then I was stuck making up all these incompletes. It's very embarrassing to admit: I felt like a failure...Now I know that I need to work at a slower, steadier pace and resist all pressures to make me go faster.

The need to work at a slower pace than some other students arose, in part, from a common problem—impaired ability to concentrate. Problems with concentration manifested themselves in many different forms:

> I get dizzy spells and my ears make funny popping noises, and I can't get rid of them. If it happens in a test, it really slows me down...Once something sinks in for me, I'm really good at it, but it's hard for me to learn it in some contexts—like a group. I can't focus clearly enough to get it: I have to work on it first on my own or I get messed up.

> I'm one that has a hard time concentrating when I'm in pain. I try to psych myself out of it—convince myself that its doesn't really hurt. But it only works for so long, then I crash. All of a sudden, you just hurt so bad you can't think straight. It takes a lot of emotional energy and I've very limited time—perhaps just enough to get through the test. Then you crash. And it's all over for the day. The worry is, Am I going to crash before the test is over? Will the adrenaline run out part-way through?

Pain and fatigue were common factors in both impaired concentration and the need for a slower pace:

I have time constraints because I get real sore from sitting. I get all cramped up and uncomfortable and I cannot concentrate. I have an inner time constraint: I know about how long I can sit, and I schedule my classes so they all happen in that time-frame.

With my disability, I tire more easily—and a lot of it comes from really trying to pack a lot into a short time period...I've always loved math and reading, but, since this happened, I get really exhausted after a hard day's studying. It really hits you physically. Then the concentration just evaporates.

I was having difficulty sitting there and doing the stuff—because you lose your concentration and then you can't do the work. The doctor says I should get up and walk about every half an hour. I talked to the instructor and he said, 'Well, you can bring a chair right up in front of the class.' But it's hard to stand up and pace about in front of 150 people...The professor didn't recognize that. He thought I just didn't know the material.

Because of their disabilities, many students had problems with the physical characteristics of classrooms. As indicated in some of the above extracts, sitting for long periods, especially in chairs that were uncomfortable, and seeing the board clearly enough were issues for some. For hearing-impaired students, particular room acoustics, their seating position in the class, and the teacher's delivery and accent, all affected how much of the lesson they could hear. Some aspects of lab work presented challenges for students with damaged or prosthetic hands. However, the largest number of concerns expressed by students with mobility impairments related to physical aspects of the campus. Despite what these students saw as the university's good attempts to address mobility problems, they still had to negotiate a campus with long distances between buildings, some of which lacked elevators:

I can make it down to Williamson Hall, but I trudge along slowly. I can't go anywhere fast because my lungs can't handle the burden...I get down there and I ask for a transcript. They tell me, 'Oh, we printed one for you; you can collect it from the Coffman Union building—it's just a block away.' A block, to me, seems like ten miles. To someone else, it's no big deal.

An elevator in all the buildings that still don't have one would be nice—especially the mechanical engineering building...When you register, you have to go all the way back to the river. For most people, it's just a few blocks—a pleasant walk. But it's a very long way for people like me—plus, when you get there, there's no elevator in that building either.

When I register, I guarantee that I am going to have to hoof it from the registration building back to the department to get my over-ride, and then back to the registration office again. I have a friend who walks with a cane who often gives me a ride—but the parking is a mile away from campus. That's hard on him too.

42

They send you to Coffman to pick up your registration materials. You get to push the wheelchair up the ramp. Have you ever tried pushing a wheelchair up a ramp that steep? I have limited muscle strength. Sometimes it's sheer hell just to get across campus. The whole campus is like that: it's built for healthy young white males.[16]

This group of students cited a number of different but related problems where their own physical limitations collided with the university's administrative limitations. Broadly, these were: getting to campus; parking close to classes, libraries and labs; getting around campus; getting access to certain rooms in certain buildings; and dealing with physical problems in classrooms:

On top of the problem of getting there, you've got a problem with the seating. It's disruptive if I get up and move around a bit, plus the fact I don't want to miss getting any of the notes. And it's embarrassing being put down the front of the class, so I just use one of the folding chairs and pack a pillow into it. It means I've got the desk part pushing against my stomach, and it's uncomfortable. But at least I can sit in the middle of the classroom where I can see the whole board. That's one of the problems at the front—you get reflections off the board, and, on a white board, the markers don't stand out if you are looking from a sharp angle. I need to get straight on.

If you have a wheelchair, the only place you can sit is either the very front or right at the back. So I always ended up parking my chair wherever I can, and writing on my knee on a clipboard. It would be nice to have a decent surface to write on. You can't concentrate so well hanging onto a clipboard—especially for exams. There are some auditoriums where they have a table near the back which I can wheel up to. Those are great.

Compared with the variable constraints of some other disabilities, the difficulties dictated by visual, aural and mobility-impairment were more constant and predictable. For those who could not drive, the adequacy or otherwise of the bus services and the metro transit service for people with disabilities dictated the class schedule that this group of students could undertake. The five students who were dependent on the public transit system reported that bus times and class times tended not to coincide:

---

[16]Registration accommodations are available upon request for some students with disabilities, including those with mobility impairments. This was not, however, known by these students. This illustrates one of the frustrations of Disability Services who are able to accommodate a number of the difficulties which were described to us by the participants, but who experience problems in conveying the relevant information to those students who could benefit from it. We noted that mature students whose mobility impairments were acquired as a consequence of work-related injuries were among those who sought to deal with difficulties on campus without help from Disability Services, and who, as a consequence, often did not know what was available to them.

For this last quarter, I found there were only three classes I could take that would fit within my transportation time-frame. So I ended up taking a class that's no use to me, just to keep my credit load up for my financial aid...So I'm kind of bouncing between when my classes are offered and when the buses allow me to get to them. I can't get here before 10:00 a.m., and the last bus I can catch home is 2:38 p.m., which is pretty early. So I've just got this kind of four-hour window, and I have to pack everything I need to do on campus into that time.

If I had lost my driving license, I would have to walk three-quarters of a mile from where I live to catch a bus at 6:30 a.m. There are only two buses back—at 12:00 noon and 3:00 p.m. That would really limit the time I have on campus. (Visually-impaired undergraduate)

To augment the bus service, students with disabilities organized a complex system of 'rides' and emergency back-up arrangements with family, friends and class peers. Those who drove reported: delays in getting handicapped parking stickers or spaces;[17] difficulties with the high cost of close-in parking when denied a permit or space; no provision for booking a particular parking space near a building where they had to take an examination; and time limits on parking. Arriving late for classes, labs, tests and appointments was a constant source of anxiety:

That walk across the river—a ride would be nice there. If you park on this side, just recently, they posted a three-hour maximum. Many a time I've spent all day here, and then I have classes at night—that's 12 or 15 hours on campus. And there's no way that I could walk there and move my car every three hours. I parked there one day, and they got me.

Because of the parking restrictions, I had to get here at 8:00 a.m. for an 11:30 a.m. appointment. If I had a place to park that I could count on, I could have arrived at 11:00 a.m.

It's really stupid! They've got these small handicapped spots scattered around the campus. And you can never assume one spot's going to be there, or how close you can get to your exam. They should have a central parking location—preferably a weather-proof, underground lot—and just give one whole damn floor over to however many mobility-impaired students there are. You shouldn't have to worry about whether or not you can find a place. You end up driving around checking every spot, working further and further away from where you need to be. And, at certain times—between about 10:00 a.m. and 2:00 p.m., the central spots are always full...I missed one exam three times running, through a combination of three blizzards, and the lack of anywhere at all to park.

---

[17]Some students expressed the belief that employees with disabilities had priority over students with disabilities in the allocation of designated disabled parking spaces. Disability Services refuted this belief. They also clarified that regular, contracted parking spaces are available to students with disabilities. However, spaces marked "handicapped parking," which are closer to teaching buildings, cannot be booked.

On a large, spread-out campus, negotiating longish distances between buildings was physically and emotionally stressful. Some students used wheelchairs, walkers, crutches and canes; some used no aids, but were constrained to go slowly or were limited in their range of movements. A number of problems could make the difficulties inherent in their physical conditions more painful, tiring or stressful. Failure to adequately maintain the physical facilities which were installed specifically to aid access was a common source of frustration:

> I can go over snow, but (name) can't. On the bridge, it's really messed up—it's dangerous. It's really risky, because there's not much room, and then you've got a curb.

Never knowing in advance which elevators would and would not be locked, or which wheelchair ramps and paths would be cleared of snow, meant that in bad weather especially students with mobility impairments arrived in class tired, wet and muddy after dangerous encounters with paths, bridges, ramps and stairs:

> It's just a solid leg from the knee down. I can do almost everything except stairs. I wish I had a key to every elevator in the mechanical engineering building...Lind Hall has a nice elevator. Akerman has one too, but you have to ask for the key.

> After it snows, they shovel the ramps, and then at the top of the ramp, they quit shoveling.

> In the winter, in bad conditions, it's difficult if a building is far away. It varies how quickly I can get along on snow. But it's awfully messy, because the snow sticks to your wheels and rubs off on your arms. So you end up being wet and covered with dirty snow. Winter, ick! I'm glad it's over.

The university has, for some years, allowed students with disabilities to register by computer, however, we found that many undergraduates with disabilities did not know this, or were not told this in encounters with registration staff. Those who had discovered computer registration thought it was a recent concession. In default of this information, the registration process involved long journeys between widely-spaced buildings, and obliged mobility-impaired students to push their physical abilities to the limits. Too, unwittingly, administrators and faculty could place these students under stress by assigning classes to inaccessible rooms, and by starting classes a few minutes early or running them over-time:

The classes are supposed to last 45 minutes. Generally, what happens is they start putting notes on the board five minutes before the class starts, and they usually run five minutes late—so the class ends up running almost an hour. Then, if you've got classes back to back, you get to the next one late. But they started that one five minutes early too, and so everyone has been scribbling for 10 minutes before I can get there.

Less mobile students also lost out on the chance to talk to faculty or to class peers at the beginning and end of classes, given the time they needed to get to work or the next class.

Being assigned to an inaccessible room for a class, lab or examination is also is a problem which Disability Services can resolve. Again, the difficulty lies in conveying this information to those students who need it. Where a classroom was entirely inaccessible, students who had taken the problem to the Disability Services reported they had been helped to negotiate a room change with the department or professor concerned:

The law says that the class must be accessible to all students...And they've generally been good about moving classes for people. I only had to do it once, but I had disabled friends that have also had classes moved without much problem.

Getting a place to sit where they could see and hear adequately, and to appropriate seating or writing surfaces, were common issues for the visually, aurally, and mobility-impaired students. The social embarrassment of arriving late, disrupting classes to get to reserved places, being placed by faculty in a conspicuous, isolated spot or of having to get up and move periodically to relieve discomfort, added to the difficulties they faced in getting to class.

The University System of Accommodation and Support

As the discussion of mobility-related problems suggests, it is difficult to understand the problems of students with disabilities solely in terms of the constraints which arise from the nature of their disability or its treatment because condition-related problems inevitably draw the student into conflict with certain physical, institutional or attitudinal aspects of the university as a social organization. The university has sought to meet the problems of those disabling conditions of which it is aware by changing aspects of its architecture, facilities and administration. To meet needs created by all types of disabilities, the University of Minnesota has established a set of policies, processes and services administered by Disability Services (DS). The system is intended to accommodate whatever condition-related constraints on educational progress which students with documented disabilities bring to this office. Before continuing to consider other types of problem referenced in Table 2, it is important to discuss the scope and efficacy of the university's formal provisions for students with disabilities.

The assistance of the Disabiltiy Services staff and other services are available to all students who have documented disabilities. Unfortunately, as is suggested in Table 2, some students did not know Disability Services existed and did not know what it offered. This was most likely to happen when an illness or accident occurred after entry to the university. Nine undergraduates who reported late-onset disabilities were, until invited for interview, unaware that the university offered any services to students with disabilities, and were surprised to find that Disability Services knew about them. Two of these did not know that they had been registered and assumed this must have been done directly by off-campus agencies. None of this group were using the services available to them, although they had unresolved problems with which Disability Services could have helped. Two more students had documented their disability later on because, initially, they got the help they needed by informal negotiation with faculty and only went to Disability Services when these arrangements broke down.

Another group knew about Disability Services, but experienced difficulty in getting the formal documentation required for eligibility for reasonable accommodations. Nine undergraduates reported that the high cost of professional disability evaluation was an absolute bar. Five of these students, with conditions requiring a complex testing process, reported the cost of professional evaluation to be approximately $1,000. Eight other students described the difficulties they had experienced in getting their doctors to give a sufficiently clear diagnosis of their condition for registration purposes. This kind of problem arose for disabilities (such as post-traumatic stress syndrome) which were less well-known to the family doctors they initially approached. Four others reported that they used their documented disability to get help with problems caused by a second, non-documented, disability.

Late diagnosis was reported as the cause of registration difficulties by 17 undergraduate and graduate students: their conditions encompassed learning disabilities, illnesses, surgeries, accidental injuries, and mental or neurological conditions. Some students with learning disabilities received no formal diagnosis of their condition until after college entry. In high school, they had learned to compensate for their difficulties in various ways. Once at university, however, they were unable to circumvent complex writing tasks, or the foreign language requirement. Some with mental and neurological conditions, and with slow-onset chronic illnesses, had been unsure that they had a "medical" problem, or had found it hard to come to terms with their disability. For some, formal diagnosis came as a relief. Because of late diagnosis and registration, this group had experienced delays and set-backs in the early stages of their undergraduate education, difficulties in getting financial aid, and flawed academic records (especially failed or uncompleted classes) which they felt reflected their difficulties rather than their abilities.

The majority of the participants who both knew about Disability Services and used them reported that a record of their documented disability had been automatically transferred from high school, community or vocational colleges, or that they had been predisposed to use Disability Services because of good experiences with disability services in community colleges.

A different reason for either not documenting a disability, or not using Disability Services, was the pervasive issue of fear of disclosure. Twenty-four of the undergraduates described disclosure of their disability on campus as the "price that they paid" for getting the accommodations that they needed. Those who were able to "pass" (visually) as not having a disability would have preferred not to disclose their condition on campus, but knew that faculty were (quite reasonably) likely to ask them to present their request through formal Disability Services channels. Although using these procedures made the granting of an accommodation more certain, what these students feared were adverse faculty or peer comments about the "unfairness" of test accommodations. To protect themselves from the adverse reactions of class peers, I.T. faculty might arrange their accommodations in such a way that other students could not know of them. This was (as we shall later discuss) not always done. Some students with more than one disability, chose, when asking faculty for help, to disclose only one condition; that is, whichever disability they thought faculty would accept as a "valid" reason for their request. On the other hand, disclosure to Disability Services staff in a "safe," confidential setting was described as a great relief to students who had otherwise sought to keep their condition private. We found no evidence to support Ellis' (1992) suggestion that the increase in numbers of students reporting a disability between freshman and senior years was caused, in part, by an increased willingness of students with disabilities to identify themselves over time. Most students expressed a strong preference for non-disclosure (where feasible), except as a means to get accommodations. We discuss the participants' experiences with stigma, and the dilemma of disclosure to current or prospective employers later in this report.

Overall, as Table 2 indicates, the problems arising from difficulties of knowing what services are available, and disclosing and documenting a disability in order to gain access to Disability Services, account for 8.2% of all problems reported by current and former I.T. undergraduates. Not using Disability Services, and failure to overcome personal difficulties about asking the Disability Services staff for help, accounted for a further 7.5% of reported difficulties.

Disability Services is only one of a number of agencies with which students with disabilities negotiate the help they need in order to complete a degree. On campus, the most important of these is the financial aid office. As Table 2 indicates, and as we shall later discuss in detail, problems in securing adequate financial help (from all sources) was the participants' second most frequently-cited type of problem. Off-campus agencies which governed the level of students' financial support were: the state Vocational Rehabilitation Service, and the Social Security and Workman's Compensation systems.

Students pointed to a number of problems with off-campus financing agencies which had negative consequence for their educational access. Prominent among these were the discretionary nature of the financial aid decisions made by the state Vocational Rehabilitation agency, and a general difficulty in finding which agencies offered what kinds of provisions to which students with disabilities in what circumstances. They looked to Disability Services for help in dealing with the gaps and inconsistencies in what often appeared to them as an incoherent, often unfair, jumble of off-campus agency provisions.

There were also 51 complaints about what students saw as the university's lack of a coherent, comprehensive, accessible system of information and aid to students with disabilities, including financial aid. Knowing what was available in time to make the best use of it was a recurrent theme in this type of complaint. For example, a number of students with disabilities did not know, at the time of interview, that they could register early for classes by computer or that they could get "over-rides" for particular classes. (This was especially important where students needed classes at particular times of day, or in particular locations, for reasons related to their disabilities.) The participants strongly recommended that the university produce a handbook giving a clear statement of its policy with respect to students with disabilities, a comprehensive and coherent explanation of the services offered, and of the formal procedures to be followed in relation to accommodation. The DSCC participants suggested that handbooks should be sent to all students with documented disabilities, be readily available at the Disability Services office and at other locations (such as the Students' Union, the Disabled Students' Cultural Center, and departmental offices). A copy should also be sent to every faculty member, and to all administrative and departmental staff.

This common complaint is a source of considerable frustration to Disability Services, which has, since 1980, produced brochures and newsletters describing their services, and has sent these to all students with documented disabilities, and displayed them in Admissions, and other administrative and collegiate offices. Despite these efforts, the problem of reaching students with a consolidated source of information and guidance clearly remains.

Many of the problems which students took to Disability Services were those which they had been unable to resolve themselves, and which required negotiation between Disability Services staff and other agencies. On-campus negotiations undertaken by Disability Services staff were mostly with individual faculty or deans concerning accommodations, or with university administration (e.g., to secure the availability of particular classes or rooms). Both the success of Disability Services staff, and of the students themselves, in getting their requests to administrators met is reflected in the very small number of complaints (N=4) about the university administration. The positive contribution of university staff is indicated in Table 3 as 4.0% of all sources of help cited by the participants.[18] A comparison of the Disability Services-related items on Tables 2 and 3 also indicates a high level of satisfaction with Disability Services, its director, and staff, who are credited as the source of approximately one-third of the help which they had received, and only 2.0% of their dissatisfactions. (The other, non-financial, sources of help which are summarized in Table 3, are discussed in Chapter Three.) Students with experience of other institutions of higher education reported they had found fewer (or no) services for students with disabilities at other colleges or universities. As is suggested in Table 1, the university's good reputation of support for students with disabilities was a factor in some participants' choice of this institution. Only those with experience of one local community college (Normandale) reported more extensive institutional services than those encountered at the University of Minnesota.[19]

---

[18]Table 3 shows the relative importance of different sources of non-financial support as reported by the current and former undergraduates with disabilities interviewed for this study. Some of these are commented upon in this chapter; the balance are discussed in Chapter Three.

[19]For example, Normandale College's provisions included a free diagnostic service for all students who had, or suspected that they had, some form of learning disability.

Table 3. Sources of (non-financial) help in completing undergraduate degrees: by number and percent of all sources of help reported by all disabled students in the University of Minnesota sample (N=65).

Sources of Help	N. of Times Reported	% of All Times Reported
UNIVERSITY SERVICES FOR STUDENTS WITH DISABILITIES	**(136)**	**(28.9)**
Disability Services (help with accommodations)	70	14.9
Disability Services ("counseling")	48	10.2
Disability Services career/job placement	12	2.5
TRIO (General College) services to "students at risk"	6	1.3
PEERS/STUDENT ASSOCIATIONS	**(119)**	**(25.3)**
Disabled students cultural center	63	13.4
Peers with disabilities	30	6.4
Class peers without disabilities	18	3.8
Mature student peers	6	1.3
Other student organizations (honors society, fraternity)	2	0.4
ACADEMIC SUPPORT	**(81)**	**(17.2)**
SMET faculty generally helpful	19	4.0
SMET faculty sometimes helpful, sometimes not	15	3.2
SMET faculty offer qualified help	13	2.8
Faculty advisors	12	2.5
Liberal arts faculty generally helpful	10	2.1
Tutors (university, I.T.)--especially learning disabilities	7	1.5
TAs (I.T.)	5	1.1
PERSONAL SUPPORT NETWORK	**(72)**	**(15.3)**
Family-of-origin/family-of-marriage)	44	9.3
Friends	16	3.4
Mentors (disabled graduates, friends)	12	2.6
UNIVERSITY: SYSTEM & STAFF	**(17)**	**(3.6)**
Practical help from the university or department administrative staff	7	1.5
Improved physical access to buildings	4	0.9
Class registration system for disabled students	4	0.9
Usefulness of particular facilities available to all students	2	0.4
OTHER SOURCES OF HELP	**(46)**	**(9.8)**
Department of Vocational Rehabilitation counsellors	14	3.0
Doctors, therapists/therapeutic groups	14	3.0
Societies for people with specific disabilities	5	1.1
The law (existence/implementation of ADA)	4	0.9
Lawyers (with appeals against refusal of financial help)	3	0.6
Community college faculty and advisors	3	0.6
Community services (e.g., transport)	3	0.6
TOTALS	**471**	**100.0**

The two most-valued aspects of the Disability Services' work were, help in getting appropriate test accommodations and regular, supportive relationships with specific Disability Services staff members. With respect to tests (and other forms of assignment), what students with disabilities mostly needed was extra time and a quiet place in which to complete the work. In response to requests for test accommodations, the Disability Services staff followed a formal procedure. Requests commensurate with the limitations of particular disabilities, and with accommodations given to other students with similar difficulties, are presented to faculty by the student who must give sufficient notice for the accommodations to be arranged. Their requests are accompanied by a letter from Disability Services stating the exact nature and conditions of the accommodation required. Students can take tests for which they have been granted extra time (or other accommodations) at the Disability Services testing center, where they are strictly monitored. Faculty are asked to send test papers in a sealed envelop to the Disability Services proctor, who returns the completed exams to faculty, and affirms that the conditions governing the accommodation have been met. Accommodation requests to faculty do not reference the nature of the student's disability—only that he or she has a documented disability, and that this request has been approved by Disability Services in accordance with university policy. Where faculty are reluctant to grant some or all of a Disability Services' accommodation request, a Disability Services staff member seeks to negotiate its terms with the faculty member directly. Where the test accommodation process worked smoothly, students expressed considerable satisfaction with the system. Taking their tests in a quiet room at the Disability Services offices circumvented the problem of faculty arranging separate tests in unsuitable or disruptive settings. (Students described occasions when they had been required by faculty to take tests in their offices, or those of TAs, general departmental offices, photocopy rooms and storage closets.)

Other services and accommodations arranged by Disability Services, and which students with disabilities cited as of special value to them, included: arranging priority registration for particular classes; pre-registration (which allowed greater pre-planning of class schedules); changing inaccessible or remote class or examination rooms; arranging the services of a scribe (with particular knowledge of the subject matter and related symbols) for students in need of temporary or permanent help in written tests and examinations; arranging readers (also subject-specific) to assist with tests and some lab work for students who were blind, or who had low vision; arranging interpreters for deaf students; getting text books recorded before the start of a new class (a service used by students with disabilities of several different kinds); helping students withdraw from classes that presented more problems than they could deal with, by assignment of "incompletes" (rather than Fs), which they could redeem the following quarter; help in locating particular forms of assistive technological aids (e.g., closed-circuit magnification devices, computer screen monoculars and screen enlargement programs). Some technical aids (e.g., a voice-activated computer) were not yet available, but students had found it more productive to search for them with the help of the Disability Services staff than on their own. Some other services suggested by the students included: organization of car-pooling between different areas of the university on a quarter-long basis; and tutoring in keyboard/typing, and use of computer adaptations and special computer programs.

A common need for students with learning disabilities was help from tutors with knowledge of the mathematics or science needed for a particular class. The university offers general tutoring services, but these were reported not to be geared to the needs of those with learning disabilities. Students reported confusion between separate campus-wide, departmental and Disability Services tutorial services, and difficulty in getting the particular kind of help they needed. Nine of the undergraduates reported they recruited and paid for tutors themselves. Students suggested organizing paid or volunteer tutors from among other students with disabilities with the same or similar discipline.

An additional source of free tutorial help was provided by the university's General College to those students who fit the criteria for the TRIO program (i.e., those who are learning-disabled, first-generation undergraduates, and with low incomes). This program also offers study sessions, and negotiation of test accommodations with General College faculty. The six students with learning disabilities who reported using TRIO had been pleased to find that the tutors understood their specific difficulties, and that access to tutorial help was relatively simple and straightforward. It was not, however, available to SMET majors in the Institute of Technology.

Disability Services also offers a Career Connections program, as a three-course career development sequence for graduation credit available to students with documented disabilities. It offers career exploration and planning, and teaches job seeking and job keeping skills, followed by an internship experience (which can also be undertaken independent of other elements in the program). Participants are connected with a mentor in their field of interest, with whom they meet regularly, and from whom they also learn about career opportunities. The program also assists students looking for employment, whether as students or graduates, discusses with them the job accommodations they may need, and how to go about getting them. Disability Services has, however, experienced some difficulty in promoting awareness of the program, and getting students to take advantage of it. They recently added an on-line computer service which allows students to learn of job opportunities offered by employers who wish to encourage application from graduates with disabilities. The relatively small number of students reporting that they had tried this service had found it valuable, because it avoids the dilemma of whether or not to disclose their disability to a prospective employer. (This issue is further discussed in Chapter Four.)

The most serious and frequently-raised problems with Disability Services concerned what one student described as "faculty sabotage" of test accommodations that had already been arranged through the official process. Students described instances where: test papers were not sent to the Disability Services proctor; the wrong test paper had been sent; last minute alterations or corrections to test questions were communicated to students in the main test sitting, but not to those at the Disability Services test center; where faculty had insisted that they take the test under their direct supervision or in a room where they were subject to noise or periodic interruption; and where deans or departmental chairs over-ruled accommodations that had already been set up. Seven students with average or above average performance scores reported that faculty who had reluctantly granted them test accommodations had subsequently encouraged them to drop the class or change their major. Most students felt there was little that the Disability Services staff could do when faculty refused outright to give the accommodation requested, delayed granting it, sabotaged it or gave a lower grade for work done under accommodation conditions than for the same level of work done by students without disabilities. This belief was widespread, despite the actual power of Disability Services to insist on the implementation of an accommodation they have determined as reasonable, and where the request was presented in a timely manner. Students also felt that Disability Services might not have the power to rectify computer errors in their academic records or, in two cases, accidental dis-enrollment, including loss of student medical insurance. They also noted some variability in the quality of Disability Services staff, difficulties in getting appointments (with presumptions of under-staffing, given the high level of demand), and uneven treatment of apparently similar requests—depending on which staff member one happened to see on a particular day. As a comparison of Tables 2 and 3 indicates, overall, the total number of concerns or complaints about Disability Services were far outweighed by students' appreciation of the Disability Services system and staff. The contribution made by other aspects of the work of Disability Services to the persistence of SMET majors with disabilities is discussed and illustrated in Chapter Three.

As Table 2 indicates, the two major types of difficulty which, taken together, affected all participants to some degree, were financial difficulties and problems arising directly or indirectly from negative attitudes of I.T. faculty towards accommodations for students with disabilities. A considerable proportion of the time which Disability Services staff spent in helping students with disabilities appears to be focused on seeking ways around one or the other of these two kinds of problems. This emphasis is ironic: the formal powers and duties of Disability Services specifically exclude a financial aid function,

56

and the formality of the university's accommodation procedure makes it hard to predict that so much time would need to be spent on dealing with faculty attempts to undermine the efficacy of the official university system. In the following sections we discuss the source and nature of these two types of problems.

Sources of Educational Funding and Financial Difficulties

As Table 2 indicates, financial problems in completing either undergraduate or graduate degrees at the Institute of Technology were the second most commonly-cited form of difficulty (alongside those created by the disabilities themselves) and accounted for 11.2% of all types of problem in degree completion. Table 4 summarizes the sources of financial support of current undergraduates and graduate students in the Institute of Technology (N=45). Though students drew upon different sources of income to meet their education and living costs at different stages in their higher education, the most common long-term source of funds (i.e., 40% of all reported funding) was their own paid work. Approximately two-thirds (N=25; 62% of the 41 current undergraduates) were working at the time of interview. Eleven of these were employed full-time (i.e., 40 hours or more); 10 were employed part-time; and four were self-employed. Three of the four graduate students were working: two (both with low vision) were doing work-study jobs for the university; one was self-employed; the fourth (who had cerebral palsy) was supported largely by his family. A total of 12 current and former undergraduates and graduates had started their own businesses—six of which were still in operation—as a way to support themselves through school.

All of the working undergraduates with disabilities faced the problem of balancing their working hours with the demands both of their academic work, and of the agencies offering them financial assistance. These problems are familiar to many undergraduates. They are, however, exacerbated by disabling conditions which restrict the type of work and level of remuneration students can command and/or the percentage of full-time academic work which they can realistically undertake:

Table 4. Sources of financial assistance with costs of completing SMET majors: by number and percent of all sources of income reported by undergraduate and graduate students with disabilities at the Institute of Technology, the University of Minnesota (N=45).

Sources of Financial Support	N. of Students Reporting Type of Support	% Contribution Each Type of Support
STUDENTS' FULL-TIME OR PART-TIME EMPLOYMENT	(28)	(40.0)
PUBLIC FUNDS	(22)	(31.4)
Educational (i.e., financial aid, Department of Vocational Rehabilitation); state scholarship	17	24.3
Social services: unemployment/welfare benefit, social security	5	7.1
FAMILY MAJOR CONTRIBUTOR	(10)	(14.3)
WORKMEN'S COMPENSATION	(5)	(7.1)
MINORITY SCHOLARSHIP (university)	(2)	(2.9)
VETERAN'S ADMINISTRATION BENEFIT	(2)	(2.9)
DISABILITY SOCIETY SCHOLARSHIP	(1)	(1.4)
TOTALS	70	100.0

Right now, the only source of financing I have is me working and paying my tuition, paying my other bills. And I also have to support my family outside of school. So it's been pretty rough...Right now I'm taking some pretty tough classes, but I try to work 40 hours. When I first got here, I was working 50 hours a week.

I worked two jobs, three jobs, and was...paying out of pocket. I think that hurt my grades. It sure didn't help. I ended up with them dismissing me...They said I could come back in a year.

Some have chosen to go to school full-time and take on a load of debt...Some choose to work full-time and go to school part-time. Others choose to work part-time 'cause the salary is okay, and to go to school full-time. Then there's a group of us who just have no choice: we have to work full-time and go to school full-time…And I find that's pretty consistent when you get to the older students.

That so high a proportion of the funding for students with disabilities comes from their own paid work and so little from funds ear-marked for them because of their disabilities is, perhaps, surprising. Only four participants had been given scholarships: one received a state scholarship for high academic performance in high school; a second received a scholarship from a trust fund for blind students; and two students of color received scholarships which targeted minority (though not disabled) students with good high school performances. The five participants with low vision were the only group who reported relatively trouble-free access to disability-related funds: one (as above) had received a disability scholarship; all had received tuition waivers offered by the university to students with blindness and low vision; and the state services for the blind gave them some help with living expenses. The two blind participants who entered graduate school found that this provision ceased after completion of their undergraduate degree.

Other sources of disability-related funds were: Workman's Compensation, and Veterans' Administration (VA) disability benefits, which were received by seven of the participants who had been injured in the course of their work or military service; and discretionary grants of variable size and duration from the state Department of Vocational Rehabilitation (DVR). Undergraduates who received Workman's Compensation or a VA benefit saw themselves as financially better off than most students with disabilities. However, the five Workman's Compensation recipients described hard fights (including legal action in two instances) and many delays (up to two years for one injured worker) to establish their entitlement to compensation, and some restrictions in the educational costs for which the fund would pay. Two of this group also reported difficulty and delay in getting the insurance companies who control disbursement of Workman's Compensation funds to meet the medical bills arising from their injuries.

Funds for tuition and books were provided by the state Department of Vocational Rehabilitation to some undergraduates with disabilities who had sought their help. The main problem reported by the

19 undergraduates who had approached the DVR for financial assistance was the discretionary nature of their awards—including considerable variation in their amounts and duration. Whether or not an applicant was granted some level of financial help with their higher education costs was thought to depend on the counselor to which they were assigned, and on the nature of their disability:

> It seems like they just gambled a little bit of money on me in the first place, and then, toward the end, I was getting more than at the beginning.

> I learned my very first quarter that what people received in the long-term is totally arbitrary. It has little to do with needs and/or qualifications. And much more it seems to be a personality issue between yourself and whichever counselor you're dealing with.

> It's really strange...Some people are only allowed $100 every quarter, but they're paying me $1000 for one quarter for books, fees, tuition, bus passes and stuff. I feel this isn't really fair. Maybe they pay me more because my only other alternative is loans—but I guess lots of other people are in that situation, too.

DVR counselors were believed to discriminate against students with certain types of disability, especially mental, emotional and learning disabilities, and chemical dependency. We discovered that one undergraduate with epilepsy had received DVR help with her university tuition, while a second received no indication from her DVR counselor that she might be eligible for aid. Three students who had originally been denied or given minimal financial help by particular DVR counselors got more assistance when they changed counselors. Two students reported that DVR counselors had refused to give them any financial help; a third had won a lawsuit for discrimination against the DVR and was now receiving tuition assistance:

> The net outcome of what began that fall was a lawsuit that I pressed against the DVR which was settled two years later...The best thing was that I received a change of counselor and the awards got much better. But it was an incredibly difficult first year.

Students also complained that the help they had been offered was for very short periods. DVR counselors advised some students to choose less academically-rigorous institutions (particularly, community and vocational colleges) regardless of good academic performances. One student who disregarded this advice lost her DVR tuition grant when she transferred from community college to the Institute of Technology.

The DVR did not offer help with living expenses: these were left to the financial aid system or to the student's own earnings. In matters unconnected with the disbursement of funds, 12 students reported practical help from DVR counselors, including encouragement to enter higher education and help in discovering or co-ordinating services offered by other agencies. One student had been enabled to document her disability with the university because the DVR had paid the cost of medical examinations.

With respect to financial help from other public sources, four undergraduates were receiving assistance from Social Security. They had found the process of establishing a claim to be slow and difficult, and described their problems of financial survival until entitlement was established:

> Right now I'm working with Social Security people trying to qualify for Social Security under disability. Unfortunately, they're giving me the big run-around on that, too. The biggest problem I've got to solve right now is getting money to live. I own a house, but I can't afford to live in it any more.

Five undergraduates had found "informal" ways to get financial help from public funds: three were receiving Welfare payments, not because of their disabilities, but because they were single mothers with small children; and two students, who had been laid off by their employers for reasons unrelated to their disabilities, were drawing unemployment benefit. All of those receiving public funds reported they were inadequate to meet basic needs. They needed to work to supplement their benefits, but risked losing their aid if the fact of their employment were known to the public agency. This also limited the kinds of work they could undertake:

> Of course, once I'm on Social Security I'll have some support whether I go to school or not. But, if I make more than $500, I run the risk of losing it. A part-time job would knock me out. So I can't work at all. It's kind of the same trap the Welfare people run into. Either you have to be completely dependent or you fend entirely for yourself. There's no in-between.

> If you make $500 in any month, then you're considered working, and you're no longer —according to Social Security—'disabled'. Disabled means you make less than $500 a month; 'non-disabled' is anybody making more than $500 a month.

> I do things on the side to keep me going—unofficially. Unfortunately, that's the only way, right now, I can survive...They put limits on what you can earn. And that makes it very difficult to live and work and to go to school.

The main difficulty of students who sought financial help through the university's financial aid office was that the rules under which this system is administered make no allowance for the difficulties which students with disabilities face in trying to undertake the full class load which is required of all financial aid recipients. The nature of their condition, its variability or unpredictability, the effects of particular medications, problems of fatigue, and difficulties of transportation and mobility, conspire to make a full compliment of classes very difficult or impossible for many students with disabilities. Taking a full load in order to qualify for financial aid very commonly creates a pattern of "incompletes," failures and withdrawals, which has a number of negative consequences, including refusal of the student's next application for financial aid:

> I was granted a student loan...But they required a minimum of 12 credits for course work, so I took three classes this fall. Unfortunately it proved to be too much and I ended up having to drop all three classes.

> To get the full quarter's loan, I had to take twelve credits minimum, which proved too much for me...So thanks to some of the harder times with my condition, I'm also making up incompletes —that is, I have to start over from scratch. So I'm trying to take six credits and do those back ones too. And I need to do that for financial aid. It's that or trying to work when I'm really not capable of that. With this disability, I just can't do that.

> You may not be able to handle the full load. And, if you have to work too, that makes the burden even more difficult.

> It's a Catch-22. If you don't go full-time, you have to start repaying student loans. So I'd have to have a second job to pay off the loans at the same time as I was going to school and paying for that schooling. If I could get the full loan, I wouldn't have to be doing that...At one stage, I ended up with three jobs, and it just nickels and dimes your time away.

> I'd go to the financial aid people and I'd say, 'But don't you understand? I have two children that I care for...I can't do what you're asking me to do. And even if I could, your funding only covers maybe 40 percent of overall need.' And they'd say, 'Well, that's just the way it goes. Struggle on.' And so I did—borrowing from friends, and working when I could. It's kind of hard talking about it right now. It brings back some old pain.

The students who described this dilemma argued they could have maintained a "clean" academic record, and would have spent less time, energy and money in repeating classes, had they been allowed to work at a pace commensurate with the constraints of their condition.

The financial aid system also created problems for those mature, returning students who had received aid for higher education at an earlier (pre-disability) stage in their lives, but who were preparing themselves for a career shift appropriate to a recently acquired disability. Three students in this situation were refused financial aid, one of whom had registered a formal appeal. Dealing with flaws in their academic record (some of which were a consequence of trying to meet financial aid requirements) and disputes with faculty over lower grades given for work done under accommodated conditions, were typical of the problems which students described in relation to financial aid.

Ironically, none of the 23 participants (i.e., approximately one-third of the sample) who described these types of problems was aware that Disability Services can, as a matter of reasonable accommodation, determine that some extra educational costs encountered by students with disabilities can be met by financial aid.[20] Also, where a student cannot take a full class load for disability-related reasons for which they can offer documented support, a part-time load can be defined as a full-time load for financial aid purposes. In such situations, the award for fees, tuition and living expenses is proportionately reduced. However, as part-time students still have the same living expenses to meet as full-time students, the amount awarded for living expenses can be negotiated between the student, Disability Services and the financial aid liaison officer. Only one of those students who had experienced difficulties with financial aid had received assistance from a financial aid officer in arranging a financial package for a part-time class load. She did not, however, know this person was acting in an official role. The other 22 participants were unaware of the existence of a liaison officer within the financial aid office. Again, a combination of: reluctance to disclose a hidden disability to university administrators; the general lack of knowledge of existing services which we encountered among students with disabilities; their isolation from each other; diffidence about "bothering" Disability Service staff with problems which were believed

---

[20]Only three of the blind students, none of whom had experienced difficulties with financial aid, were aware of these provisions.

to lie beyond their scope, coupled with a preference for coping independently; and the commonly-expressed belief that Disability Services did not have the power to insist on the implementation of whatever accommodations they had determined to be "reasonable," may explain why the university's provision in this regard was not working as intended.

The graduate students, and some of the graduates considering a return to graduate school, recounted the longer-term consequences of the problems they had experienced as undergraduates in keeping a clean academic record during periods of ill-health or when attempting more classes than they could manage in order to get financial aid: it was more difficult to get into graduate school, or to secure a teaching or research assistantship with a flawed academic transcript. None of the graduate students thought there were any specific financial aid provisions for graduate students with disabilities.

The students reported that the officers of the financial aid system appeared to be aware that the rules within which they had to work did not meet the special problems of students with disabilities, but that they seemed powerless to waive, adjust or amend them:

> They are aware of this, but they can't do anything about it...The effort required to solve the problem is too great for anybody to want to tackle it...They throw up their hands and just say,'I can't do anything about it.'

As already indicated, the most commonly-expressed general concern of students with disabilities about the services that might be available to them was the difficulty of finding out who offered them, what they offered, how they should apply and whether they qualified. Financial aid was seen as one part of an incoherent, piecemeal, non-system for the disbursement of public funds, in which the particular needs and constraints of students with disabilities had not been acknowledged. Students were frustrated by the apparent thwarting of their attempts to get reliable information about what might be available to them, and sometimes suspected deliberate obfuscation on the part of financial aid officers. They found the demand for repeated applications and presentation of documents exhausting, and assumed it was intended to discourage them from persisting:

I guess the whole area is still kind of a mystery. 'Cause they say there's all this money available, but I was never really able to find it...It just never really materialized.

It seemed like the only way I could get to hear about the resources that might be available to me, was if I was in crisis. And then he would tell me about something. I don't know why he has to wait that long, or why it's such a secret...They were doing tests to determine who could qualify as learning disabled. And, because the funds were so tight, they raised the qualifications as to what you had to get on the test in order to be considered learning disabled. That doesn't mean the person has any less need. It just means that they're not going to help that person. It seems to me that there's a lot of secrets and they really only want, you know, a few people to take advantage...That's a strong supposition.... I mean, realistically we don't know that's exactly going on. But it sure looks like that.

I don't know why it's such a secret. It seems like they're so afraid of people taking advantage, or finding that there's too many people that actually need financial aid.

Finally, it took going to the head of the financial aid office, and saying, 'I've done what you've asked of me. And I've done it repeatedly. Here are the letters...You've either lost them or your people have chosen not to act.' Going to see her improved things in the following year. But it was only temporary. They send you through it over and over and over again, until you're so exhausted that pursuing it further seems meaningless.

It's the people who are the most persistent, or just damn lucky, who get the money. It's like they're pitting disabled students against each other in a contest for funds.

The financial aid system was also viewed as out of touch with the needs of the current student population, which contains an increased proportion of mature students, including those with disabilities:

It's geared towards an 18 year-old coming out of high school, living with parents that are not too badly off, where you work mainly to increase your level of comfort, not as a matter of survival. And the whole university system in the country is based on that assumption.

In order to be able to plan their progress through a degree program at a pace commensurate with their condition, students with disabilities felt that they needed a clear, coherent, accessible and flexible system of provisions which disburses public funds in ways that accommodate the different ages, life circumstances, needs and constraints of disabled undergraduate and graduate students. In default of such a system, 80.5% of the disabled undergraduates (N=33) and three out of the four graduate students, described themselves as being in serious financial difficulty, including two students who were temporarily out of school, in part, because of financial problems. Their specific concerns included the institutional costs of undertaking the degree, which, as they pointed out, are often higher for students with, than without, disabilities. This is partly because they may have to work at a slower pace or repeat classes, and partly because of the extra costs of study aids (e.g., computer software), alternative format materials for private study and special services (especially tutors), which they meet from their own resources.[21] Medical bills, and medication costs were also an extra cost for which six students with disabilities who lacked, or had lost, medical insurance were paying directly:

> The big factor right through my education has been economic. It's like $35 to $50 a month, easily, in medication costs...That's probably the biggest concern...The cost of that particular medication was $156 a month, which was a killer. I had to give it up—even against my doctor's recommendation—simply because I couldn't afford it...And then my blood pressure got elevated, which affected my ability to work and earn money. So I was forced out of college for a time...I remember doing financial aid forms when I first went to college and they'd send them back to me saying, 'Are you sure this figure of $2,400 a year for medical care is correct?' But it was right.

> The things you have to spend your money on are so expensive. When you go to a neurologist, you're not talking $10 an hour, you're talking from $100 to $200 an hour.

> I dis-enrolled from one class, and even though I was still taking summer school, the university computer dis-enrolled me from medical insurance...I told them, 'I have to have this school insurance.' Before I found out what had happened, I had got treatment from the Boynton (university) Health Services. The first I knew, I got a bill for $700. The university doesn't feel it's their fault, and Boynton doesn't either. So besides losing my home, and going on welfare and accepting charity, I also have this $700 bill which I have no hope of repaying. Disability Services can't help me. As far as I can tell, there's nobody who can help me....I can't even pay my rent, and right now, I'm living for free at someone else's charity...If they didn't do that, I'd have to give away everything I have left and be homeless. I spent all my resources on my health and on going to school. I had $20,000 when I came to Minnesota, and I don't have anything now.

Two of the graduates also pointed to a long-term risk of managing without medical insurance because of temporary or contracted employee status. Those undergraduates who had been laid off work for reasons unrelated to their disabilities, emphasized the special vulnerability of displaced disabled workers to loss of medical insurance:

---

[21]With the exception of tutors, if Disability Services deem any of these to be "reasonable accommodations," the costs will be met from institutional funds. Again, most students were, apparently, unaware of this.

I wasn't eligible for medical assistance, because I'd just got laid off, and you have to be without health coverage for three months before you can get medical assistance, so I was in that three-month waiting period.

As financial aid was the only source of help with living expenses available to most of the students with disabilities, and, for reasons explained above, students with disabilities found it especially difficult to get, the majority of our informants reported that they were largely dependent on what they could earn or borrow to finance their university education. Some students with disabilities were unable to work at all because of constraints imposed by their conditions. Those who worked, but were limited in the types of work and pay they could get, worked longer hours than students without disabilities to earn comparable amounts of income, and were, thus, forced back onto an even greater reliance upon student loans than were students without disabilities. The burden of debt awaiting them on graduation, whether by loans or borrowing from family and friends, was a pervasive source of anxiety:

> I've had no income for the last five years and very little for the last 10 years. So my parents have supported me the whole way. They've gone through all the money they had saved for 60 years and....I've borrowed tons. *Tons* of money. I'm very deeply in debt. So that's why it's pretty important that I do really well.

> I don't have the money to spare. Since I've been here, my credit rating has gone down...because of the financial pressures.

> I'm going to have to go to work right away...I'm so...deeply strapped financially that it's a surprise that I'll be able to finish. And that's part of the reason I'm going through this so fast, is because the money is just not there.

> I guess, right now, I'm so poor that I can't even see out of the hole...I went that far under. (Engineering undergraduate temporarily out of school)

Nine of the undergraduates and one of the graduate students cited their families as major contributors in meeting their educational and living expenses:

> I consider myself very lucky. If I had a different family, or my family were in a different financial situation, I wouldn't be here. I would not have had this opportunity at all. I think money is the critical issue for most disabled people...I'm getting minimal help from other sources. Without my family, I'd have to worry whether or not I could afford the book for this or that class. They make the difference that's just enough to get me through. The line between making it and not making it is very fine.

I can't carry a full load of classes because I can't learn as quickly as others. So right there I lose some financial aid...The money issue is probably the saddest part because, most of the time, you can't do anything with that. Money is the most critical issue—it's the most difficult to work out. I have to admit, I wouldn't be able to be here if I weren't getting help from my family. I couldn't do it on my own.

Among male undergraduates, over half (N=16; 55.2%) were mature students, and wives were a more common source of financial support than parents. Two-thirds (N=8; 66.6%) of the female undergraduates were mature students, of whom five were divorced and three were single parents. These women described the negative effects of late-onset disabilities on marriages. Only one of the 14 female undergraduates was receiving financial support from a husband.

Not surprisingly, many students saw insufficient financial help with educational, living and (in some cases) medical, expenses as the most serious barrier to university education for students with disabilities. They described—often in terms of anger and humiliation—their difficulties in navigating the qualification and application processes of all types of public funding agencies—the state Division of Vocational Rehabilitation, Social Security and welfare, the financial aid system, Workman's Compensation, and the Veterans' Administration. Recurring themes in these accounts were: these agencies' failure to inform them of the financial options open to them; delay; the over-use of discretion in granting provision; and forcing applicants with disabilities through administrative processes not equipped to deal with them:

Nobody ever told me I could apply. Then, finally, one counselor said to me, 'This is a disability—you can apply for a disability grant. I have all kinds of money and can let you go to school for free and take one class a quarter.'...If I had known this, instead of falling behind for that whole year, not being able to complete a whole quarter, getting all messed up with financial aid, struggling so hard, and then having all these incompletes to finish...(begins to cry) I could have just plugged away one course at a time.

As far as the service is concerned, their idea is to keep their costs down as low as possible, and make sure no one is screwing them over in regards to a supposed disability...The government looks at you as though, 'Well, he's just a worthless piece of trash now. We used him for what he was worth, and we'll see you later. Have a nice day.'

When you apply for general assistance, you go into a poorly-funded, poorly-staffed system of people who are over-burdened and think you just need to go out and work. You get to stand in a lot of lines. You wait for long periods of time next to people who haven't bathed—and worse. And you can spend hours or days being sent to the wrong person, the wrong place at the wrong time...It was beyond humiliating, beyond demeaning...I was very nearly suicidal at that time.

At a personal level, financial difficulties were often closely interwoven with issues of time and pacing in the student's academic work. However, the participants felt that the greatest single cause of their financial difficulties was lack of a coherent, accessible, fair and efficient system of public financial provision designed to meet the needs of students with disabilities as a group.

Problems with Science, Mathematics and Engineering Faculty Attitudes

As indicated earlier in this chapter, students with documented disabilities who use the formal, university provisions for accommodations administered by Disability Services reported that the system would have met most of their accommodation needs had SMET faculty not commonly resisted, or refused to grant accommodations, or sabotaged accommodations which had already been arranged. None of the undergraduates recommended changes in the accommodation system itself: when it worked as the university's policy intended, it met their needs. However, as Table 2 indicates, by far the largest proportion (N=282; 20.3%) of the specific problems and complaints raised by undergraduates concerned the actions and attitudes of faculty which, in effect (though not necessarily in intention), impeded academic progress. This finding is not an artifact of the research method. All students were asked about the responses to accommodation requests which they received from faculty both in SMET and non-SMET classes. There were only a handful of complaints about non-SMET faculty, most of whom were reported to be co-operative in following the formal accommodation procedure. It is important, therefore, not only to understand the nature of the problems which students with disabilities encountered with SMET faculty, but also to ask why faculty in these majors tend to resist the granting of accommodations which are accorded by the university's policy and provision.

When undergraduates meet resistance to a formal request for an accommodation from I.T. faculty, the responses they describe are not idiosyncratic, but follow particular patterns which the students have learned to expect and prepare themselves to face with each new encounter. The same set of faculty reactions, arguments, and conditions imposed on accommodations are repeated over and over in individual student's accounts. A response which students had come to dread, was faculty insistence on being given details of the nature of their disability. As explained earlier, the Disability Services letter of request which students take from Disability Services to faculty does not mention the nature of their disability—only that the student has a legitimately documented disability which has been formally recognized by the university and for which the student is legally entitled to receive accommodations. Despite this, students find themselves forced to offer a description of their condition, its cause, and consequences for their academic work. They find this process embarrassing, painful and humiliating. They are also obliged to defend their right to accommodation:

> In some cases, there has been outright hesitation on the part of the instructor...They say, 'Well, I'm confused about this. Why is it that you are requesting these accommodations? Do you get them for your other courses? Did this effect you in your education in the past?'—all of which is disturbing to me, and something I shouldn't have to go into.

> 'Well, I think an hour should be sufficient,' was the reply that I got. Another time it was something about, 'Why should you have more time than everybody else?'...I was often asked, 'Do you have documentation? Do you have written proof of this? Is this on record?'

> My experience has been that they usually want to know why. Sometimes I'll tell them 'It's a chronic illness. It effects my concentration. I have to take medication for it,' you know, if they need some explanation. Because any psychiatric illness, depression, whatever, you get real negative reactions...and if you say you have a psychiatric disability, you know, most people assume you're crazy and you're going to go out and kill people.

Clearly, the whole purpose of this close questioning appears to be to allow faculty to evaluate the student's condition by their own criteria of what constitutes a "valid" disability. This necessarily involves discounting formal professional diagnoses, and replacing them with the professor's lay diagnosis. This relabeling process has two related latent functions: it allows the professor to reach a decision on the 'worthiness' of the student's request; and it provides a moral justification for refusing an accommodation, or for interfering with its effectiveness by limiting or redefining its terms:

> He was okay with the accommodation, but he wanted me to take the last test with the class.

I think in some cases the instructor does a double-take after reading the terms of the accommodation. They say things like, 'Well, gee, you don't *look* disabled,' or 'In my class everyone gets treated the same, so why should you receive these accommodations?'

I'd say half the I.T. faculty I've had, when there are hearing-impaired people in the class, they won't slow their speech down...One particular professor was really awful. He didn't like using the interpreters. They made him nervous. He spoke really fast, and then he wrote really sloppily, so there was no way that I could keep up...I would have no idea what was going on because he would be talking so fast. He just wouldn't slow down. So the interpreter kept missing things. Normally, I just copy off the board whatever is written. But no one could read his writing. And he wouldn't change that either...I tried to talk to him using the relay service. And he said, 'I don't like to use the relay: contact me through e-mail.' I told him I didn't have e-mail. Then he said, 'Well, then we'll have to talk later.' And he rang off. Boom. He was just really hard to work with...I sometimes had no idea where we were or what number of problem we were on, so I start looking really stupid in the class. Then he started questioning whether my interpreter was interpreting correctly, or maybe she wasn't qualified to do a math class. It was really ugly. In all my other math classes I got As, but in that class I got a C. It's really suspicious that my grade would drop that much.[22]

I just want to say, 'That's it. I give up.'...I told her before the class began, 'I am most likely going to need to do some special form of testing to pass this class because I don't think I can do it the regular way.'...And she said, 'Okay. Let's see how it goes to begin with, but if you need it, we'll do something.' But the only thing she did, just on the final exam, she allowed me to look at the test 40 minutes beforehand. And she supposedly gave me 50 extra minutes. But, then she walked in before the end and said, 'I think you've had enough time.'...I'm just so sick of this scenario.

I was not allowed either open-book or notes—just certain types of definitions on formulas, but that's it. There is no way I could pass the course. I couldn't do it. Period. The instructor did not see it as a memory issue—knowing how this formula is related to that formula. And even my psychologist couldn't talk to him. The instructor felt that in order for him to be able to make certain kinds of accommodations, I needed to bring him a person who had both an engineering and a psychologist's background...I'd say *that's* pretty non-existent.

The biggest problem was that they would either forget or just not bother sending the test over when I was supposed to take it. Or there would be errors and mistakes in the tests. If you were in the classroom, people would spot them right away, point them out to the professor, and everybody got that cleared up. When I have a mistake on my test at the testing center, I'm sitting there poring over it, you know, wasting all my time trying to figure out, 'What the heck are they looking for here?' Nobody would bother to call and say, 'Hey, there's an error in this problem.'

---

[22]Every student at the University of Minnesota has an e-mail account. This student was either unaware of this, or did not have a home computer with e-mail capacity.

Students who had known the faculty prior to an illness or accident noticed a strong change in their attitudes towards them now that they had to ask for particular accommodations. Even though the faculty knew their work and level of ability, they acted with suspicion, expressed doubt about the validity of their requests, or conceded them with reluctance.

Students report a number of arguments commonly used by faculty in justifying their refusal of accommodation requests. These include, reframing the student's condition in a way that 'normalizes' it, that is, sets it within the normal range of human problems. Faculty then use their redefinition of the situation as an argument by which to discount the need for accommodation:

> I can see it in their eyes. 'You don't look sick. You look fine. You don't look like you're disabled.' 'Okay. I have both arms and legs and stuff, but if I stay in this classroom, they're not going to work for very long.' (Laughs.) It's difficult, I think, in a lot of cases, for people to accept that there is a disability when you don't look like you have one. And I can understand that. (Undergraduate with an immune system impairment)

> And if you say you have depression, they say, 'Oh, yeah. Everybody gets depressed.' But this is different from that.

> I was having health problems...And so I went to talk to him to tell him that I was concerned that I had missed a class right before the first mid-term because of this. And, right away, he tried to get me to drop the class. He was totally unsympathetic. And he was saying stuff like, 'Well, hey, I think I'm a fair guy. And we all have problems.'...I guess we all do have problems, but ours are a magnitude greater than most other people's.

> Took the first test and did really well on that. But the day before the second mid-term, I had a change in my medication and was really, really sick the day of the mid-term. So I called the professor four hours before the test, and I said, 'Look. I'm having some serious side-effects from my medication...I'm really too sick to come in and take the test. I'd really like to go the doctor.' (Laughs) What followed there is really kind of funny. He said, 'Well, I don't mind students coming in and taking tests early. But I really don't like to give tests late. If you'd come and told me earlier this week that you were....' And then he stopped. 'Cause he was actually going to say, 'If you'd come and told me earlier that you were going to be sick, we could have scheduled it ahead of time.' And then he stopped because he realized that was a dumb thing to say. And I said, 'Well...I could take the test I guess. But, I'm feeling terrible, and I need to see a doctor.' And he said, 'Well, we all have constraints in our lives.'

> I usually say that I have a sleep disorder and it's difficult for me to get somewhere by 10:00 a.m. And, I...I don't care to go into it. I'd have to explain that, 'Well, sometimes it's because of medication, that I just can't get up.' However, if I just say, 'Well, I have a hard time getting up,' then they say, 'Well, so do I some mornings.' And it's like they make it just an everyday occurrence, and suggest that I don't have the stamina or the drive, or I must not care about

school. So they put it back on me, as if it's just my attitude that's the problem—or my laziness...Then he shifted ground and said, 'Have your doctor write to me.' But, it's like, 'Disability Services already wrote to you. Why do I now need to go back to my doctor? It's just more running around!' And so I gave up on that class.

The corollary of this line of argument is to find an alternative explanation for the student's problems by redefining them as evidence of moral flaws, such as laziness, making excuses or seeking special advantage over other students. Students were very familiar with such imputations:

> In my case, they don't really know whether I have a learning disability or something else, so they're probably thinking, 'Oh, this guy is just a slacker, and he's trying to get away with something,' which, given my grades, is obviously not the case.

> Getting instructors to understand that I'm not some lazy, irresponsible person who just can't get up in the morning, that's the difficulty....

Using this rationale, professors place themselves on high moral ground as the defenders of all honest students against those "slackers" who would seek to succeed by gaining an unfair advantage:

> They were like, 'I'm not aware of this. You have to talk to the dean.'...I think a lot of it was, 'I've never had to deal with this before.' And I got a feeling that, 'You are really trying to get away with cheating.' You know what I mean?

Another common argument, used to justify refusal of accommodation requests is that graduates with disabilities will have to function in the working world without help from employers and colleagues. It is, therefore, argued to be short-sighted to make concessions to students with disabilities. Accommodation refusal is presented as a benign form of discipline—a kind of 'tough love'—which forces students with disabilities to compete with other students, and better prepares them for the rigors of a competitive world:

> With the competitive nature of business today, and the stresses that are involved, they think that people with disabilities are just not cut out to handle the strain of the program here, or of employment. I guess that's part of it. I think they also think that this is a highly competitive program and that, somehow, it's not fair to the other students...I guess a lot of the professors also feel that somebody with a disability just doesn't belong in a technical field. That they'd never be able to cut it...When I told my counselor what this professor was doing, he would say, 'Well, don't worry. You're not the only one. We have a lot of students who have a lot of trouble with some of the faculty in the Institute of Technology.'

It should be my choice whether I could or couldn't do it, and I confronted faculty when they raised it. I'll ask, 'Why would you make that assumption?'...But, see, they couldn't come back and say, 'Well, you can't compete,' 'cause I had a 4.0 average. So they didn't know what to do.

Another faculty ploy is to feign lack of awareness of any university accommodation provisions for students with disabilities, and force the student to explain both the system, and their need to use it:

You have some that have gone through it in the past and are knowledgeable about how this works. So when you come in and you...present the form that says, 'I need this kind of an accommodation,' they say, 'Okay, fine.' And they'll work out the details with you. No problem. On the other hand, you'll get other faculty that haven't done it before, and they are unaware of it. I mean, I can't assign blame. But they'll say, 'Wait a minute. Why do you get this? This is unreasonable.'...All kinds of judgments are being made, I think, in the classroom by a faculty who hasn't any insight to...well, let's just say, disability awareness.

He says, 'I don't know anything about this disability stuff. I haven't had any disabled students before, and I've never heard anything from the department. I'm not going to sign anything before I know.' Okay. So I told him, 'If that's the case, then I want you to call this Disability Services counselor who will give you some information. And then I want another appointment with you.' He says, 'No, I can't give you an appointment because I don't have time.' I said, 'I can't come at the same time as other students because I don't want to disclose my disability to them.' And he said, 'Well, you can come or not. If you don't, that's your problem.'

We noted that a minority of undergraduates with disabilities reported that some, most, or all I.T. faculty were normally helpful in meeting their requests for accommodation. What distinguished the accounts of this group of students from all others was that faculty either did not ask "what was the matter with them" or on receiving an answer, conceded the accommodation without further argument or questioning. The salient issue appeared to be that SMET faculty 'approved' certain conditions as 'genuine disabilities', and exercised various degrees of skepticism about all others:

I see a big division between attitudes towards students who have physical disabilities which are visible—or knowable—compared with disabilities which are hidden, and seem apparently mysterious to faculty.

If somebody has a disability that is not hidden, it's simply more apparent that this person is going to need some help. But when their disability is hidden...I think there is probably some wonderment as to whether or not this person is really worthy of receiving help. It's an automatic kind of response. It's simply the first thing that pops into their mind, 'Well, this person doesn't look disabled.'

> Students with a disability that you can't see don't get the help, and the other ones do. That's part of the battle. I don't know if people have always been good to disabled people—I don't think they have.

The characteristics of conditions which SMET faculty either approved or disapproved does not, however, simply follow the distinction between 'visible' and 'hidden' conditions which has traditionally been used to explain the phenomenon of stigma, although those conditions which were most clearly 'approved' were all visually obvious at first encounter:

> The problem with my vision is pretty obvious from, basically, just looking at me. So they can kind of tell that I'm not bluffing.

Only six of the 41 undergraduates described attitudes of unequivocal approval in their accounts of encounters with SMET faculty: one had cerebral palsy; two had serious mobility difficulties; one had an artificial arm; and two had low vision. Three of the four graduate students whose disabilities fell within this same set of physical conditions, also reported no difficulty in getting their accommodation requests met by SMET faculty. With one exception, all of these students seemed unaware that other students with disabilities face difficulties with SMET faculty over accommodations. This undergraduate had epilepsy, as well as mobility impairment. When she approached faculty for help, she described how she allowed them to assume that her obvious mobility difficulties were the cause of her request, and never mentioned any problems related to epilepsy.

Some non-hidden disabilities which we found to be treated with greater faculty skepticism were: mobility impairments which did not require either a wheelchair or a walker; hearing and speech impairments; visual impairments short of legal blindness; injuries to limbs, back, hands or feet; and burn injuries. Hidden disabilities towards which faculty expressed more leniency were: cancers, heart conditions and injuries acquired by industrial accident. (We noted that students who described their problems as caused by "tumors" reported less helpful faculty attitudes than those who described them as caused by "cancer.") The types of disability towards which SMET faculty expressed least tolerance included some systemic conditions and chronic illnesses, notably: epilepsy, diabetes, immune deficiency and neurological disabilities. No fine distinctions were drawn, however, for students with any form of emotional or psychological disability, chemical dependency or learning disability. All were treated with disapproval. Discrimination against students with learning disabilities is particularly ironic because, as indicated in our description of the participants in Chapter One, students with learning disabilities saw it as more congenial to select math-based, rather than language-based, majors.[23] The group with learning disabilities were, by disability type, the largest single group (28%) of I.T. graduates and undergraduates with disabilities. They were also among the most highly-achieving students in the sample, and included the post-doctoral fellow, and one of the four graduate students.

The constraints of particular conditions experienced by these students made them more liable to transgress SMET faculty norms about acceptable student conduct. For example, those students who missed, or were late for, classes, or who had to absent themselves from part of a class period, for reasons directly related to their condition, or its treatment, were treated as inherently 'deviant':

> I can't attend...probably close to half my lectures. This class was early in the morning when I have a lot of side effects from my medication...Luckily, I also get so much more out of text books than out of the lectures...I don't seem to need the professor to interpret it. And I think maybe they resent me for that—the fact that, although I don't come and listen to them, I do as well as I do...I got one call on my answering machine from a professor who said he was really concerned that I wasn't attending class...He wanted to change his agreement with me regarding test accommodations...So I called him back the next day...He started to try and talk me into dropping his class. And I said, 'Well, you know, I always have this medical problem, but it usually doesn't cause me a problem with my work.' So then he tried to talk me into switching to another section. And he was getting more and more agitated—he just didn't seem like he wanted me in his class.

Students in this situation reported instances where faculty refused to give them accommodations which they saw given to students without disabilities who also had problems with attendance:

> During that bad weather I missed...the first quiz...She said, 'Oh, don't worry about it. A lot of people couldn't make it in today. It's no problem. We'll just have you come in and take it on Monday.' So I was pretty relieved. But when I went to take the test on Monday, the first thing I noticed was that she had written this really long note to the proctor on the envelope containing

---

[23]We have no information to indicate whether, at the level of ability represented by the students with learning disabilities in our sample, there is a tendency to choose math-based, rather than language-based, majors or careers.

the test—something like, 'When you get this test, check it carefully to make sure that it wasn't tampered with. Please sign here, and return it to me stating that it wasn't tampered with.'...It seemed like she was questioning my honesty or reliability...Then, when I got the test back, I got a 49 out of 50 on it, but there was this note attached to it—kind of a threatening note almost, saying something like, 'Students are allowed to miss exams only for extreme reasons. Please be aware that I may not be so understanding next time.' Which I thought was really strange because she had been so understanding about it when I originally called in and talked to her, and she seemed willing to accommodate all the regular students who missed the test because of the blizzard.

But, towards the end, when I got sick...He just didn't want to give me an incomplete, although they give incompletes to students right and left around here. But he didn't want to give me one. He just wanted me to drop the class. So I did.

In a number of ways, all forms of disability appeared to be inherently deviant to SMET faculty.

They found it particularly hard to contend with the variety and variability of disabling conditions,

especially within the same type of disability:

It's like they want to be able to categorize people. Like, 'Gays are this way. And disabled people are this way. And Blacks are this way.' You know? It's just not the way things are.

She was talking about the situation in her class with two people who knew each other well, but who had different kinds of deafness, or different stages. This really threw the professor. She just couldn't sort out who was deafer than whom. Why this would matter, I don't know. But it was an issue to her.

I guess what confuses them is that I really need a power door, but [addressing his friend] although you're in a wheelchair, you can probably handle most doors. (from a focus group discussion)

The seeming impossibility of defining 'disability', of creating a lay taxonomy, or of finding uniformity

in a complex array of variable conditions, may be one important source of frustration among those faculty

who feel professionally obliged to make moral distinctions between 'valid' and 'invalid' claims for

suspension or amendment of traditional disciplinary norms in order to provide accommodations:

With this instructor...it's very important to be there every day, be on time, and stay for the whole class, and not leave early. And he has a way of talking to you about it that makes you feel guilty...When I've tried to talk with him about why I wasn't in class—and I don't know how he does it—I usually end up leaving him feeling just awful. Like I'm a horrible person.... That's really hard.

> I think this one professor was doing it because he just didn't think I...because I could walk around, he thought that I was just faking this stuff. And really didn't believe that I had a disability. I had that impression throughout the course.

Students with disabilities are, above all, seeking some flexibility commensurate with the constraints and variability of their conditions. The implications of their requests are, clearly, alarming to faculty who see such concessions as a threat to the established order of their disciplines. Students with disabilities, however innocently, essentially call into question the moral rules of progress through SMET majors, of which faculty see themselves the primary guardians:

> Most of the professors that I run into in E.E.[electrical engineering] make a long-winded speech that they're going to offer this final at one time, and one time only, and if you can't make it or you're not there, you'll fail the class. Period. And I've only known one of those types of professors who's ever had to change that rule for a disabled student. That was a special case, and the department head apparently insisted that he give the accommodation requested for the final. It would have to be something awfully serious, I think, before I would dare risk having a professor remember my name (laughing) in that kind of connotation.

> I said, 2Even if I do have extra time, if I haven't studied the stuff, I'm not going to get done.'...I mean, you could give me three days to do an exam, but I'm only going to take the time I need. I'm not going to somehow do better just by sitting with the exam longer...'Cause I'm only going to be able to do what I have in my head.

> And one of the things about being a recovering alcoholic is you have to spend a lot of time going to meetings, doing service, being available for other recovering alcoholics. I had a suicide in the middle of the quarter, and explained to this professor that was why I missed that one test. So he gave me a D for missing a grade, and I had to retake that whole course. You know, how do you get somebody like that to understand that a friend of yours who had eight years of sobriety, relapses and blows his brain out in the back of a car? Apparently, you can't.

In our earlier (1994) study of why undergraduates leave science, mathematics and engineering majors, we described some of the moral rules which govern progress through undergraduate and graduate school, and which ultimately determine the recruitment of a relatively small number of survivors into the professions of science and engineering. Some of the rigors of this process appear to have little to do with academic issues *per se*, but are regarded by faculty as an appropriate way of testing for fitness to belong to the academic and professional communities based on SMET disciplines. Fast pace, work overload, competitive curve grading, limited support from teachers, dull class material which is poorly organized and presented, all appear to be pedagogically dysfunctional both to those who leave SMET majors and to those who suffer through them in order to stay. However, faculty justify these practices in terms of their presumed (though unproven) efficacy in selecting the best students. By the start of junior year, SMET faculty have (on a national basis) effectively engineered the weeding-out of between 40% and 60% (with variations by discipline) of all freshmen (and of larger proportions of women and students of color) who had intended to major in these disciplines. Though many of the features of this process and its consequences are currently being called into question, what is not at issue is the fairness by which SMET faculty exercise their gate-keeping function. The overt aim of faculty is to treat all students alike—that is, toughly, but equally.

> Some of them are real understanding and are quite concerned. And I've run into others whose attitude is, you know, 'Tough. Everybody's got a problem. Live with it.' And, you know, it's been...zero assistance from them. And I don't think it's me that they're targeting. They would treat any student in that manner.

Treating everyone alike—that is, in a manner which is in line with the prior educational experience of white male students—has unequal consequences for whole groups of students for whom this treatment is unfamiliar and less appropriate, namely, white women and all students of color (see Seymour & Hewitt,1997; 1994). It is clear from this inquiry, however, that students with disabilities inadvertently challenge the traditional system more than any other group by openly asking for suspension of, or exemption from, some of its moral rules. The essential question raised by every request for accommodation is, whether, in granting it, a student with a disability would be given an 'unfair' advantage over other students, and whether some form of cheating is being condoned:

> When I ask for flexible deadlines on an assignment, I'm told, 'Well, you could get the answers by then.'

> They do not want to be unfair to the other students in the class. And that is perfectly reasonable. By giving the open-book and open-notes (accommodation) they say this: 'Any student who had their books and their notes could do better on these tests.'...But these same instructors say to the class, 'I have found that when I give open-book tests that the students do worse than when they are closed'—just completely opposite statements...They tell me that an open-book is an advantage to me, but tell the class that it's a disadvantage.

I get a lot of questioning that I will cheat—that I'm asking for things that aren't fair to others...Those are the biggest problems, I think, when I talk to instructors about accommodations...Once, when I was having problems with my disability, I said, 'I'd like to take the exam a day later, as outlined on this accommodation request.' And it was, 'Oh, no, no. I can't do that. It's just not fair. You could have the answers by then.' He's calling me a cheater! There's no doubt about that. He doesn't believe that I need that accommodation. He doesn't think that it's a fair, and besides that, he thinks I'm a cheat!

An older person like me is not doing this because they want to cheat their way through the system. An older person comes back to college because they *need* to know this stuff. And they've grown beyond the idea that they want to get away with anything just to get through.

I feel like I am frequently treated as someone who is cheating and lying. You get that feeling from both the professors and the graders....He said, 'You did not do that lab. You couldn't have gotten this data.' I did do the lab. That was my data. I should have written a note that, 'The write-up of the experimenter's results may not be standard because of the problem with my hand.'

I kind of paved the way through engineering. I had to fight teachers. Everybody thought I was cheating. Everybody thought that I would open the test envelope beforehand....And I can say, 'Okay. You send the test to the Disability Services office. They have proctors sitting there.' But, I still had teachers thinking I was cheating, because they think that all engineering students cheat. So here comes this student in your room saying, 'Can I have extra time to take this test because I have a disability?' And he thinks, 'Well, you look just like everybody else. This is just a scheme to cheat.'

And when you ask for something from a professor, they look at you like you're trying to get away with something. What they don't understand is, is that it took me *years* just to be able to ask for help.

In situations where accommodations are granted at the insistence of others (by Disability Services staff or departmental heads), students report that faculty may (as already indicated) sabotage their efficacy by holding the test under inappropriate conditions, sending the wrong test, or changing aspects of the test without informing the Disability Services proctor. They may also delay the granting of an accommodation, delegate the decision to a departmental administrator, or to an assistant who lacks the knowledge or authority to arrange it. Students also described a number of more serious negative responses which they experienced as forms of punishment. These included: giving explanatory information on the content of the test to students who take it in class, but not to those who take it at the testing center; insisting that a sick student take the test with the other students; lowering the grades given for work done under accommodated conditions, exposing the identity of students with disabilities who are granted

accommodations to their class peers; refusing to interact with them; trying to persuade them to drop the

class or the major (regardless of their performance level); and forcing students to be physically present

in classrooms which present them with health risks:

> She made this big production in front of the class: 'I'm going to hand the test back, but we don't have one person's score yet, but I'm not going to mention their name in class. So I'm going to hand 'round this piece of paper so you can check your grade.'...And she came towards me, and, with 100 people in the class, literally, yells across to me: '(Name), your's is the test that's not there. I don't know if they told you over at Disability Services, blah, blah...' and she starts to launch into this big mock apology—right in front of the whole class. And this is a *highly* confidential thing.

> These instructors, they're the ones who make me feel defective because they kind of punish me for being disabled—punish me for needing accommodations...They think that I should not get accommodations and be forced to do without them. They think that I'm really a C or D student and that getting accommodations is what give me these As. And I know that's not true.

> He wanted me to re-take my exams that I had gotten As on, because I had been given more time. I got a C on the first exam because he put me in that room that was real noisy. I completed one question, and got a perfect score on that, but I didn't do the other question at all because I couldn't concentrate. And that's why I got a poor grade. He wanted to show the two exams that I had As for to the mechanical engineering department head and prove to him that I was getting an unfair advantage over the other students. I mean, it really scared me. He wanted me to give him the paper that I got an A on, but I wouldn't, so he gave me a B. I just avoided him after that until the class was over. Now, when he sees me in the hall, he acts like he doesn't know me: he just turns away. It's real obvious.

> I wrote a grant for a research project, and they wanted a copy of my transcripts. And it just rubbed me so bad because I don't feel that my transcript reflects what I've done. And a lot of it is because of the attendance problems, or missing a pop quiz and being told, 'Well, you can't make this up.'...I've got very good homework grades—and they are supposed to help your grade. But when you don't get that counted...I feel like I've gotten a lot of punishment in grading.

> I had two instructors who were totally against it. My counselor had to contact them several times and practically force them to give me the accommodation I needed. It was very hard to be in the class 'cause it was like the instructor hated me. What he did was, instead of giving the top 10 percent As, as he usually did, he cut the As off just above me so I would get a B. Maybe I'm paranoid, but I think he did that on purpose.

> The buildings on the university campus are old and dusty. I don't think they could clean it up to the point where I could tolerate it for long...My inhaler keeps me going to the point where I can tolerate short trips on campus—I can take a test, then wait three weeks, and manage another one...But I've tried going to class in that bloody building I don't know how many times, but every time I do, I get sick. I tried taking quantum mechanics there, and had to drop it. I get

in there, and I'm sick immediately...Wanting us to be present in class is a real issue—particularly if you are a bright student who does well. It seems to threaten people...They say, 'Can't you study something else?'...I always go to the book store, get the books and read ahead of the class. The first quarter, the professor didn't follow the book. I couldn't go to class, but I still got a B....I called and asked him why he had picked a brand new $60 book and wasn't following it. He gave me a list of references for the library—all of which I followed up—I mean, I love this stuff...Later, when I told him what I'd been reading on quantum chemistry, he said, 'Well, you didn't really need to know all that stuff.' He was just trying to put me off—to scare me I think...And when I tell the professors that I can't be physically present—that I will become ill—the response is disbelief. And they are not impressed with the diagnosis on a piece of paper...I tried going to class with a mask on, but it didn't help...That professor was a real stinker. I don't know why his attitude was that way. I wanted him to fax me the homework, so I could fax it back to him every week. I went up to talk to him and the man ignored me for a full two minutes. Other people came up after me and he talked to them first...I also went to his office to talk to him. I saw him coming down the hallway. He saw me, and I saw him starting to turn in the opposite direction....They expect me to come to class and don't accept that, when I'm there, it jeopardizes my health and my job. I can't afford to lose that: I'm the only support my daughter has...The last time one of them insisted that I take a test in that old building, I went into anaphylactic shock, and my doctor pulled me out of school.

A dominant concern to prevent dilution of academic standards by acting as gate-keepers for the rules which are believed to protect these standards, makes faculty vigilant against attempts at rule evasion by any student. Students with any kind of disability are treated as having the potential to undermine the integrity of science education in so far as they seek exemption from particular rules. Students with disabilities expose and test the limits of the rules by which university science education traditionally proceeds. Often, this is unwitting, but some students were aware that this was the implication of their requests, their protests and their assertiveness about accommodations:

I'd crossed some boundaries that it wasn't okay to cross. It was like it wasn't okay to say what I saw happening out loud...The end result was they didn't really like me and didn't want to interact with me at all.

The rules which faculty insist that students follow may be facets of a more important, but unspoken rule: students may, thus, have difficulty in understanding the nature of the resistance which they encounter. For example, it may not be immediately obvious why SMET faculty should react so negatively to students with disabilities who perform well, although they may not always be able to get to class, need to learn from home, miss some tests or ask for extra time on exams. Demonstrating their level of knowledge and understanding is clearly not enough. The norm which underwrites faculty insistence on a high level of class attendance and on uniformity in test-taking, requires all students to show that their knowledge and skills were acquired in the approved manner. Students with disabilities are, understandably, distressed when a good performance is discounted or a particular piece of work accorded a lower grade than a similar level of work by other students. Their 'fault' lies in attempting to succeed—even worse, actually succeeding—by non-approved means.

We cannot assume that faculty are aware of the implications, dynamics or consequences of their encounters with students requesting accommodations. They may, quite appropriately, see themselves as reasonable, compassionate people. However, an accommodation request poses an unexpected and direct challenge to a normative system into which they and all their colleagues have been profoundly socialized, and which they reinforce and perpetuate by their normal teaching practices for each new generation of students. Their immediate, negative response appears, as several students noted, to be quite automatic. Faculty attempts to reconcile accommodation requests with the norms of their professional pedagogy, give rise to further behavior which students with disabilities find distressing and perverse. By attempting to create a taxonomy of approved and disapproved disabilities which is consistent with their moral duties as disciplinary gate-keepers, SMET faculty also find themselves in conflict with university accommodation policies, with the law which these procedures reflect, and at odds with those non-SMET faculty whose disciplines do not operate by these moral imperatives.

In summary, the moral function of SMET faculty as gate-keepers for their professions (which is deeply learned as part of their professional socialization [c.f., Seymour & Hewitt, 1997; 1994]) can be seen as the underlying cause of faculty resistance to the granting of accommodation requests. It is also the source of faculty attempts to classify students who make accommodation requests into those who do and those who do not 'deserve special treatment', to undo accommodations already granted, and to respond in a manner perceived as punitive by those students who have been formally granted them.

CHAPTER THREE: RESPONSES TO DIFFICULTY AND MODES OF PERSISTENCE

In this chapter, we describe how students with disabilities feel about their experiences as undergraduates, the role played by affective responses in increasing or reducing their chances of survival in their major, and the part played by other factors in the persistence of students with disabilities.

How Students Feel about their Educational Experiences and about Themselves

As readers will by now have noted, the accounts of difficulties experienced by students with disabilities are permeated with strong feelings. Dealing with the emotions prompted by the experience of a level of difficulties that are much greater than those faced by most students in SMET majors can become a problem in and of itself. Students may also be distracted from their study, and employees from their work, as they deal with feelings prompted by aspects of their condition, by struggling with administrative problems, or by the attitudes and behaviors of others. To clarify the impressions gained in the interviews, we tagged and tracked expressions of feelings throughout the data set: these are summarized in Table 5. By far the most frequently-mentioned affective issues were those bearing upon self-esteem. Taken together, expressions of damaged identity, denial, self-doubt and guilt, accounted for approximately one-third of all the expressions of feeling which were embedded in the text data. Other feelings, which were most commonly-expressed in reaction to specific difficulties, were (in rank order) stress, anger and a sense of powerlessness, fatigue or weariness, depression and anxiety, frustration, fear (e.g., of faculty reprisal) and cynicism or distrust.

Issues of self-esteem

The problem of 'managing a damaged identity' (cf., Davis, 1961; Goffman, 1963; Freidson, 1966) has been described in the classic literature on disability as a special form of 'deviance'. As Everett Hughes (1975) originally observed, a status such as race, gender, or having a disabling condition, operates as a "master status" which overshadows all others—despite the best efforts of those in these status groups to avoid or deflect such typifications. Bearing this in mind, we specifically asked women

Table 5. Types of feelings expressed in accounts of undergraduate and graduate experiences in SMET majors: by number and percent of all expressions of feelings reported by disabled students in the University of Minnesota, I.T. sample (N=60).

Feelings	N. of Mentions of Feelings	% of All Feelings Mentioned
NEGATIVE	(337)	(85.7)
Issues of Self-Esteem:	(144)	(36.6)
Damaged identity	75	19.0
Denial	34	8.7
Self-doubt	24	6.1
Guilt	11	2.8
Other Emotions:	(193)	(49.1)
Stress	49	12.5
Anger/powerlessness	37	9.4
Fatigue	25	6.4
Depression/anxiety	24	6.1
Frustration	23	5.8
Isolation	19	4.8
Fear (of faculty punishment)	14	3.6
Distrust/cynicism	2	0.5
POSITIVE	(56)	(14.3)
Pride (in self/achievement)	30	7.6
Relief/gratitude (for help received)	10	2.5
Confidence	9	2.3
Generosity (towards faculty)	7	1.8
TOTALS	393	100

and students of color with disabilities what (if any) issues related to gender and race/ethnicity had been raised for them by their undergraduate experience. In contrast with the SMET undergraduate women and students of color interviewed in our 1994 study, SMET undergraduates with disabilities seemed little concerned with issues of gender or of race/ethnicity *per se*. Their main preoccupations were, indeed, with issues related to disability.

One underlying cause of problems with faculty which we have already described and illustrated, is the tendency to assume that students who exhibit 'deviant' behavior (i.e., by asking for rule exemptions) possess other undesirable traits (cf., Becker, 1963) which faculty assume to be the root cause of such requests by any student. As we have already illustrated, students who ask for accommodations risk imputations of laziness or dishonesty because faculty have been socialized to expect, and to exercise vigilance against, certain forms of student 'deviance', to interpret behavior that looks like 'advantage-seeking' in terms of personal moral flaws, and to punish those who 'get away with it'. They have no learned professional guidelines for making a more appropriate response to students whose conditions force them to break the unwritten rules by which SMET education has traditionally operated.

Being the recipient of inaccurate and damaging representations of one's character is, in and of itself, upsetting:

> Over time it wears on you, because there *are* people who cheat. If I knew their names, I might turn them in, but I don't. I'm busy, and I've got to go home and study. But you know cheating goes on. And you get to the point where you feel like, 'Look, I'm one of the good guys. I'm doing what I'm supposed to. I'm one of the few that's sticking to the rules.' And sometimes, when you ask for a reasonable accommodation, you feel like you're punished for them.

Anticipating these responses, encountering them on a regular basis, and finding ways to rebut them, are an inescapable part of being a student with a disability in these disciplines. Simply knowing that one is not a cheat, a liar, a shirker, or someone seeking an unfair advantage, is not enough to keep the 'labeling process' at bay, that is, from causing damage to the student's sense of self-worth. However students respond to these imputations—by denial, confrontation, system-playing, faculty-avoidance, tact or stoicism—their actions and self-presentations are, inevitably, changed from what they would have been otherwise. These interactional distortions can make those who encounter students with disabilities impute a further set of character traits which are seen as 'typical' of students with disabilities—for example, that they are "demanding," "aggressive" or "over-sensitive."[24]

Students often found themselves cast into roles which constrained, discounted, or denied their abilities and achievements, and were forced to "manage" the impressions made upon faculty, advisors, administrators and counselors in order to get what they needed. Goffman (1963) called this developing a "spoiled" (or damaged) identity, and described it as a major personal consequence of the stigmatizing process. We found that almost one-fifth (19.0%) of all manifestations of feelings evident in the text data were either references to, or expressions of, damaged identity:

> After you've proved you have a learning disability, you shouldn't have to prove it over and over again. Because it hurts your self-esteem intensely. It makes me feel stupid...It's like, 'Okay, you guys want to slap me now? Go ahead! Why don't you hit me?' 'Cause it feels that bad sometimes. It's like, 'Yeah, I'm not capable of certain things'—or, at least, I'm incapable in your system.

> One of the biggest frustrations with the whole thing is feeling stupid. You feel like an idiot. I don't know if I'm torturing myself, or if I should keep doing this degree, but it's been painful recently to deal with.

> He gave me shit to begin with, and finally he said something about my being dumb. I said, 'You know what? It's hard enough for me to have confidence in myself when I have to deal with this on a daily basis, and when you say that to me, it really doesn't feel good. And, if you don't have to, I'd appreciate it if you didn't do it any more.' And he said, 'You know, you're right.' He's a pretty blunt guy....'Cause I don't need somebody dumping it on me every day...you know, I call myself stupid every day, and it's horrible—nobody should. But that's how I feel... And I think it could push people right over the edge.

Rather than cope with interactions in which their condition was part of the conversational agenda, students (and also job interviewees, and employees) with disabilities preferred, whenever possible, to restrict disclosure of their condition(s) to those whom they could trust. Those with the most obvious physical disabilities described the embarrassment which they noted in interaction with faculty. This,

---

[24]Lemert (1975) calls this phenomenon "secondary deviance."

however, was not necessarily very different from the response they were accustomed to in many other (non-academic) encounters:

> Most of the time, all you want to do is to fit in. You don't want to be looked at as being different. And a lot of times, no matter how good your grades are, if you tell someone you have a disability, they're going to look at you differently. People have this tendency, even if you do well in class...I just want to be myself.

It was students with less obvious (and especially those with 'SMET faculty-disapproved') forms of disabilities who were obliged to divert energy into coping with the discomforts raised in dealing with those faculty who acted toward them in a negative manner. In these instances, the issues go beyond those of everyday interaction, and are specific to the SMET undergraduate context in which students with disabilities have to operate.

Self-doubt and loss of confidence was one commonly-experienced response to repeated exposure to difficult encounters with faculty. It was particularly marked among those with learning disabilities, but was also expressed by others with 'less-approved' disabilities, including neurological and mental conditions:

> I really don't want to believe that I'm an idiot, but it makes me feel like an idiot participating in this system.

> I've been feeling really dumb lately...It really kills your motivation, and it obviously kills your self-confidence...It's very frustrating. I hate it. I *hate* it! And one of the main reasons I stopped out of physics this past year was because I had that every single day. I had that feeling, and I just couldn't take it...The pressure is incredible.

It would be quite erroneous to suggest that negative faculty attitudes towards students with disabilities are the only source of lowered self-esteem or self-confidence among undergraduates with disabilities. Many of the participants with disabilities of longer-standing described pre-college experiences which had undermined their sense of self-worth:

> So I feel incapable, compared to most people. And it's an over-riding thing that goes on all day long, every day. Even when I was at home, I'd feel like I wanted to hide all the time. Even when I was at school. So (sighs), you know you just don't feel normal compared to everyone else. And that makes everything harder.

My family perceives me as being very bright, but just a little disorganized, and, um, scattered and lazy...And my self-esteem is about an inch high. It makes me question and doubt myself—and my abilities.

For some students, lowered self-esteem was linked to perceptions of their condition as stigmatizing, and to their difficulties in accepting a diagnosis:

And when you have a disability like mine, it's so hard, 'cause no one can see it, and I can't quite explain it. At the beginning, you think you can handle it, but eventually you become overwhelmed—and you can't.... (Deep breath and sigh.) If it was physical, it would be a lot easier—for them and for me. It's so hard to admit to myself that I have a mental problem (laughs). You know, when you want to be an engineer, you're suppose to be all rational.

In my freshman year, I hadn't admitted to anyone that I had a learning disability. I did an incredible job of hiding it from everyone—from the seventh grade on—just 'cause I hated that label.

I haven't taken any use of some of the things that are offered...You don't like to necessarily admit that you need help. You feel too vulnerable. I'm not exactly sure why that is, but I think it kept me somewhat from seeking help.

I look like I am healthy and I want to say, 'I'm not sick; it's fine.' But on days when I am doing only 40 percent of what I usually can do, and I'm walking very slowly in the street, I just have to admit that I have cancer...You have to make your own little standard—just to go your own pace—and that's very hard for me, because I have been healthy until now....One thing I would like to know is, how many disabled people feel good about themselves in this society?

I think it's demeaning—for me it was. I think most of us like to think we're pretty liberal about mental health. But we don't want it to be us. You end up going down a really long road before you figure it out, and can sit back and say, 'I've got a problem. It's just medical.'

I thought of a handicapped person as someone in a wheelchair, and I never thought about myself in those terms. I was in therapy for five years learning to cope with the idea of having a disease that I couldn't ignore or get rid of. When I started to wheeze, I'd tell myself, 'Nope, sorry. This is all in your head. It doesn't exist. I'm not going to the doctor.' I just wanted to believe it was all psychosomatic. It took a long time, and a lot of tears, and a lot of rage, before I calmed down and said, 'Okay, you are disabled. And you have to deal with this and go slow and take care of yourself.' I'm a Type A—'Let's work till we drop' sort of person.

There was a whole year of sort of coming to terms with the fact that I had a real problem, although, at first, I didn't know what it was. Eventually, I got the help I needed to get it identified—which was an agonizing ordeal in itself. That was probably the worst 12 months in my life...And then I had a real wrestle with myself before I said anything to the people here at Disability Services. It was easier to pretend that there was no problem.

Students who had experienced a period of denial of their condition, and of the self-doubt, depression, shame or guilt associated with its recognition, were particularly vulnerable to further depletion of their sense of self-worth by negative experiences in college:

> You run into situations on campus where you feel like the Lone Ranger. I have a difficulty accepting that I have a disability. I like to think, 'Dammit! If I try harder, I can do it.' But it sometimes doesn't happen, and sometimes I have to ask for help. That's a hard step to take. But I think if people knew that help *was* available, and that they do have a Tonto some place, I think that would help a lot of people. (Mature student with an accident-acquired condition)

Some students also expressed guilt at seeking or being offered forms of help which were not available to other students. They had, in effect, internalized the norms which SMET faculty set for all students:

> I want to make it through college without a lot of special help—'cause I feel kind of guilty if I get extra time in classes...So I don't think I've ever told an instructor about my problem.

> I've tried to figure this out a fair way. I mean, I need to be timed. If that's the premise they've established to be fair for all the other students, then I should have to work under the same time pressure, you know. Otherwise, it's like they're not grading me on the same skills that they are grading everyone else on.

Students with disabilities also had their own sense of which people with which kinds of disability 'deserved' help the most, and often placed themselves well down that scale. This, too, made them feel guilty about getting help:

> I see other students come into the Disability Services office in wheelchairs. They're much worse off than I am, and I sometimes feel, 'I don't need to be here.' You know? But they're visible, and I feel bad about accepting help for something that's not visible to people.

> 'Cause I wouldn't have gone for help otherwise. I thought Disability Services was for people that really—I don't know—that *really* had problems.

On the other hand, being accepted into the university, especially by the Institute of Technology, doing well there, and achieving the degree were also important in the discovery (or recovery) of self-confidence and a sense of self-worth. This, too, off-set the difficulties that students with disabilities often shared with women and/or students of color and helps to explain their greater determination to persist:

> Once I got myself declared as a disabled person, I have been working on myself rather, and not pretending I can do it all alone like I had been. 'Cause a lot of my identity was lost during all this and I thought if I could get my degree, then I would feel whole again.

Getting the degree validates all these feelings that I've had for a very long time now—instead of people telling me I have poor character.

I don't think I had a high degree of confidence when I was going through school, and that inhibited me from going for internships. I think if I were to do it again, I would absolutely go for the internship, regardless of my lack of confidence. (Engineering graduate)

For so long I've been saying, 'Well, if I just get my degree, I'll be okay.'

I spent about a year at fairly menial tasks to try to return here to the university and gain a measure of self-esteem that I'd felt I lost all those years before by not graduating.

Stress

Beyond issues of damaged identity and self-esteem, stress was the second most commonly-expressed feeling. Its most commonly-cited sources mentioned by two-thirds (i.e., 28) of the undergraduates were their battles with public agency staff and faculty (and in some cases with employers) in order to get the accommodations they needed to continue in school and to survive financially. Again, like many of the students interviewed in the 1994 study, students with disabilities saw SMET majors as inherently stressful. However, the constant need to anticipate, negotiate and argue for most of the help they required, was an additional layer of stress for students with disabilities:

I made it through that quarter, but there was a lot of stress involved in getting the accommodations and it really disheartened me. I didn't really work as hard for a while and I dropped back down to a 3.0 just for that quarter. I'd been at 3.48 cumulative, and that dropped me to a 3.38. And I'm not used to going backwards...But I figured, 'Well, finally, that quarter is over. At least I won't have to deal with that any more.' But the winter quarter, it was the same thing—same set of problems with different professors. They were just as rude.

Like I said, I'm pretty pushy. I was very good at getting people to give me what I ask for. But its very wearing. It's hard on them, and it's hard on me, and it would be nicer if there was someone that was supposed to handle accommodation requests without my having to do it in person every time.

As the last speaker exemplifies, the need to be "pushy" is stressful in itself—particularly for those students who are shy, dislike confrontation, are resigned to not getting their needs met, or who are afraid of disclosure (which is another intrinsically stressful part of these encounters):

I get so damned sick of this, you know. You have to stand up and fight for your rights. They force you to make demands, and cite the law, when you'd rather just ask.

I get weary with self-disclosure—of forcing (county) administrators to follow through with their own policies—and to be accountable.

A blind student came into the computer center and found that the network wouldn't work with JAWS, which is the screen reader. So he just said, 'Okay,' and left. I feel that's what a lot of students with disabilities do. They have become used to things not being accessible to them; and they accept it, and don't push the point.

The need to be constantly assertive also attracts the risk of 'secondary deviance', by which students with disabilities come to be viewed as inherently demanding (or over-demanding). However, as the next speaker illustrates, "being pushy" is an essential strategy: students with disabilities have more to lose than other students in terms of long-term economic survival by not completing their degree, or by graduating with a poor GPA:

The thing is, if you have a disability, you have to push. Because if you play the game by everyone else's rules, you'll lose it. The world is set up for people without disabilities, so you have to find out the unwritten rules, seek out the exceptions, and exploit them. You have to work the rules somehow, because if you don't, you lose. And if you're disabled and you lose, you're on skid row.

The participants also described as "stressful" the recurrent effort of trying to "educate" public agency staff, insurance company officials, faculty, etcetera, one person at a time. Their weariness with this effort tended to diminish their resolve to take on further "battles," and had negative effects on their health and academic performances:

And you only have so much energy, and there's a point where you cannot go beyond it. It's too much to fight sometimes.

He had a letter for this test accommodation—to have a quiet place and a little extra time. And the professor wouldn't sign anything. And he went back and back, and he wouldn't sign. And, finally, it was two days before the test, and he went back, and asked, 'Are you going to sign this? Am I taking this test, or what?' But, like he said, for the rest of the quarter, he didn't feel he could go to that professor for anything...that one battle was enough. You only have so much energy to fight these things.

He could tell I was mad, because I wasn't saying anything. I've never done anything to any one of these professors to antagonize them. I'm the most even tempered person you're likely to meet—especially considering what I've been through. It takes a lot to get me excited. But when I do, I internalize everything, and that takes its toll.

One undergraduate typed out the following observation on his speech synthesizer:

I need help with the reading, and I have to organize it well ahead of time. It's a hassle...You have to keep explaining what you need over and over again...They are always asking, 'What's it for? What's it for?'...So they give it to you this time, but they say, 'Next time, you've got to go higher up to make this request.' I've done this for three years, and I'm tired of it. They make it very hard. It's a constant battle every day. It gets really, really hard.

Another aspect of the stressful-ness of these experiences was fear of faculty reprisal, especially if the student had been successful in getting an accommodation. Students reported that they sometimes held back from making a request rather than risk "punishment":

So when you get somebody who just has no idea about the system, or who has an attitude, you don't keep going back there and trying again. It would be masochistic of you to go there and say, 'Just punish me.' (Laughs.)

Interviewer: Do you feel punished?

That's how I feel. That's exactly how I feel.

The following speaker (a mature student with a 3.44 GPA and a disability towards which some SMET faculty had expressed disapproval) described an instance of what he defined as "faculty reprisal." It happened at the end of a quarter in which he had pressed for and received permission not to attend particular class sessions for health reasons:

We had to give a presentation at the end of the class. There were three of us in the group, and we had some difficulty with the synthesis. I was aware of that and knew I was going to have to explain to the class that it didn't quite work, so I said this up front. But after the presentation, when we asked for questions, she just launched into me right in front of the class. And she would not back off: 'Well, why didn't this work? What's the problem? Why didn't you understand?' And the two other guys in the group were just standing aside, and not having anything to do with this. She directed her questions entirely at me and seemed to be trying to catch me out in my answers. It was just dreadful. I'd sat there and watched all the other presentations, and no one else got questioned like this. And it was very unsettling to some of the class—and especially to the presenter in the next group. When he got up, he was so nervous he couldn't talk...And I thought, 'That was totally uncalled for.'

If the "price" for getting their needs met was felt to be too great, students might abandon their request:

He was just totally unsympathetic. He refused to give me an incomplete when all I had to do was to finish three assignments at the end of the class. I'd done both mid-terms and the final, and all the other assignments....Disability Services went back and forth trying to negotiate an incomplete, but he just wasn't interested. So I finally said, 'Let's drop it. I don't need all this stress.' It had been going on for a whole quarter.

Dealing with chronic financial problems was, as already indicated, a major source of stress, too. For some of the mature students, coping with family problems—often related to low income—was also stressful. For those students with limited mobility, unresolved access problems (including elevator availability) in certain buildings, parking problems and coping with the sheer size of the campus in all weathers, were major stressors. Seven of the undergraduates also reported that, although they greatly enjoyed the intellectual stimulation of their classes, their educational experience had been tarnished by the stress involved in trying to secure the various kinds of help they needed.

Anger

Some of the issues which provoked anger were strongly reminiscent of those raised, with similar depth of feeling, by SMET students without disabilities in our 1994 study. As is reflected in Table 2, 9.3% of the problems cited by students with disabilities referenced the discomforts of the "weed-out" experience of introductory SMET classes. For example, the following remark might easily have been made by any SMET freshman:

> It's definitely rejection. It's definitely, 'I don't want to help you. Your problem is not important.' And, more importantly, 'Aren't you stupid because you came here to ask that dumb question, when you should have known where else to go and ask.' It's just infuriating! No, I didn't know. I didn't have a clue how to start.

However, as Table 2 also indicates, the negative consequences of problems which all SMET freshmen and sophomores tend to encounter are often exacerbated for students with disabilities. Although (as we shall later discuss) anger could be a potent element in the motivation to succeed, anger could also become a problem in its own right in so far as it diverted creative energy, wore students down, and prompted them to become over-engaged in fighting with faculty, or pursuing their complaints with Disability Services or campus administrators. Students who had realized the potential for fatigue in fighting every battle, advocated other ways to deal with these feelings, and chose to conserve their energies for academic work:

You can never go in and say, 'I hate this school! I hate this system! I hate this office!' Because, I guess, it serves you better if you try to stay upbeat...Which is really a bit sad.

He wouldn't take me on as a grad student because of the mess-ups on my GPA. I was shocked when I talked to him about it, and I was thinking, 'What the hell are you talking about? We just wrote a paper together and got it published with that NSF grant. I just wrote this whole paper for you, and you're asking me about my fucking GPA?' I couldn't believe it...But, then I thought, 'He's one of the top people in the field and having his name on my paper may help me one day'—so it's a trade-off, I guess...You suck the anger down and hang in. I couldn't believe it, but you know, it's part of the game.

Frustration, cynicism, and distrust

Frustration was a common reaction to the difficulty of getting a workable compromise between the limitations and set-backs of their health condition, the value system of SMET faculty, and the system constraints of public agencies. Pressures to take on a fuller class load than they knew was realistic, under classroom or assessment conditions that were difficult or impossible to manage, were major sources of frustration because they destroyed the possibility of working through the degree process in a way that reflected their actual intellectual capacity. Almost half (N=19; 46.3%) of the undergraduates described frustration caused by loss of control over the pacing of their work and the consequent distortion of their performance records. Making up classes which they had been unable to complete and dealing with a grade record which under-represented their ability, work, comprehension or skills, reflect the mis-fit between the students' health-related limitations and the expectations of SMET faculty and agency staff disbursing educational funds:

I would like to get that stuff done because there shouldn't be any need for me to have to repeat any of those classes. And I wouldn't have done, but for the disability. That's what held me back. I'm so frustrated over losing all the classes that whole winter and spring.

I'd been doing real well, and then I had to miss some classes. First they told me they didn't want to give me an incomplete. They just wanted to give me an F. Then I explained about my health, so they gave the incomplete with the stipulation that I did the whole lab over. So it's like those eight credits that I'd just done were just psshitt! Gone! No credit at all. There's an awful lot of that—doing things over and over and over.

Students with learning disabilities reported frustration with performances which under-represented their knowledge and abilities, and with former high school teachers, and with faculty, who had made no allowances for their limitations:

> I remember having screaming battles with English teachers, threatening them with lawsuits and things like that. I'd take an essay test and they would take off marks for my spelling. And I would say, 'Look, I have this neurological disorder. I can't spell, and I can't do much about it.' And they would basically say, 'Well, this is an English class, so tough.'...I knew the materials as well or better than anyone else in the class, but because of the idiocy of the teachers, I didn't have a prayer. I could be the most knowledgeable and articulate student in class, but when it came to a written exam, they'd still give me a D because I couldn't spell. My feelings through all of that ranged between frustration and fury. (Second-year graduate student)

Both they, and students with other disabilities, described the instances where class-mates whom they judged to have lower levels of knowledge and skills or who worked less hard than themselves, and who received higher grades; and where faculty did not believe how hard they had worked:

> When they were out last night having fun, I was up late studying like an A student, but I got the Bs and Cs...And there's no way you can prove to the professor that you spend all your time studying. If I get a C-, it's assumed I didn't work hard enough...And yet, there are a couple of the girls who do better than I do who are amazed because I can explain all the questions to them that they got wrong.

> I know for a fact that some of the students that I've sat down and explained the material to end up with a higher grade than I do.

> I've heard other students with learning disabilities also tell me, 'I'm the one that's tutoring my study group, but I'm behind in my grades.' My group comes to me for help and yet I'm not performing. I don't get the As—the guys I show how to do things get the As. It's very frustrating.

Some of the graduates, and some approaching graduation, described the limitations on their career aspirations wrought by grades which under-represented their abilities:

> At graduation, you will be judged largely by your GPA by those people accepting you into the world that you plan to go into. And your GPA gets trashed by things which are not your fault—things out of your control—which do not reflect your true abilities. So you're put at a tremendous disadvantage.

> I think the real sadness for me was that I had lost my original career hope which had held up well during some difficult times—and that was my ability to teach. Over the years, I've coached soccer and taught skiing, and had a lot of out-door teaching experience with younger people. And I had really hoped to go all the way through education, and teach in a small environment

somewhere. But the grades I've received won't be enough for graduate school. So that's probably my biggest disappointment. I'm in the 2.6 range—just a little too low. And a lot of the early grades—you know, you get beaten down so quickly that it isn't worth the effort of trying to go back and trying to get them fixed. I know I could have done, but there's the money involved in that, and I just wasn't willing to risk it.

Knowing the consequences of ignoring their flawed record, the more assertive, action-oriented students struggled to "set the record straight." However, four of the undergraduates with depleted grade records described how frustration with their academic record had turned into fatalism, and thoughts of abandoning their degree or their career plans:

> I would never advise another student to come here...You have this great hope that all this wonderful education is going to be yours—I thought that when I came back here three years ago. And I still have to deal with that fantasy. I keep hoping that my experience has been abnormal.

> I was pretty excited to come here—I was pretty fired up. I always enjoyed learning. I enjoyed school, and I always wanted to come to the U. But it's not been a very pleasant situation, you know...I feel they're doing everything they can to discourage me.

> They fail to communicate what they expect just with this reward and punish system...You have to guess what rules they are playing by—and what they expect of you. Without that, everybody's always guessing—trying to figure out what the faculty want...and when to break the rules. The response can take your breath away—it's just vindictive. It's vengeful...What would I tell the faculty here? Learn to become human beings again.

For two other undergraduates, frustration and disappointment had turned into cynicism and distrust:

> How do I know if that's true or not? Because it's this institution that's telling me that.
> And so, when you push, and refuse to be put off, you get pushed right back down again.

Anxiety

Feelings of anxiety came from two dominant sources. They were expressed across the sample around the issue of how to survive financially—both in the present, and in the face of a high level of debt after graduation:

> I wasn't able to take classes in the winter quarter, and so they canceled my financial aid for this quarter. I had to use some of the living expenses money they gave me to pay for car insurance, so now it's gone, and I'm unable to work, and I'm getting scared.

> I'm about to be dumped into the working world and it's like there we are with anything between $5,000 and $30,000 in loans to repay, and expected to compete in an environment which you may not be familiar with or suited to. I worry about that a lot.

Anxiety was also expressed by students with more severe forms of physical disability about their ability to cope with aspects of the working world:

> I think the unemployment rate in the blind community is somewhere around 75 percent. I know many people are going to school, but when they get out, they're not being employed. And right now it's incumbent on the blind person to figure out what the hell they need to do to be competitive. There's no program to give good advice about that, but we obviously need some help with this.

> I keep wondering, will I be able to get a full-time job, and just do it—just live a normal life? I don't know if other people wonder about that, but I think about it an awful lot. I worry about being evicted or them taking my son away from me. People tell me it's not really that bad out there. But I worry about getting to a point where I'm not able to do my job right or take care of us both.

> I've had this all my life, and it is really hard for me sometimes to think about myself in an actual work place. Sometimes I think about all the limitations that I have. It's kind of depressing to think about. Then other times, I think, 'You can do it.' So some days are up days, and some are more down—but it's always at the back of my mind.

Anxiety about the present or future was often accompanied by a sense of being overwhelmed by trying to cope with so many different kinds of problems simultaneously:

> I did get a scholarship once—I met the criteria. But I've been so overwhelmed with my health problems, making up my classes, correcting my grades, dealing with accommodation issues and everything, I haven't had the time or the energy to make a formal application...sometimes I wish I could have used a bit of help just to get on top of all of this.

Isolation

Finally, isolation was a feeling which increased the risk of abandoning the major or leaving the institution for students with disabilities. Feelings of isolation were expressed by all three of the undergradutes who were temporarily out of school, and by most of the ten students who described themselves as having considered leaving. The tendency to isolation often arises because the nature of the disability places limits on campus sociability, and because some conditions are perceived as shameful, stigmatizing or likely to frighten other people away:

> Mental illness is very isolating because, well, for me, there's the shame. And when you try to explain how it works to other people, and they don't know what you're talking about, the shame doubles...I get guilted and shamed...and then what happens is the part of me that I fight terribly—and it's a terrible bad habit I've gotten into—I disengage—pull out completely.

When I discovered the tumor, the first doctor gave me six months to live...But I insisted on seeing other doctors and having more tests...But through the whole process, I had to do it alone. There was no one to help....I was not able to speak with my parents, because they couldn't deal with it. And that was a whole nine months...I mean, I was completely alone. And that's not something anyone should go through...And here, it's hard for others to connect with people who are chronically or terminally ill. I mean, people would rather not know about us. It scares them.

And the natural reaction—not the intellectual, but the emotional reaction—is that we make people feel uncomfortable, and because of that, they are likely to ignore or reject us.

I'm not the most social person in the class room, just because of my vision. It's hard to identify people and say, 'Hello, John or Frank.'...I've only made a couple of friends—not close friends—mostly because of the transportation problem...I mean, I get here, I take the classes, and I go home immediately. So I really don't have much time at the university to be sociable with anyone. In fact, my social life at this university is about non-existent.

As the last speaker explains, students with disabilities may find their opportunities for social contact more restricted than other students. Tight transportation schedules, and getting from class to class in a short time frame, limits the social contacts of students with visual or mobility impairments; some of the mature students felt "too old" to socialize with the younger students; and the extra hours spent by students with learning disabilities in studying reduced their sociability:

I'm very isolated. And yet I'm a very sociable person...But I have to spend all my time studying.

I've never gotten together with other handicapped people—there's not a lot I can do, and I'm in such a hurry. I've got to make it to the next class myself.

I'm uncomfortable being around these young kids. I'm more serious than they are. It's silly, but it's there...You know, when you're an older, returning student, you tend not to have those relationships that young students benefit so much from—that camaraderie.

As one student with a hearing impairment reminded us, it is difficult to find other students with disabilities, let alone disabilities similar to one's own:

I was really disappointed because I thought there would be a really good deaf community here in campus. And there's not. It's terrible...It's really lonely. The deaf students are isolated from each other.[25]

---

[25]This observation points to a general problem for students with disabilities who wish to contact each other. It is especially pertinent, given that the University of Minnesota has one of the highest proportions of deaf students in comparable research institutions.

Students with disabilities of long-standing were aware of the dangers of isolation, and sought

opportunities to counteract them:

> Being able to sit down and talk to somebody about all your interests and all the things in your
> life and theirs, and your concerns—that's the biggest single thing that I *never* got here. (Graduate
> student)

> People are very important in my life. When I don't have people to talk to, and bounce ideas off,
> I get more withdrawn—more isolated and depressed. It's a downward spiral. Then it takes the
> right kind of person to talk to me and pull me out of that. So I try not to let myself get to that
> point. I try to stay in contact—even staying home from school for a day—weekends are really
> hard for me.

Overall, students with disabilities contend with an emotional burden which is quite different in

character from the emotional difficulties which we found increased the risk of switching to non-SMET

majors in our seven-institution study (1994). The feelings described above, and the sources from which

they arise, are, qualitatively distinct from those expressed by white male and female undergraduates and

by those of several different ethnicities in SMET majors. However, what these emotional difficulties

share with those known to undermine the chances of persistence of SMET majors in other under-

represented groups, is their potential for damaging the student's sense of self-worth.

Some of the emotional stresses described above arise from the students' struggles with definitions

of disability which are common in the world outside academe. However, it is clear that an extra layer

of emotional problems is added by attitudes and practices generated within the university and within the

Institute of Technology. Because (as discussed in Chapter Two) SMET faculty responses to disability

which create problems for their students are adaptations of attitudes which derive from the wider society

or arise from deeply-socialized aspects of the culture of academic science and engineering, they are

unlikely to be peculiar to this institution—particularly considering its pro-active policy and procedures

for accommodation. We predict that this set of emotional difficulties, and the problems to which they

are a response, will play a significant role in undermining the determination of higher education students

with disabilities in many other institutions, but particularly those in SMET majors.

In the next section, we consider some factors which aid the persistence of students with disabilities, including the role of attitudes and feelings.

Factors Contributing to Persistence

Despite the greater degree of difficulty that they face, in some ways, students with disabilities can be regarded as more likely to persist in SMET majors than some others. As already illustrated, students with disabilities demonstrate a high level of commitment to their majors for reasons known to predict persistence, namely: a high degree of intrinsic interest in the disciplines and careers they have chosen; well-grounded, realistic, non-materialist (sometimes altruistic) career foci; and (as we shall discuss in more detail in Chapter Four) a high degree of clarity about what they want to accomplish, and why. As a group, students with disabilities are highly self-selected, so as to include students of somewhat above average abilities. Because of inherent difficulties which mitigate against their chances of achieving university entry at all, those students with disabilities who are at greater risk of non-persistence seem less likely to have entered the university than students with comparable academic ability who do not have disabilities. Notwithstanding a distinctive tendency to periods out of school, students with disabilities appear to have a better-than-average chance of success, so long as their health states remain manageable.

In this section, we draw together some supports for persistence which are reflected in three different tables: Table 3 (on sources of help, p. 51); Table 5 (on feelings expressed, p. 84); and Table 6 (on coping strategies and attitudes; following page). Table 6 summarizes the students' view of their own contributions to success in their majors. It reflects students' direct responses to questions about what had helped them to persist. The 'positive' feelings shown in Table 5 were more indirectly gathered from their answers to other questions or from spontaneously-offered comments. Table 3 lists all the external sources of support which graduates and undergraduates cited as important to persistence in their undergraduate degrees.

Table 6. Coping strategies and attitudes reported as important to persistence in undergraduate majors: by number and percent of all coping techniques reported by all disabled students in the University of Minnesota sample (N=65).

Coping Strategies and Attitudes	N. of Times Reported	% of All Times Reported
ORGANIZATION STYLE	(128)	(31.8)
Working with/around the disability	43	10.7
Good organization/forward planning	33	8.2
Effective use of what's available	31	7.7
Early registration with Disability Services	21	5.2
USING GROUP SUPPORT	(119)	(29.6)
Student association activities and support	65	16.2
Small group; working together and mutual support	54	13.4
ATTITUDE AND ORIENTATION	(102)	(25.4)
Persistence, assertiveness, goal-orientation	78	19.4
Attitude adjustment/acceptance	24	6.0
OTHER STRATEGIES	(53)	(13.2)
Playing the system	19	4.7
Enlisting the help of doctors/therapists	14	3.5
Self-presentation/management	13	3.2
Making strategic choices	7	1.7
TOTALS	402	100.0

The importance of the University of Minnesota's commitment to support for students with disabilities is strongly reflected in Table 3. Approximately half of the sources of support cited by students with disabilities are directly or indirectly attributable to policies, programs or improvements in access to facilities initiated by the university. Most notably, help given by Disability Services represented 31.7% of all help cited by the students. A second, very important source of help (i.e., 19.1%) was that received from disabled peers or mentors, of which the largest single source of help was the Disabled Students' Cultural Center. Also of note in Table 3, faculty, faculty advisors and TAs., taken together, provided 17.3% of the help which students cited. Given the depressing picture offered in the last chapter, it is important to note that help from some SMET faculty could generally be counted upon (4.4% of all help cited) and that others were prepared to give help in a more qualified way in some situations (6.5%). The students' personal support network of family and friends contributed 14.0% of all sources of help cited. On campus, the Disabled Students' Cultural Center provided both a setting and an organizational structure for mutual support which was not otherwise met.

In the next three sections, we discuss the contribution made by Disability Services, peer groups and the Disabled Students' Cultural Center to the persistence of undergraduates with disabilities.

Disability services

As described in Chapter Two, the assistance of Disability Services (DS) staff in arranging accommodations—which is the Disability Services's staff's main official purpose—was described by students as central to their ability to persist. However, the contribution of Disability Services to persistence has a number of other facets. Prominent among these were the establishment of regular contacts between students and particular staff members. These relationships were a highly-valued source of help:

> She's my counselor at DS. She's just terrific. She's patient, and she took a lot of time to explain everything—from what the accommodations might consist of, about the interaction faculty would have with me and the implications for later on—having to admit to the fact that I used accommodations, and so on. Every question that I had was answered. And most of the questions

that I had, I didn't have to ask because she had already given me the answer—just the whole process.

That many of the Disability Services staff (including the director) were themselves people with disabilities, or had a professional level of understanding of the constraints imposed by particular disabilities, was a greatly appreciated aspect of their service:

> I came here, in part, because I knew that this campus had a really good quality Disability Services office that was run by women with disabilities. Other Disability Services that I had encountered were not run by people with disabilities. That was a big deal to me.

> It was like a breath of fresh air when I met her. It was marvellous—somebody with that type of disability helping others with the same type of disability. It was fantastic. Not only can she empathize, she can feel it, you know. So I thought that was really marvellous. It spurred me along knowing how much she has achieved, and how respected she is now.

Although the Disability Services staff do not refer to themselves as "counselors," and do not offer therapeutic counseling, students regarded particular Disability Services staff members as "their" counselors. They were described not only as sources of information and practical advice, but as active listeners, role models, mentors, advocates and a valued source of emotional support:

> My experience of disability services? Wonderful! It's hard to get in to see the counselors—they're busy, but when I get to talk to her, she's like the only person in the world who knows how I might be feeling and struggling. She gives me direction on things to try; helped me with letters to community resources and to the professors. And when she writes me a letter, it's like gold. I am suddenly a responsible adult being taken very seriously, right here and now.

> When I've had problems dealing with the stress load, my DS counselor has said, 'Come in and we'll talk about it.' I mean, she's there for anything—just someone to talk to. That's particularly valuable when you have so little time to cultivate friends...I feel confident that I can go back to the DS office and work on any problem with them. I don't feel like I'm alone with my problems.

> It's hard for me to describe some of the run-ins I've had without getting emotional—like I've had run-ins with bus drivers a lot. I was describing all that to my counselor. And she was trying to get across to me, 'You're not asking for something special. You're just asking for something you need.'

> I had gone through a divorce, and it was kind of a difficult time in my life. I had sold my business and everything else to go back to school. So really, the DS counselor really helped me get through to graduation. I really appreciated that.

Students stressed the importance of continuity in their relationship with staff members who came to know their history and their issues. Those who had not developed working relationships with DS staff members appeared much more vulnerable to despondency in the face of set-backs. Students stressed the importance of making contact with Disability Services staff early and seeing them regularly:

> I mean, there's nothing worse than sitting in a class and feeling powerless because you can't see the blackboard. If I'm not getting any of the notes, I'm not going to learn anything...After seeing what that did to me in high school, I made sure it didn't happen in college. So right off the bat, I went to see a DS counselor before my first class.

> I always go back to the same one—I assume that's assigned—but it's best to do that 'cause they know about your specific case and about you as a person. They can't put everything in a file.

> I keep in touch with my disability counselor regularly—I probably talk to her much more than to my faculty advisor.

> You need that continuity. I think it's really important to have someone who has seen you all the way through.

Arranging, providing or directing students to special forms of help and acting in liaison with other agencies, and as facilitators, resource managers and problem-fixers were other aspects of the Disability Services staff's work which students cited as important to their persistence:

> I've used the taped books previous quarters, but this quarter the Student Services for the Blind and the Recordings for the Blind didn't have the law books I needed. So my DS counselor arranged for a lady who is taping for another blind student to tape books for us both. So that's a really great service. I'd have been stuck without her.

They gave practical advice on academic planning and how to get help with study skills:

> I didn't know where to turn. I needed someone to tell me where to go and the counselor directed me to a group on how to study. And it was a life-saver, really.

Also seen as important was the Disability Services staff's knowledge of how the university and off-campus agencies worked, and their ability to tap into and co-ordinate help from different sources:

> I was having financial troubles 'cause I couldn't take any classes in the winter quarter, and so they canceled this quarter's financial aid. And I really needed the money 'cause I'm unable to work. I was getting scared and feeling down about it. So my DS counselor referred me to someone in financial aid who works with disabled people—I didn't know there was anyone who did that until this happened—no one in financial aid ever mentioned it. Anyway, she was able to cut through the red tape and get me some emergency money right away.

They taught coping skills, helped students deal with their feelings and supported them through crises. They also helped students feel that it was "okay" to ask for help, taught them appropriate ways to approach faculty for the help they needed and encouraged them to accept help without self-blame:

> The counselors say, 'Now, don't feel bad. It's not you. We've had problems from many of the professors over there with our students. And we'll work with you. If you have difficulties with them, let us know and we'll intervene.'...So that's what I've done. I've never spoken a word in anger to a professor—never had a negative conversation with them. I've just had the DS counselor contact them and work it out.

Above all, students cited the importance of the Disability Services staff's readiness to be their advocate for reasonable accommodations with faculty and others, and to persist in pressing that students' legitimate needs be met:

> And she's encouraging me to stand up for the terms of the accommodation as stated. And that there's nothing wrong with going back to the professor, and telling him that I appreciate his effort, but that the environment isn't quiet enough and I'd like DS to proctor the exams for that course....And if she spots a problem, she'll make good suggestions as to what we might do about it together.

> What helps is her official position at the university. She has the materials from my doctor. She knows what the disability is. She's an expert, and she can tell them, 'This is necessary, and that isn't.' And she will—even if they don't want to talk to her.

> DS counselors are powerful people on campus because they enforce the law.

> He was a fairly new instructor who refused me, so I asked him to call my DS counselor and he did. And she read the riot act to him—that he was a required by law to do this. In the end, there was no real problem—he just didn't know.

> So she would pick up the 'phone and talk to the professor if there was an issue...I would say, about 30 percent of the time, I had to get her involved.

> She just explains it in very clear terms, '(Name) has a condition such that she has these needs and, if you have further questions, just call me.' She's really great—she has a way with these difficult instructors, getting them to co-operate. She's a real expert in that. I'm glad she's my counselor.

The difficulty in getting an appointment was one of the few complaints offered, and some students used e-mail as a way around the difficulty of reaching their over-extended counselors. Overall, as Table

3 clearly indicates, Disability Services was a very important source of aid to the persistence of graduate and undergraduate students with disabilities.

Peer group learning and support

Both our 1994 findings, and those of many other researchers, stress the value of peer groups for study, co-operative learning, emotional support and the transmission of practical information and advice between peers, and from older to younger students. We asked all the participants in this study about their experiences with peer learning and support and found them to be somewhat divided on the issue. About one-third (32.3%) of the whole sample (i.e., 17 of the undergraduates and four of the graduates) reported that they found it helpful to study with class (or other) peers—usually peers without disabilities—and to keep these relationships going through different classes over time:

> I had one person that I went all the way through with. She was a TA, and had keys to some rooms. So, on Saturdays, we'd go and lock ourselves in the one room with three walls of blackboards and I'd start in one corner, just cranking through the physics. And she'd sit on a table in the middle and watch what I was doing, and she'd run up and check errors, and change things. She was responsible for the arithmatic, and I was responsible for the application of the physics. It made a wonderful team. (Physics graduate)

> Part of the process of group-learning when it works really well is that, as you go through different materials in the course, the strengths of different people will come out. Somebody leads one week because they understand that piece of the material better. And, as they explain it to the rest, their own understanding gets clearer too...And those that get it, try to explain it to those that don't in different ways—so everyone hears it from several angles until you've all got it. When that process works well, it's fabulous. It lifts everybody's level from wherever they started out—the As and the Cs alike, depending on how active a part they played in the group's discussions that week.

> A thing that's helped me through a lot is taking classes together with friends every quarter. The grade I get in class depends a lot on whether I'm working on my own or with a group of people. On my own, I usually get a C, but if we meet as a group and really set up and study regularly, I really do well. I even work harder with the group—we pull each other along.

> I hooked up with a friend and the areas that I didn't understand, he understood, and vice versa...I could have never have made it without the guy, and we ended up being pretty good friends. Without us working together, it just wouldn't have happened. I would have changed degrees, or gotten out of school altogether—it was that important. (Blind graduate)

As the last speaker indicates, developing a good study relationship could be critical to persistence. Some of those who stressed the importance of group study were mature students who joined with other mature students (whether or not they had disabilities) for mutual academic and personal support:

> We've just kind of clicked. We had all started in community college, but we met here and started this study group together. You know, like at midnight, there's the three of us sitting at the table working. And we'll just kind of look at one another and go into this hysterical laughter for no reason at all—other than we're all mentally fatigued or at the wall with the math...But it's great to have that camaraderie—not everyone finds it—lifesaving really.

However, not all the relationships which students described were symbiotic in nature. For students with learning disabilities especially studying together sometimes meant getting help from friends with types of academic work they found difficult, rather than working with class peers as equals:

> I have a lot of friends in liberal arts majors, and they come over and help me—and it really works well—I like active learning.

> I'll ask the TA or other students if I need some help.

Some students with physical disabilities sought practical help (e.g., with lab work, as note-takers, readers) from students without disabilities and used the student network—including the electronic network—for information:

> I always used a reader in the labs, unless I had a lab partner. Initially, I would bring in a reader, and then if my new lab partner turned out to be co-operative and understanding, I'd ask them to work with me instead. (Engineering graduate)

> I ask friends to take notes or act as readers—either from the dorm or the building—or just friends.

> Most of the information I've gleaned about how things work around this campus came from other students, not faculty or advisors.

However, those who did not work with other students—whether by choice, or not—explained why it is often more difficult for students with disabilities to develop or join peer groups. As already discussed, fear of disclosing their disability tends to isolate students with hidden disabilities from their class peers. Students with disabilities who share the same classes tend not to know each other, may not seek to find each other in a class context and may even avoid each other for fear of disclosure. Some students who have been granted assignment accommodations express fear that other students will learn

of this, and behave unpleasantly towards them. This risk is felt to be enhanced if they associate with any

other students with disabilities in the class:

> He and I found we were in the same class. And it was like there was a camaraderie. But yet,
> you know, 'Maybe we shouldn't sit together'—it felt rather dangerous to do that.

For some students, this fear promoted the avoidance of any obvious association with other students with

disabilities in their classes. Concerns of these kinds are an absolute barrier to the establishment of close

working relationships with class peers.

Some students with more obvious physical conditions reported instances of embarrassment,

awkwardness and avoidance among their class mates, all of which limited their social encounters to

superficialities, and prevented the development of useful working relationships. A participant with

mobility and speech impairments raised the issue with other members in a focus group discussion:

> My professor had the class get into groups for a project, and I didn't have a problem with that.
> I wanted to be in the group that he set up. The problem is the group didn't want me—But they
> didn't want to tell me that there was no more room in their group. So all last week they were
> avoiding me—all four of them—the same people who were in my class last year...And now the
> prof wants me to work on my project on my own....

> It's fear. I think you are describing fear.

> I've heard research that people are afraid because they think we're contagious.

> I want to comment on what (name) was saying about groups. It's different with hidden
> disabilities—and it's not just disabilities—it's being a woman in engineering too. My condition
> fluctuates, and if I start to let my partner down because I don't feel good or can't be there, I feel
> bad—my self-esteem gets low, and I'm ashamed to go to class. I have a real hard time with labs
> and lab partners.

As also discussed earlier, students with mobility and visual impairments often found it difficult to meet

other students, either in a regular or in a spontaneous way, because of their constraints of time, access

and transportation. In addition, those with learning disabilities often had difficulties with peer group

learning because of the way that their own learning processes worked:

It got very difficult to stay in the group because I was going much slower than the other people...a lot of people don't have the patience for that.

Once something sinks in, I'm really good at it, but while I'm trying to learn it, it's hard for me to do that in a group. Once I have it down, then I can work with a group. But I have to work on my own first, or I get pretty well messed up.

Seniors and graduates who had found peer study groups valuable were less concerned about disclosure issues than were some of their juniors. They had found that, over time, class peers were more accepting of a group member with a disability. However, as the next speaker indicates, there was an initial problem of stigma to be overcome:

In I.T., everybody died off until you just had a few people left in the class. And everybody knew everybody else, and they didn't care any more if I got extra time, or if I took the test in the next room. And they would work along with you and they didn't care, because they knew you had passed all the same areas and that you were good enough to be with them.

Two students with obvious physical disabilities, who liked working in groups, but who noticed the disinclination of others in the class to invite them to join, found ways around this. As one of them explained:

The lab class won't break up into perfect pairs—there will be some threes. Making a third is a great trick—just to be the third man. It makes for a little extra brain power. I hold my own—I do my share of the work—no question about that—especially when it comes to writing up the report. But by being the third person, I can pick the work I offer to do, and let one of the others do the lab work that I can't manage so well.

Students with disabilities might choose to work together, if they knew each other as friends, or seek out others with similar disabilities:

My room-mate is disabled too, so if I'm frustrated with something I'm working on, I can talk it over with her. And I have other people who are visually-impaired in some of my classes and we talk about how it's going. And I just have my own network—but not others in the class really.

A couple of my friends that also qualify for disability services would sometimes get together and study with me. We were doing the same subject, so, anyway, that felt okay.

110

Study groups formed of class peers who had different disabilities were also not thought not to be particularly useful:[26]

> And the guy in the wheelchair isn't going to understand my point of view, except that he's been ridiculed and so have I...But as for my special needs, can I sit down and study with him? Probably not. Because his mind isn't going to have the blocks that mine does.

> Those bonds are not going to form just because people happen to have disabilities—particularly if they are of very different kinds. There problems just aren't the same.

However, in the case of learning disabilities, students with the same types of disability were particularly reluctant to work together:

> It is very difficult to get people with learning disabilities to come and support each other, or to make bonds with each other, because there's such a barrier of shame.

> Most other people with learning disabilities in classes I've had refused to take tests with me. They want to take them solo, because in the past, they've been ridiculed. People are very embarrassed about this...The department told me there were others with learning disabilities in my class and suggested I seek them out, and work together. But it didn't go down too well...She was a sophomore and I was in my senior year, and in her shoes, I don't know that I'd be comfortable...I tried to offer my help to her, coming as a senior—you know, 'I know the ropes. Can I give you some help?' It was no go. I tried several times, and always it was 'No.' My guess is she never made it. It was hard enough for me to make it.

For one-third of the undergraduates and graduates who had found ways around these difficulties or were less troubled by them, regular contact with class peers—largely for study purposes, but sometimes for support and sociability—was cited as important to their persistence. For the majority of the participants, however, peer group support was not accessible through normal class contacts. However, as we discuss in the next section, the context in which group support is made available to students with disabilities makes a considerable difference to whether it is accepted and reciprocated and, thus, to its contribution to persistence.

---

[26]By way of comparison, in our 1994 study, we found that SMET majors who belonged to particular ethnic or racial groups were not comfortable with institutional initiatives which encouraged or arranged study or support groups composed of individuals from several different ethnic or racial groups.

The Disabled Students' Cultural Center

For reasons discussed above, it is harder for students with disabilities than for other students to study or socialize with other students, whether or not they have disabilities. The Disabled Students' Cultural Center (DSCC) was conceived and established by students with disabilities, and is entirely run by them. Located in the Students' Union building, it provides a comfortable, relaxed setting in which study and social groups can form, and meets many other needs of students with disabilities that are not easily met in other ways.

The DSCC had been in existence for approximately three years at the time of the interviews. It was founded with the strong support of the current Disability Services director, by a group of current and recently-graduated members, and arose, in part, from a series of discussions prompted by Mary Litsheim's (1993) dissertation study (see Chapter One). With help from Disability Services, this group developed a proposal requesting a grant from the Student Fees Committee, developed the constitution required by the university for officially-recognized student bodies and secured an accessible space within the students' union building. Funding requests are repeated annually. Students use the DSCC as a place to meet informally, for organized social gatherings and meetings and as a drop-in center for information and practical advice. All students with disabilities are welcomed, including those who have not officially documented a disability with the university, as well as students visiting from other campuses. The DSCC is entirely student-run. Below its elected governing body, the DSCC has developed a structure of committees, each of which works on issues of dominant concern to members (e.g., academic issues, assistive technology). Funding for day-to-day running expenses is awarded—as for all accredited student organizations—from the student services fee paid by all students. The DSCC committee raises extra funding (e.g., for special services to members, conferences) in various ways.

The DSCC was described as valuable to students with disabilities in a number of ways. As we have already noted, social isolation, fear of disclosure to class peers and problems in developing study group and support group relationships, are common among students with disabilities. Students who feel stigmatized, marginalized or "disapproved of" by faculty because of the nature of their disability, as well as those who fear disclosure, reported the significance of the DSCC as a place to meet, develop friendships, give and receive academic help, find acceptance and support and have fun:

> And it was good for me, that coming together with people who were kind of dealing with a lot of the same stuff as I was. But, more importantly, who had this new experience—to have a conversation, you didn't first have to educate them. There's a high level of givens. You could just start at that point and move right on.

> I was pretty shut in with my disability, and I don't think I could have come out in a completely non-disabled environment...I don't think I would have been as free to talk about it, and to sort out some of my behavior that was a result of my disability...And I'm learning to interact...I think patience and understanding has been so much greater here. As a result, I feel so much more assertive and confident. I really don't think I would have made it without this Center.

> If there wasn't this Center, there would be no place to go and have fun. You'd be going to tell your troubles to a counselor perhaps—but that would be focused on just fixing things. That's why the social aspect is so important.

Students who sought contact with others with a similar disability were able to find each other:

> The Center has been a good place for the deaf students to get together. It's a real obvious place, and there are people here they can call to make contacts. We have a TTY they can use, which is really good. Without this Center, I don't think the deaf students would ever have got together.

Some of these linkages were made by electronic mail for students for whom the campus is less accessible.

Given the constant burden of being required to explain themselves and their problems from scratch, students valued the opportunity to relax in a context where other members understood their situation, and where no explanations were necessary:

> These people are so laid back—I mean, their perspective on the world is so different. They are really supportive of each other. They are a lot more accepting of diversity. I mean, it's a lot easier to come in here and say, 'I'm having a problem.'

> For me, I'm really well organized, and I know some people are threatened by my knowledge and my confidence. But the Center is a place to come and get one's ego boosted. (Typed on a speech writer by a focus group participant)

> If it wasn't for the people at the DSCC, I'd probably deny that I had a disability.

I felt before that I was kind of a shut-in. I feel it's brought me out a lot, and helped me develop some inter-personal life. It's given me experience in interacting, and I was kind of retarded in that...And, then, it's a place to be comfortable in—I don't have to hide.

The DSCC was also a safe place to talk about common difficulties and feelings about them, and to share information, resources and ways around problems:

It's a kind of a hook-up for people with disabilities to help each other and, I guess, be advocates as a group for disabled students, and a way to deal with practical problems as they come up.

You can learn from one another what works and what doesn't.

It's an extremely important place to me. I can go in there and complain or just talk about my issues, and they understand. They're great people. And I can go and fret to them—even if I can't see solutions, just to talk. Just them understanding helps.

When one student had a "victory" in getting an accommodation granted, others learned from this, were encouraged, and cheered each other along.

The DSCC had emerged as a congenial place to seek information and advice. Those who had tapped into its collective know-how on the operating systems of the university and other pertinent agencies reported its volunteer advisors to be knowledgeable and resourceful:

Students feel really comfortable coming here and asking us questions that, maybe, they're not asking their counselors, although we always send them back to their counselors too...I always felt that help was a secret—especially financial help—'cause they didn't want too many people asking for it...It seems like they're afraid of too many people taking advantage, or just finding there's too many people that need it.

There's a great strength here, because there are a lot of people that have strong knowledge of the various resources available. And that's hard to come by. There are people here who will just say, 'Oh, we'll try this.' And that's just so beneficial. The best way to describe it in my mind is community-building.

As the last speaker suggests, its committees and active members had become adept at inventing ways to get around problems or system rules to get individual or group needs met.

Notwithstanding its contribution as a resource center for the disabled student community on this and neighboring campuses, the DSCC runs itself with volunteers, and a part-time paid organizer. Those who were active committee members of the Center described how much easier it was to negotiate the resolution of particular problems with university departments by presenting them as DSCC matters, rather than seeking to deal with them alone:

> Because it's hard to get your hands on the information that's available. It's hard to know what's available and who it applies to. You have to sort of be in with the right counselor. And your head just swims with the run-around they give you. But here, we can put all these scraps of information together, make some official phone calls from the Center office, and get to the heart of it. Then we can put it in the newsletter, so everyone knows what's what.

> Oh, I find this negotiating along with each other a blessing. Because I do a lot of negotiation with the university—for example my long, ongoing effort to get the TTY installed in the DSCC office. It's been frustrating, but we made it.

They had found the administrative staff of the university generally open to such overtures, and described a number of specific accommodations for particular groups of their members which they had successfully brokered in this manner (e.g. access to/adaptation of computer facilities, getting oral or sign language interpreters for meetings). They had also been successful in raising some issues which university policy-makers had not previously addressed, or of which they had been unaware. Brokering solutions to problems is a daunting task when undertaken alone. The active members shared this work, and, as particular members tired, others took up the work and built on the cumulative successes of the organization:

> In our second year, all of the work was focused towards making the entire campus community aware of disability rights and culture issues—and that's a huge task. And, at the same time, we were trying to educate ourselves...It never ends—there's always someone else to educate.

From a focus group discussion:

> I wouldn't want to stop pushing an issue because someone tells me it's getting on their nerves. I'd rather stop because I'm exhausted and need a rest.

> It's hard to find a comfortable place to do that—that's where this Center is so important.

> I agree—because, at least you can say, 'I'm sick of working on this!' and give it to someone else for a while—or get some support to keep going.

> When you are talking about just your own disability, that's enough challenge in itself. But when you start planning and working for lots of people....

> Oh yeah—the barriers are endless.

Although there are no formal rules for joining the DSCC, those who used it as a social center on a regular basis spoke of themselves as "members." They described the relationships they had developed at the DSCC as having given them a sense of family and of pride in the accomplishments of the disabled community. They defined this community as extending beyond the campus to students with disabilities on other neighboring campuses (who joined them for meetings and social events), and to campuses nationally (with whom they were developing a network for the exchange of ideas and information):

> Our events and our people are available to the community far beyond this university. The Center is sometimes a refuge for students at other colleges in this area. The smaller colleges—apart from one good community college—tend to have nothing for disabled students at all...Then, this summer, we brought together students with disabilities from all around the country for our conference.

The DSCC had organized one conference which brought together the leaders of similar groups on a regional and national basis, and was busy with the arrangements for a local conference at the time of the interviews. The focus of these meetings was practical (i.e., addressing common problems in a collective manner), educational (i.e., learning about disability history), and focused on the development of disability awareness in the community, and of empowerment and a sense of pride among students with disabilities:

> Disability Awareness Month last year was an incredible experience. We covered a host of different issues with different speakers and panels—like a panel on hidden disabilities. And I think we take on a tremendous job. We've had two of these Disability Awareness Months now—they go on the entire month of October. It's a tremendous undertaking, and you can't adequately cover it all...People who don't know anything about us are amazed what we can fund and organize ourselves.

> I think this summer's major event—Disabled and Proud National Conference— is a good example of how we generate pride and self-awareness. Talk about empowering—it was a gathering that empowered me from the inside out. We were only allowed to invite 100 people, but more came...We addressed academic concerns, we socialized, people shared their talents in theater and in their writing. We all had different gifts and capabilities, and we learned from each other's experiences. But most of all, we had the joy of sharing, and not feeling unique.

> I give the DSCC credit for the fact that I have learned to have some pride in myself, and in my intellectual ability...Disability Services is a wonderful supplement, but we begin here. I would say that, as a student, if I had to choose between the DS and here, I'd pick here—for that pride and self-confidence aspect alone.

Making individual members aware of issues currently being debated on a wider front, as well as the activities, information and events on this and neighboring campuses, was achieved through a newsletter, computer contact and the materials available at the DSCC:

> I've gotten more things through the Disability Center—being able to get their newsletters, as well as the ones from Disability Access and Pace—that's a parent advocate group which I use for my son. It's very nice to know you can get these things at the Center.

The organization of both on-campus and out-reach activities engaged a particularly active group within the DSCC membership, including some individuals in our sample. These participants spoke in terms of a disability culture and the disability movement, which they saw as parallel to those of other 'minority' groups:

> I think the idea of a disability culture has been around for a while, but it was the students who said, 'We exist. We're here. And we need our own.' And out of that came a real student movement...But the students themselves put it together—I think that's why it's so unique, and so important in enhancing the academic experience—and our life and social experience too...just to have a comfortable place on a Big 10 college campus is pretty cool.

In pursuit of disability awareness, this group involved themselves in community education, including presentations to local groups and on local radio and television. Collectively, the DSCC had become a repository of expertise on what needs to be done to make this and other campuses accessible to students with disabilities:

> Speaking about disabilities is almost a small business in itself.

> And then, there's consulting. We suggested that architects undergo a training session with members of the disabled community around issues of access, because even highly educated people don't understand what's needed, and not needed.

Requests for their services as consultants (to local employers, public bodies and community groups) were increasing, and the members who undertook this work saw it as an expanding role for the organization. As they had also discovered via their national network, they (and other similar associations) were having to consider asking fees for these time-consuming services:

> People are already beating a path to our door. Like with the decoder—finally the university came to us and said they were finally entertaining the idea of getting a decoder, and wanted to know

what we recommended that they buy. But we had to spend the time doing the research. It's good that they have realized that you need to consult with the people who will use a system, but, on the other hand, many such requests make for an unreasonable amount of work. I have my studies, my work, my home and my social life. I don't have time to be a consultant, and put together panel discussions, do research and answer all the questions any business or agency sends along to us. It's something the disabled community in general has realized—you have to ask for some funds to break out the time to do all of this. Otherwise, each of us has to decide rather carefully if we can afford to donate our time to any of these requests...No one at the DSCC has been offered payment as yet, but we are going to have to start asking.

One interesting facet of the development and operation of the Center was the bringing together of people who would not otherwise have much opportunity to meet. In the two focus groups held with DSCC members and elected office-holders, it was clear that the group had, collectively, learned much about the kinds of problems that people with different types of disability encounter:

> She and I walk, but we both have mobility impairments. But, for me, it's much easier to use ramps, but it's very hard for her—but she can use stairs better than me. So we have to find a totally different entrances. You would think people with mobility impairments, or immune diseases—or whatever—would have similar needs—but we have to learn that's not so, just like everyone else.

> It's been a real learning experience, and interesting that she and I are president and vice-president. We have really had to learn to work together. I mean, she needs to look at me when we're walking down the hall to have a conversation, and I need to avoid the bright lights so I don't fall.

> It's a big thing, I mean, we have to lead the way in learning about each other's disabilities and how to make this Center accessible for all.

Their behavior toward each other in the focus groups, and in their general office interaction with people who dropped by, was courteous, thoughtful and sensitive, and was clearly founded on a good understanding of the nature of the difficulties posed by disabilities other than their own. Such learning had not, necessarily, been easy. Members described how, in setting up the Center, they had experienced conflicts of needs between members with different types of disabilities. These may be seen as paralleling the conflicts which SMET faculty face in balancing what they see as the competing needs of students with and without disabilities. The group had found itself reinventing democracy in order to meet, in an equitable way, the wide array of needs, concerns and perspectives which the new organization embraced.

Ironically, the members had to work through some of the misunderstandings which they encountered with people without disabilities among themselves before they could understand, and take into account, competing definitions of the organization's priorities. In common with the non-disabled world, initially, the organization found itself dealing with more obvious problems of physical access. Attention to more subtle needs came later:

> It seemed for a while that more of the attention of the DSCC was paid to people with access problems, and people who needed alternative format. I can remember one discussion about one particular publication. And what it came down to was that people with learning disabilities needed a different format and structure from other people. And, because it wasn't a right out front issue, those of us with physical disabilities had sort of over-looked it, not realizing that it needed an accommodation from us. So our focus was a bit lop-sided at first.

> Like how do you get something on the agenda? You fill out this form and put it in that box. I mean, that's a simple structure. But, when we started, some people wanted a free-form meeting with no set agenda, and people speaking whenever they wanted to. But there's a lot of people that are used to being shut-ins, and they are reluctant to speak up. So if the chair knows that they have asked for a little time to say something, they can sit back and know their turn will come, and not worry about how to get into the debate. When we realized this was another access issue, it was amazing the respect that it got.

> For a while, there was some conflict between hidden and physical disabilities. Whenever there was an event of some kind, it felt like the hidden disability people were there to run the errands, and do the able-bodied things. But once it was brought out in the open, I think that straightened it out.

What policy-makers, especially, may note about the Disabled Students' Cultural Center is that it works so well precisely because it is a grassroots organization, founded and run by students with disabilities to meet needs which they define and refine themselves.[27] It does not displace the need for Disability Services: their professional knowledge, and role as the implementers of legislative provisions and provider of services for students with disabilities, were clearly invaluable to students. However, for the same kind of financial outlay accorded to other student organizations, it had developed into a resource

---

[27]We made a similar finding in the 1994 study with respect to women's support systems. All of the seven campuses on which we interviewed had official women's programs, established and run by SMET departments with the intention of supporting and, thereby, seeking to improve the persistence rates of women. However, few women were aware of, or used, these forms of support, compared with those who knew of the women's professional association chapters (e.g., AWIS, and SWE) which were run by the women themselves.

center for students with disabilities on this and neighboring campuses, for the university administration, and for the local community.

Coping Strategies, Attitudes and Feelings

Table 6 highlights four main facets of the students' view of their own contributions to success in their majors. They are labeled as "coping strategies and attitudes" because the students typically spoke of how they "coped with" certain issues rather than "how they persisted." This distinction is not merely semantic: it stresses their greater focus on how to surmount difficulties which are not self-generated. The largest group of items thought to contribute to persistence—one-third (31.8%) of students' responses—stressed the need to be well-organized, both in working around the more predictable constraints of their own health states, as well as those created by educational, financial, employment or other external factors. Organizational items focused upon planning ahead, and making good use of whatever help was available. A second pair of items—joining in collective action, and turning to others for support—which also accounted for about one-third (29.6%) of reported coping strategies—were discussed earlier in this chapter. About one-quarter of the students' responses (25.4%) reference the importance of particular personal attitudes and of actions based upon them. Important among these were tenacity, assertiveness, focus on particular valued goals and willingness to make attitude adjustments in order to achieve them. Finally, students advocated a set of other practical strategies (i.e., 13.2% of their coping strategies and attitudes) which reflected realism about the situation of students with disabilities in a non-disabled world, and their knowledge (both individual and shared) about how best to deal with particular practical and interactional problems. One can reasonably argue that a set of pro-survival attitudes lies behind all of the actions and strategies the students offered—and we shall comment on some of these. However, it is also clear that knowing how systems work and acting upon this knowledge is regarded by the students as critical to their success.

Being well-organized and planning ahead are, of course, important factors in success for all students. However, the constraints and consequences of particular disabilities make this an even stronger imperative for students with disabilities:

> I'm just streamlining my study methods—a blind person can never be satisfied with their methods. You can always find ways to improve them. You can never sit back...I'm definitely not organized by nature, and losing my sight has kind of forced me to be more organized than I would have been otherwise. The best thing is to go out and talk to other blind students and find out how they do things.

The most basic component of "being organized" was knowing the constraints of their own condition and figuring out ways around them—sometimes with help from Disability Services or from other students with a similar condition. These adaptations had to include working around patterns of change in their health, some of which were known and expected, some of which were unpredictable—including those wrought by changes in medications:

> I write big and messy, and my head's down in the table, and I have a hard time reading my own notes. So after the class, I convert them into my computer...And I make tapes too. I find that's a very good way to ingest the material.

> I mean, I'm still learning about my own pattern, and with the medication, that does alter everything—so there are still things to learn.

> I record the lectures—and they don't even notice the machine. It's very useful to listen to the lecture again at home.

Having alternative strategies, and being ready to re-evaluate goals and time-tables in the light of health set-backs was seen as an intrinsic part of learning to work with one's disability:

> Everything I do, I find five ways to do it. And then, one of those ways, I won't run into a problem...And I do that because, with my type of learning disability, there will be certain things I won't be able to conquer. I just won't be able to get around them, so I have to take another path.

> I've gotten where I can write almost as well left-handed—though not, perhaps as fast. So I can write with my left on the days that my right hand hurts.

> You have to realize that you may not be able to achieve your original goals and set new ones—but not to lower your expectations. You've had a set-back. You've got one with your life, and you deal with it as best you can.

As we have already discussed in relation to the students' use of Disability Services, being ready to find out what sources of help are available, being willing to use them (rather than trying to do everything alone and unaided), and making contact with Disability Services early in one's undergraduate career, were cited as other important facets of coping by "being organized."

> I knew that I wouldn't make it without help, so I immediately went in there—like the second or third week of school—well before any tests. I went through the rigmarole to get into the program, and then I just plowed my way through pre-engineering.

Developing a network of informal sources of information—largely other students—and being pro-active in finding out what is available in systems that often appear confusing and obscure were also cited as important to survival:

> I run into people who tell me about such and such an organization and service. Then I go there and ask and find about other things too—eventually, it's like you get a network of who can answer what questions, or help you with what...I've always been a good person to go find help.

Some of the most difficult and subtle personal accommodations to disability were those made by students with learning disabilities, attention and memory deficits, and other neurological disabilities. Perhaps, more than any other type of disability, successful management of these conditions implies an understanding of what 'learning' entails, and what aspects of learning processes are affected by their particular disability. These students also need to understand (at least in an experiential way) the theories of learning on which faculty (usually tacitly, rather than overtly) base their pedagogy and their methods of teaching and student assessment, in order to compensate for their own inability to learn entirely by these means. They must understand what aspects of faculty expectations they can and cannot meet without accommodation:

> I have to increase my study time, and continually practice on speed—and try to increase it all the time...I try not to work at night—my concentration is better if I have enough sleep before the class—and that helps my speed too.

> You have the ability to learn—but in a different style...You can't just assume there's only one learning style without wasting that talent...I get very micro-focused, and that tends to be one area where my problem is. I need to focus on grasping the concepts, not, 'How do I solve this

particular problem?' I need to keep asking myself, 'What's the main issue in this problem? What is it trying to teach me?'...It's a struggle trying to think, 'Macro, macro....'

I think in ideas. So you take an idea, and put it into words. So I read something, and have to translate it from words into ideas for me to think about it. Then I have to translate the new idea back into words to write about it. So I'm going through my disability twice every single time.

I can recognize, but not memorize. If somebody reads a list of words to me than reads them again, I know if they change a word, or mis-pronounce a syllable. I'll catch it—because it's auditory...Reading is harder. I have to read word by word, and then I have to double-check each word I read. I can't sound out words. If someone will say the word for me, then I get it, and I can read on. Or I just skip that word and fill in with the context.

A reader would read the textbook onto the tape for me; then I would read the book line by line while listening to the tape. Then you can really see where your faults are—I could miss a whole line without the tape. You can also go back and clear up discrepancies between what you heard and read. Then finally, you hear what you know, and you read what you hear. (Science graduate)

For those working with physical limitations, being organized includes figuring into their choice of a class schedule the days or times when they cannot get to campus, their transportation options and the time they need to move between particular buildings:

I have to look at my possible options and get on the computer and plot out all the different combinations. Then I kind of mentally go over the university working out the travel times.

The only difficulty with that class is going to be having to show up on campus. That's going to be tough. It's going to have to be carefully orchestrated...I have to think, 'When are the tests? Will he follow the text book?' I get the books well in advance, and ask for lists of extra references so I can brush up over the summer.

Time to locate new classes—that's a big one. You get a list of new classes, and, before the quarter starts, I'll walk it through with a sighted friend. We'll locate the buildings and the rooms and I'll memorize my way around.

I'm very near-sighted. After a while, you get to a point where you know all the bus lines and almost all the connections—so you can predict....

If students need taped or large-print books, signers or interpreters, note-takers, lab partners, adapted equipment, room changes, special seating and/or test accommodations, they must be arranged well in advance of the start of classes with Disability Services, faculty, and the relevant on- and off-campus agencies. They must also give both Disability Services and their class teachers periodic reminders of test

accommodations. All of this involves good forward planning and attention to details:

> You have to be really organized—like I have to set up interpreters for every single meeting that I have—I have to know at least a week ahead. And I end up having to do a lot of writing to people, too—to arrange things.

> I start making accommodations in November for a class that starts in January.

> One thing I do have in my favor, I'm good at following through with the details. It's really saved my neck in this institution.

> You have to call, every day if necessary. And you have to put it in writing, what you need and when...You've got to be more organized than everybody else.

> I tell my counselor that I have a test in two weeks with such and such a class...He types up the accommodation letter to take to faculty with all the dates, and we both sign it. Then I go and see the faculty. Then a week before each test, I go over to remind them to send the test to Eddy Hall. I have to make sure that I get there to tell them to turn the test over because if I don't, they usually don't.

As the last speaker indicates, students had learned to expect other people to be less well-organized, less

forward-thinking, and less reliable than themselves, and planned for these too:

> Expecting the worst helps me deal with what often happens when I get there...I mean, I come into the class or the test prepared to have to do all this stuff on my own from scratch. (Undergraduate with low vision)

> You have to go to the professors two or three months ahead of time, and just needle them—find out what text books they are going to use and then find out how you can get hold of them.

> And the profs are almost never set with their syllabuses, and what the course will entail, and when...It makes it almost impossible to plan. And I have certain seasons of the year and times of day that are better. So last semester, I took a 1:30 p.m. class. But then he decided to collect homework on Mondays at 10:00 a.m. And I'm saying, 'Wait a minute. I didn't sign up for a 10:00 a.m. class!' But I just plan around my disability, although sometimes my best efforts get undone.

Students with disabilities which constrained their learning options in classrooms or labs or their

methods of private study, developed both mental and practical strategies to address these recurrent

difficulties:

> I realized I could give a piece of carbon paper to a neighbor in class and have them do a double set of notes. It's better to do that than to bother somebody for their notes later.

I can talk and write at the same time—from so many people transcribing notes for me...I can tell the transcriber, 'Write down this formula because I'm going to need to use it.' And then, in my head, I can plug in some of the rest.

I work all the problems several times over, because I wouldn't have a prayer if I went into that 45 minute test if I didn't. I can't read fast enough, so I have to recognize the problem straight away...And I limit myself to 20 minutes a problem in the test.

I deliberately over-study. In the end I usually know more than most other students.

I do a lot of memory work. I listen to the lecture and kind of visualize what he's getting at because I can't really see it on the board. I just picture it. Then, when I get a chance to look at the notes after class, I can kind of associate them with my mental pictures.

I have to sit in the front row, otherwise I won't hear everything—the professors often don't make themselves audible...Last quarter, I had a class where a lot of people came early, so I had to arrive even earlier to get a seat in the first 10 rows.

Making time for work as well as for study added another need for careful time management:

I study in the morning. I get up at 2:30 a.m. to 3:00 a.m. before I have to go to work. It seems like, early in the morning, I study pretty well.

These long-standing habits of pre-planning and organization were, as we learned from the graduates, of great benefit in their post-college work:

Good time management and being organized has actually helped me function better at the bureau. I have learned to be very well-organized, so if I do get lost for a while, I can come back and pick up easily.

Being learning disabled, I have to give myself time to read things carefully. So I'll set a goal—like, 'I'm going to read this document during the last 25 minutes of my lunch today.' Or I'll take it home and set a half hour to read it. You get pretty organized in college, and it's just a continuation of that.

Despite rebuffs with faculty which were experienced to some degree by almost every student, many participants, nevertheless, advocated going to see faculty (or TAs) to seek their help, and by their accounts, were remarkably persistent in this regard:

I think for visually-impaired students keeping the communication with the professor going is the key. Definitely. Let him know you want to work with him.

I spent a lot of time going to professors' office hours. Sometimes I think I broke the record for seeing professors in their office hours the most...I think that one-on-one contact with TAs and professors helped me through college. (Mature graduate with a learning disability)

I think office hours, and talking with instructors one-on-one has helped me the most through college. This is a large university, but if you make the effort to see your professors, it makes it a lot smaller and more personal—even if some of them make it hard to do that.

With hindsight, some of those who had been reluctant to ask faculty for help regretted it:

I put in as much effort as the other students—probably more. But, looking back, I see that I should have gone in to see the instructor. This was my junior year, but a lot of times I wasn't comprehending the material. And I decided to drop the class rather than struggle through it.

As Table 6 reflects, the participants credited about one-quarter of their persistence in SMET majors to the development of particular attitudes, and to their readiness to act upon them. "Being persistent" was portrayed as having a number of distinct attributes. Firstly, it implied clarity and firmness about academic and career goals, and holding those goals in mind through periods of difficulty, and, for some students, despite opposition:

There's going to be people who tell you that you're not going to be able to do it. And if you believe that, then you're not going to be able to do it.

The most important thing is to have a goal in mind and focus on that. You can take advice, but you've got to keep the final say...If you're out to please everybody here, you're not going to succeed. (Graduate)

Don't go and ask your counselors. Tell them, 'This is what I'm going to do. Can you help me?' And if they can't, go to someone higher.

Don't listen to those counselors. Even though you're a woman with a disability, you don't have to be a home-maker. If you are interested in tools and how things work, and they won't let you work on things at school, do it at home. Don't let them tell you 'No.'...It would have been better if I had listened more to my parents instead of the people at high school, and just said, 'This is the road I'm going to travel, and if you disapprove, you will just have to get out of my way. This is *my* goal.'

"Being persistent" also required explaining specifically, clearly and "up-front" what you needed from anyone whose help you sought:

Number one—you have to be able to state your problem, and what works best for you. And you have to give some directions for the other person to be able to help you...And you've got to be independent—even pushy. You have to be ready to apply pressure, without nagging—-be independent, and say, 'These are the things I need.' And if they are not willing to accommodate you, you have to say, 'This isn't working out. Here are some other suggestions. Can we work together on this?'

I was up-front with everybody—professors, the administration—that I was legally-blind and these were the things I was going to need. (Graduate)

I always took the initiative right away to explain to the professor the first day of class exactly what I needed, so I wouldn't catch him off-guard. I think, after seeing me work in class with my monocular, they didn't have any problems with my veracity.

What I do, is, first day of class, I go in and talk to the professor. I say, 'Hi! My name is X. I have a vision problem, and I need to sit in the front. If you use overheads, I need a copy, so I can follow you in class. If you are writing equations, or other important things on the board, I need you to say it out loud too, so I can follow along.'

Effective negotiation began by seeing yourself as the expert on your own constraints and needs,

assuming that others were willing to help you if they knew how, and being ready to educate them:

Because, they don't know how your condition works—you have to tell them—you're the expert on it—and you have to teach them what works best for you. And sometimes you're not going to know that. Sometimes it's trial and error, and you're both just going to have to work on it. I've learned that through some really bad experiences.

I consistently reverse figures—like 68 for 86, and he railed on about this in class. So I went to his office hour and asked him to consider something for a moment. I asked him to write his name on a piece of paper so that I could read it, and I pointed out to him that it was upside down and backwards from my perspective. So then I wrote his name upside down and backward so it would be right-side-up for him. I asked him how he would make out if he had to write that way all the time in order to accommodate me?...And he could have gotten mad at me, but he didn't, and he did think about it. And in the end, we became good friends. (Graduate with dyslexia)

As these accounts indicate, being persistent includes learning to be assertive. For people who

had struggled with self-doubt and denial, or who had been discounted or stigmatized, this was not at all

easy. It could be hard for such students to give themselves permission to ask for their needs to be

addressed: before they could *be* assertive, they had to nurture self-esteem, and the belief that they

deserved to be treated well:

Well, here's a few things I'd tell other students with disabilities to keep in mind. That professor is not there to lord it over you. He is being paid—partly through your money—to teach you. If they have office hours, they should be there because, in a sense, they are working for you. And you have to see the teacher not as a nasty person who is out to get you. And you keep reminding yourself, you are doing this for yourself, and not for them. (Graduate student)

You're not wasting your teacher's time asking for a small adjustment...You need to walk into his office with the attitude that you both have something to gain out of this—because that person is going to learn something too. They're going to see something they have never seen before. (Graduate)

> You kind of have to take it upon yourself to talk to enough people, and to build your connections. The first step is to learn how to handle the situation—and how to talk...You have to talk to people to get any place. So you have to be willing and outgoing enough, and trust in yourself enough, I think, before you can even attempt a university degree. You have to be willing to take those risks with other people—and to take on those responsibilities which are part of being an adult—part of taking care of yourself.

They then had to muster the courage to ask for the help they needed, and to go on asking—or insisting:

> With grad school, they didn't take me right away...People who knew me were kind of surprised at that. They had said, 'You'll have no problem getting in.' But then I had to fight with them, and constantly have them re-look at my record, you know—that's how I finally got in. It came out that they were not so much concerned about my physics knowledge, but about the overall stress of me getting around, and so forth—they were factoring that into their decision. So it basically came down to me saying, 'Just give me a try. If I don't do it, then that's fine.' (Graduate student)

> I ended up taking a sophomore class my fifth year here, because I couldn't get into it any time before that. I mean, this class was a prerequisite for 15 other classes that I've taken. I didn't want to be put off for another semester. But I had to fight them to get them to do it. But they finally let me take it after I wouldn't leave them alone. (Graduate)

> I've also found out that the U is pretty much reactionary. But if the squeak gets loud and if you keep at it, they'll do it and go the extra mile. But that's true of anything—that's true of the real world too. (Graduate student)

> Whatever your disability, if you sit back quietly, you'll be left behind. I talked my way in here, and then I talked my way into graduate school—they didn't exactly open up their arms and say, 'Come in.' If you are disabled in any way, you can't afford to play by the official rules. You have to find ways around them, and push—or you're going to fail.

Becoming assertive thus involves changes in self-view, in attitude, and in action:

Persistence was also felt to require the development of some other personal qualities—tenacity, determination, self-motivation, and being willing to "plug away" at the degree on a daily basis:

> Tenacity—It's the labelling since sixth grade that keeps pushing me. (Graduate)

> I was just fed up with my poor performance, so I just kind of worked harder, and said to myself, 'No matter what happens, I'm at least going to get this damned degree—and to heck with my other problems.' And I did—I graduated well, sent out resumes and I landed this job. (Graduate)

> So I'd say to another student in my situation, 'It's okay if you get frustrated with it. Just keep plugging away.' 'Cause a lot of kids don't do that...You have to give it your best shot.

And the first quarter, I signed up for a full load, and had to drop back to one class. I barely made it through. I was so sick all the time. I would go down to the U in the morning, and drag myself home at night. And I studied all the time that I was awake because I was determined to get through.

I just thought to myself, 'I can't go under. I'm a survivor. I can't give up. I worked too hard. I worked my way through too many problems in those classes to give up. Then I would have gone through all that for nothing. So, no!'

You basically have to be extremely stubborn. They call it by different names—persistence, tenacity—but it come down to being pig-headed—stubborn. (Graduate)

Participants also described some attitude adjustments which they saw as contributing to their ability to persist. Basic among these were moving beyond denial and anger with the limitations of the disability, to self-acceptance. Self-esteem, patience with one's self and an ability to "live in the present" also made persistence possible:

When I was 18, my self-esteem was so low, I felt so bad about myself, that I never dreamed that I'd be where I am now—it wasn't even in my wildest dreams.

I just have faith in myself and accept who I am.

Self-esteem is a big part of it. Even though I've been legally-blind all my life, it's really hard to think of myself in an actual work place, because I think of all the limitations I would have. And it's depressing to think about. Then other times, it's like, 'Well, you can do it. It's going to take a little longer. It's going to take a little more work from you, but I think you can still do it.' So I just accept that some days are up days, and some days are down days.

It's very important for me to know for myself that I'm not stupid—that I learn differently, and that it's okay to learn differently. But I had to find that out. I took an IQ test and scored very highly on it. And someone might say that IQ tests mean nothing—but they meant something to me...So now I just know it—that I'm bright, and I can be patient with myself for the rest.

It really comes out of a fear of failing—learning to be okay with the understanding that I'm not the ace in the class...'I can do it all on my own' doesn't work for me any more. It's okay to be humbled and to accept I need help. So that's part of my survival process today.

When all of this happened to me, I realized, all of a sudden, that life wasn't a guaranteed thing. When I watch a sunrise in the morning, I realize that may be the last sunrise I see. And I enjoy it. And getting my degree and an engineering job—all that is very important—but so is the sunrise. And if I lose track of how important that is, then I'm going to be caught up in some things that could be gone tomorrow and won't really mean anything.

As Table 5 (p. 84) indicates, we found expressions of pride and self-confidence spontaneously raised in discussion of issues other than persistence. These feelings clearly have bearing for the students' chances of graduation, and of success in their career goals:

> Trust yourself. Give yourself more credit than you have in the past for the things you've accomplished. That's what I'd tell myself if I was starting over. And trust your reactions to things. Be optimistic, and don't feel dumb for asking questions.

> It may mean that it takes me twice as much work—and that is frustrating. And it does make me angry. But it also makes me very proud of what I've done. It wasn't handed to me on a silver spoon. I think that when you put that much effort into it, you should be proud of yourself. (Graduate)

> There's a bit of pride involved. I am a graduate student now. I have gotten into the upper echelons.

> I view myself as being a special person who really wants to do something, and I'm highly-motivated. I don't give up that easily...I mean, I was feeling really tired after I got up in the mornings. And it was hard to take 10 credits feeling like that every day. But, yeah, I was kind of proud of myself for pulling through that.

> I was the first visually-impaired student for our high school, so they didn't quite know what to do with me as far as adaptive equipment. But now that I've been through, I know they have two more visually-impaired students there now—I've talked to them both and they're doing great. I feel it was even more worthwhile for me, getting through, and then knowing that I'd paved the way.

> Well, high school never suited me. But look at me here—I'm all As here—all my classes—total As—well, just one B.

> My mom was just happy to see me graduate from high school...It's been a pretty long haul to get through this. I'll be 28. But for someone that hated high school, I'm pretty happy about it. And mom is going to come out and celebrate with me.

We also noted some survival attitudes and strategies among students with disabilities that we also encountered among SMET seniors without disabilities in our 1994 study. They are reflected in Table 6, partly as a matter of attitude adjustment, partly as strategy. We found examples of both strategic self-presentation in encounters with faculty, and of system-playing, that is, using knowledge of the procedural rules—formal or informal—to one's best advantage. Both of these increase the chance of securing what you need. They also reduce stress, and imply development of an attitude in which set-backs are not taken too seriously, or too personally:

> I take a lot of classes I suspect I'm going to have trouble with, but I've discovered here that instructors will give you the benefit of the doubt if you take the class on a pass/fail basis. If you show a good effort, but only manage C-level work, they will see that you are putting in the effort, and will give you that passing grade.

> For the last quarters, I've probably been more closely associated with the class teachers than most students, just because of the effort it takes to be diplomatic with them. I have to work at that so that I don't get into a position where somebody claims that I got something that I shouldn't have. It's a diplomatic posture.

> You just gotta keep your head and tell them what works best for you—give them some suggestions if they're unsure they can accommodate you in exactly the way you want. Work with them on it. Find alternative routes. If you get frustrated, you're going to get them frustrated, and they're not going to want to work with you.

As with other "persisters," both graduates and undergraduates with disabilities advocated letting go of the tendency (learned in high school) to over-attach value to letter grades, rather than the depth of understanding they are supposed to reflect. In the form in which it causes most damage to self-esteem, and thus to persistence, we found in our 1994 study that students who are at risk of leaving SMET majors include those who define their personal and academic worth in terms of the grades they receive—that is, if you get C grades, then, you must be a C kind of person. Many students with disabilities, who had already struggled to overcome feelings of low self-esteem for disability-related reasons, seemed better equipped than many of their non-disabled peers to deal with the sudden shock to self-esteem that many SMET freshmen experience when their college science and mathematics grades are unexpectedly lower than those to which they had become accustomed in high school:

> The test was not legitimately fair. It was intended to fail the bulk of the class. You can watch people being destroyed...I find it hard to believe that there's a good educational reason to destroy students like that. You can just watch their self-esteem getting flattened...You can get a C and that's not important. You just need to keep your focus on the education.

> Grades here at the university have very little to do with the amount of effort you put towards them—or the amount of information you have amassed. In so many cases, the issue is, 'Did you read this book, and can you recite this particular stuff back?'

Just think, 'You are in college, so you are already in the top three percent of the world,' or something—just to be in college is very good, and you shouldn't worry about getting As. That thought has helped me a lot. I mean you don't absolutely *have* to get As in college.

The way I look at it, my objective is to learn. The outside world looks at your grade, so it matters. But a C just means I had a horrible time getting through that class. In math, I'm thankful for Cs...My emphasis is on learning the material—I treasure what I learn because of how hard it is for me to get there.

I don't attach a lot of importance to the grades...I mean, you can't over-attach importance to that stuff.

Paradoxically, given all the problems of operating within a system which has developed in ways that work to the disadvantage of students with disabilities, our text data offer evidence to suggest that students with disabilities develop a greater ability than many non-disabled peers to cope with the problems traditionally encountered by students in the early years of SMET majors. Compared with the SMET undergraduates interviewed for our 1994 study, students with disabilities tend to enter with a stronger interest in the subjects they intend to study, a clearer focus about the careers toward which they are aiming, with more commitment to learning and less emphasis on grades. Although they recounted the same types of problems as other students with the curriculum, pedagogy, student advising and student assessment methods which are traditionally used in the first two years of SMET classes, references to these were more infrequent—an average of one mention of one such issue per undergraduate with a disability, compared with approximately eight mentions by SMET switchers, and five mentions by SMET persisters. Students with disabilities were also less instrumental in their approach to their degree, and expressed more joy in learning for its own sake:

It means everything. It means discovering yourself—discovering your own value—and to be able to communicate—it means so many things to have an education. There is always something good to read—to understand something is so much fun.

Just what we did in that class—how we went about the experiments—that was just the greatest (laughs). It was a great way to start the quarter. It was the most credits I've ever taken and it was quite a major load, but that one class, in itself, was enough to make it enjoyable.

The last two classes I've taken, I had the highest grade in the class—and I'm 47, you know (laughs). I don't attach too much importance to grades, but I was happy about it...The instructor and the book may do it one way, but I like to come up with things my own way—add my little twist on things—and that's what makes it fun. I mean, like I said, I'm 47 years old—maybe I'm not supposed to be having fun—but I am.

In comparing undergraduates with disabilities with those in other under-represented groups in SMET majors, we were struck by some differences in the ways in which women, students of color and students with disabilities process their feelings about the particular types of difficulties which they encounter in these disciplines. The different ways by which each group assigns meaning to their problems seems to produce very different consequences for their actions—including their decisions about leaving or persisting in an SMET discipline.

As a number of researchers have found (Ware & Dill, 1986; Arnold, 1987; Kimball, 1989; Oakes, 1990; Strenta, 1993), and as we also found in our 1994 study, the risks to self-esteem and self-confidence—and thence, the risk of leaving the major—are higher for women and for students of color in SMET majors than they are for white males. These risks arise not because SMET faculty treat these groups of students differently from young white men, but because they treat them in the same manner. The damage is done because women and students of color do not know how to interpret, or respond to, a regimen which has little meaning for them, and which was never intended to meet their learning styles or needs. The nature of the damage varies: bright women who are getting average, or above average, grades may leave an SMET major because they do not know whether their performances are "good enough" when faculty hold back from teacher-learner relationships. Many women have learned to rely on their teachers for an interpretation of their performance throughout their pre-college education. Having also learned to work for their teachers' praise and to depend upon faculty for reassurances that they are "doing okay," freshmen and sophomore women are distressed when they cannot evoke a nurturing response from SMET faculty.

When students of color encounter academic difficulties in the early years of SMET work, they may not give themselves permission to seek faculty (or other) help. They often take much of the blame for the difficulties they experience upon themselves, and leave SMET majors feeling a sense of shame for their "failures." Burdened with a sense of having "let down" a supportive home community, they often leave the institution rather than switching into a non-SMET major which seems less prestigious to themselves and their family.

Students with disabilities respond differently in the face of academic difficulty. Though they also experience periods where they "feel stupid"—particularly students with learning disabilities—they seem less at risk of under-estimating their own ability, of placing the entire blame for their difficulties on themselves, of failing to seek appropriate help and, thereby, of leaving the major or abandoning their career plans. As a group, they are much clearer about why they want to tackle an SMET major than were the majority of the freshmen and sophomore women whom we interviewed for the 1994 study, are more interested in the discipline for it's own sake than many young, white males, and have already overcome more difficulties than most other students in getting to this stage in their education. The direct opposition to requests for accommodation which many students with disabilities face on a regular basis clarifies one important source of their difficulties, and prompts actions other than withdrawal. Perceiving the sources of their difficulties as largely external (rather than within themselves) tended to provoke anger in students with disabilities rather than self-doubt (as in many women) and self-blame (as in many students of color). This way of defining their situation, and the feelings of anger this raised, were often the mainspring for an assertive response, and for their overall determination to persist in their chosen course, come what may:

> Don't take it personally. I mean, they're going to put you down. You're going to get insulted. You're going to get treated like shit. But you don't interpret how they're treating you as who *you* are. You learn to be confident in what you can do and ignore it—it's hard to do. It's hard when the professor is putting you down, but you just ignore it and go on. Because it's what you need—the education and the piece of paper. And what they say is not absolute reality. And I think maybe students with disabilities may understand that better than many non-disabled students do. (Undergraduate with impaired vision)

> Look at the money they've wasted on this building—and they can't get some of us in through the front door. Getting disabled people into some of these buildings is impossible. I'm sorry. In a

wheelchair, you just can't get there. And for someone on crutches, it's almost impossible to—just to get to all these old buildings in the time-frame you've got. Sorry, but I get a bit steamed about this. And you feel, you're damned if you'll let them get you.

I know there's a need for grading. But I find it hard to believe that there's a need to destroy students like that. You can just watch the self-esteem getting flattened...You're used to being on the top of the pile, and then someone rips the rug out from under you. As far as you know, you're at the bottom of the pile. But you're not really. They just flattened the pile to a thinner level.

And I had the guts to go in and say, 'Hey, look. You either deal with me, or you're going to have to fight this out at a higher level.' I hated doing that, but there's been some I had to do that with...There was one guy who said I couldn't take the test separately, and I failed the thing. And I brought him all my homework to see, and tried to explain why it was hard for me to concentrate when I had to take tests along with the rest. I just stood there and fought him, and I eventually got him to give me half the grade...He wouldn't let me re-take it.

I was pretty angry. I'd dragged myself out of bed, driven in, paid the parking, walked to his office, and was ready to take the test no matter how lousy I felt. And I asked for the test. But I think someone had got to him since he refused me the delay, and had told him he'd better give me a chance, so he was talking about a delay after all...But I said, 'I'm here now. I'll take it. I won't do so well, but I won't flunk it either. And then I'm going to the doctor's afterwards to document this.' He said, 'Document what?'...I think he might have been getting a bit nervous...Anyway, I took it, and I did really well on it. I was just so mad—and when I get mad, I get motivated, and I think faster.

Recognition of external sources of some problems, and readiness to channel anger and frustration into assertiveness, enables students with disabilities—despite their many difficulties and stop-go patterns of enrollment—to complete their degrees in a time-frame comparable to other SMET majors. In discussing the importance of the Disabled Students' Cultural Center with students, we again found difficulties defined in external terms, and angry responses channelled into courses of action geared to survival. The participants in the DSCC focus groups described anger and frustration as having prompted them to seek out others who shared and understood their problems, and who supported them in responding appropriately (including collectively) to their difficulties.

On the evidence available to us in this short, intense series of interviews on one campus, as well as that derived from our (1994) seven-campus study of SMET undergraduates without disabilities, we would argue that students with disabilities who, often against formidable odds, make it into higher education, demonstrate a higher personal potential for persistence than do many of their non-disabled peers. The tendency to process affective responses in pro-survival ways, taken together with their above-average ability, high level of organizational skills, willingness to seek out timely help, development of tenacity and assertiveness, their nurturing of self-esteem, confidence, and pride—both in themselves, and (in grass roots organizations exemplified by the Disabled Students' Cultural Center) in each other—give students with disabilities a greater potential for persistence than many other students. This potential can, however, only be fully realized in contexts where their financial, access, and accommodation needs are adequately addressed.

CHAPTER FOUR: CAREER ISSUES

In this chapter, we discuss the question of what influences the educational and career choices of undergradutes and graduates with disabilities. We also discuss several job search issues, including the role of work experience, the question of whether and when to disclose a disability to employers or co-workers, and the kinds of work environments which are seen as more and less congenial. Finally, we offer some observations on work accommodation issues.

Factors in Career Choices

As already indicated at points through this report, the educational and career choices of SMET graduates and undergraduates with disabilities have some distinctive features. As described in Chapter One (and summarized in Table 1, page 19), we found the level of intrinsic interest in particular SMET disciplines and their career applications to be unusually high (i.e., 38% of all motivations offered) compared with those offered by undergraduates without disabilities in our 1994 study samples (i.e., 17% of all motivations offered). The focus on intrinsic interest was also marked among the graduate students, and among working graduates, who carried it forward into their work placements:

> I got into physics because I thought I could give something new—add something to physics as a discipline...I want to get my ideas out there, but basically I do it because I enjoy it...and if I get a master's versus a Ph.D., that's neither here nor there. It's the work that matters—so long as I'm able to do what I got into physics to do.

> I like working in the field I'm in. I'm in a research area, and we're researching formulas for inhalers for asthmatic patients. I like being involved in the research aspect of it. You get to do the library research, then actually be in the labs working with the drugs...so it's intellectually interesting.

> I enjoy my job, because you get to build something, and actually see it work. You know, you've actually put something together with all this knowledge (laughing). You've learned it, and it works!

Another distinctive element in the choice of SMET majors by students with particular disabilities is, as noted earlier, that these majors offer students with learning disabilities and those with visual impairments (and perhaps others) some advantages over the arts or social sciences, where the volume of reading materials and the demand for writing skills, analysis of text materials and competence with foreign languages, are all much greater.

Because of the high proportion of mature students in this group, the preference for a particular kind of work was more often grounded in relevant, prior (and some ongoing) work experience than we found among undergraduates without disabilities. Some students with late-onset conditions (including those acquired by work-related accidents) had achieved a high level of work skills, experience and responsibility prior to undergraduate entry. As also referenced in Chapter One, such experiences had generated realism about limitations on the career opportunities open to people with disabilities, including the risks of unemployment. Participants with late-onset disabilities—especially those who had been laid off from work—described these experiences as important in their decision to return to higher education. They viewed their education as an opportunity to rethink and enhance their career options and, perhaps, to increase their job security in the longer term:

> I wasn't expecting to be able to come back to school—that's one of the happier sides of what happened...I've always wanted to learn more about math. Even in my work building bicycle frames, I used math and engineering to some extent.

Balancing the gain of higher education against the personal losses brought by disability was a fairly common theme among the mature students. Some of the younger students viewed the encouragement they had received (from counselors and other mentors) to enter higher education as an important factor in their personal growth. It also enhanced their chances of entering some kind of mainstream employment:

> After looking for a job for a year after I left high school, and not being able to find anything, they finally sat me down and said, 'Well, maybe we should think about having you go back to school'—which is something I had really wanted anyway. And, as it turned out, it was probably the best thing I ever did, because it was like going into the army. I mean, I was completely undisciplined and in disarray. I didn't have much motivation and probably wouldn't have been able to function that well even if I had gotten a job. So coming back here was really a good way to beat myself back into shape. And I pretty much consider what I'm doing right here at school as my rehabilitation.

138

We were, however, concerned to hear the view expressed by some of the students who had been given financial support for their education that, had they not had disabilities, they were unlikely to have been able to attend college at all:

> If I wasn't legally blind, I wouldn't be at the U at all, just because of other life circumstances—'cause my family's got no money—you know, they wouldn't be able to put me through school. And, being legally blind, I can get tuition at the University of Minnesota free—right up to my doctorate.

Overall, the career orientations of students with disabilities appear more focused, more informed, more grounded in experience and, thus, more realistic than those we encountered among SMET undergraduates without disabilities. As also mentioned earlier, the motivations of students with disabilities are often less materialistic and more altruistic than among SMET majors, overall:

> I was just so excited to have a job, and I just love it. Another woman engineer was hired at the same time I was, and this is her second job. And when she was interviewed, she was a lot more concerned with what this company could do for her...I wasn't looking at that—I focused just 100 percent on what I could do for this company.

> If I tell someone who wants to be an engineer that I'm going into teaching, generally what I get back is, 'Why would you want to do that? There's no money in it. And the schools are battle zones.' And, in some places, that's true! And the teachers are looked down on...It's so disappointing that this attitude is out there.

> I would love to find myself in a profession which was less interested in making new and great products, and more interested in helping people. I'd like to use my skills in that capacity—if I could find a job like that, I'd do it in a flash.

> A classmate and I—he's an older student also with a disability—when we graduate, we've discussed the possibility of doing projects that would help students in the future. We'd start with a lab manual, and write it in a terminology and sentence structure that a layman can understand—so maybe the TAs wouldn't have to respond to so many what they call, 'dumb questions.'

> I'm really proud of what I do here—and that's why I've stayed. I mean, I'm not even getting paid an engineer's wage yet—I'm still on a student's wage. But it hasn't really bothered me. The money isn't where it's at in my mind. It's more the experience I'm gaining. I get a lot of pleasure from it—there's a lot more rewards to work than money.

As was also reflected in their approach to their undergraduate work, an important aspect of the participants' approach to career planning was to understand the limitations set by their disability, and to take these into account when considering particular kinds of work or work settings. This was described

as a gradual, often painful, process of narrowing, ruling-out and refining options:

> I can rule out the skills-type jobs—welding was another one that was kind of difficult for me—or forging, or drilling—those jobs where you need a lot of two-handed machining skills. That's something I'd probably have trouble with.

> I went to the technical college for carpentry or something. Well, at that age, I wanted that sort of thing. But I soon found out that the teachers didn't have a whole lot of faith in me running power tools—I mean, a visually-impaired person running power tools?! So I kind of got the hint. And I thought, 'And what about transport home? I'd have to get to remote work sites.' So I had to stop being the typical teenager, and get real about what I would do.

> I thought, 'Perhaps your desire to become a newspaper editor is misplaced!' The truth is, with this disability, I can't spell worth a damn. I might have a tremendous way with words—perhaps writing fiction makes more sense—or some other form of writing where the strict deadlines and total technical perfection are not so critical.

> If you have this 30 degree angle over here, and another over there, and they tell you they are exactly the same—well, they're not for me. It's a completely different perceptual world for me. So I found out there were certain areas like that in mechanical engineering that I simply couldn't do—drafting. I mean, that was a major disaster...And so I just started narrowing the fields down, and chemical engineering just became my major by default—by ruling other things out.

For most participants, the process of adapting their career preferences to what they felt they could,

realistically, undertake was a personal process, worked out in discussion with family, friends or advisors.

In a very few instances, however, participants felt that an intended career path, which they saw as within

their capacity, had been unreasonably blocked for reasons related to their disability:

> I was a finalist for a four-year $20,000 ROTC scholarship for both the navy and the air force. Then I was disqualified on the basis of my allergies. It was very frustrating. I had three civilian doctors state that it would not be a problem for engineering service...And I had been on the school swimming and track teams, was active in all sports and had excellent health otherwise. But they had 450 scholarships available and 5,000 candidates, so they are kinda picky...I had very good high school grades and did well on the entrance exams—206 on the PSAT and 31 on the ACT...And when I told the air force recruiter that I had been disqualified, and he asked me my ACT scores, he said, 'Those stupid bastards!' And he advised me to apply again in two years. But, of course, that was too long to wait to get into school.

Students with an adult-onset disability, and those who were experiencing some deterioration in

their health, were faced with reconsideration of plans which had seemed reasonable at an earlier stage

in their academic or work careers:

I'd like to do what I used to do—I'd like to be in manufacturing, although now, with my health record, I suspect that I'm going to have trouble in a lot of businesses. They are not going to want someone with a health record like mine.

I always wanted to go to college—actually I always wanted to be a math or science teacher. And so I went to college straight after high school, but that was when I found out I couldn't finish a semester. This was before I was on medication, and because I didn't know what was the matter and that I could withdraw from classes, my record got into a great mess—I'd got all these Fs....Now, I'm actually aware of what the problem is—and how to cope with it—and this is the furthest I've gotten in school. But I'm not sure now that the education school will take me.

I feel bad that, because of my condition getting worse, I probably won't get the master's degree...My ultimate goal was to teach some college courses on disability and, with only a B.A., I don't think I'll be able to do that...I don't know. We'll see where it takes me.

Based on prior experience, some undergraduates worried about the impact of variations in their health

on their ability to do the work, and on their job security:

They dropped me three months before I was due to finish the project. And the problem was tardiness and absenteeism, which was due to my disability.

For some participants, concern about specific physical limitations, and the projected (or experienced)

stresses of particular kinds of work, shaped their choice both of work area and work setting:

Well, it basically boils down to the writing problem—and the services I'll need as a solution. If we don't come up with a solution, it's going to be a big problem when I get to Fermi Labs. (Visually-impaired graduate student)

When I think about what kinds of physical stresses there may be, I remember the kinds of physical things I did while I was at Honeywell. I remember doing a lot of standing, which, because of the injury to my foot, won't be possible any more...Then I seem to recall running around the building a lot—a lot of walking up and down the halls. I wouldn't manage that now.

With this seizure thing, I have to know that my job is going to be within the physical limits of what I can do.

The only thing with the asthma is I cannot go scuba diving—I tried it last summer after I graduated, because it does have some use for geologists in an undersea project we're working on with the Bureau of Mines...So it probably hampered me somewhat there.

It comes down to actual hands-on things—which are okay—versus doing microscopic things. I know I'm not always going to be able to see things in a microscope. So I would chose to do other things that require math or theory—more thinking orientation, versus looking at things and recording them.

While I was waiting to get the doctor's slip signed to get my driving license this time around, I was thinking, if I didn't get the license, I'd have to live in a city, near a main bus route. And I'd have to hope that the buses ran as I needed them to. And, in the engineering field, you're going to have to work Saturdays and you might have to work late in the evenings. If you rely on public transport, that can be really scary...And all of that feeds into my thinking about where I should try to work—the type of job and the place both.

I have to think about carpeting—it's a problem, particularly if it's wool. Carpet in the work place is a real pain for someone with asthma. I don't have any in my apartment. So I started to think about work contexts where there would be as little dust as possible—and *no* carpets.

I have to think about choosing the job and choosing a place to do it both together...I'm doing an industrial engineering minor in mechanical engineering. And thinking about industrial work takes my thoughts back to the logistics department. With that, you can do the same type of work in lots and lots of different settings.

One logical next step in this process was to choose or shift to a career path or work setting that plays to the person's strengths, makes their disability less relevant to the demands or context of their work and reduces its disruptive potential. Thinking of this kind drew some students into graduate school or professional training; others into planning, or actually setting up, their own businesses—some of which were home-based. It also encouraged some creative solutions to career choice problems:

As an undergraduate, I always hated using readers—you know, I wanted to wake up in the middle of the night and do something—and not have to get hold of a reader to do it. So I always wanted to do something that I could just do on my own using my magnification device. So I got a job as an electrical engineer writing test specifications, and that was exactly what I wanted—in the sense that it involved circuit analysis. It was hardcore mental work...And it was for a defense contractor, so it meant state-of-the-art designs. So I enjoyed the work immensely.

I was always interested in electronics, and I thought that would be an area where my disability wouldn't be as much of a disability—'cause it's a lot of brain work. So I just kind of went in that direction, and I eventually ended up in electrical engineering.

I'd like to get away from the conventional construction field, and possibly work for small, rural cities who can't afford to hire a full-time engineer.

The quality of recordings has always been an interest, as well as the music...So it's sort of a hobby that got out of control, I guess...And when I saw this set-up, and realized the power of what it could do, I just said, 'Holy Cow! This is a hobby I could make money at. I can support myself doing this.' Well, heck, that's the best of both worlds!

Last summer, I started a corporation in metal fabrication—to do one of a number of a specific projects I had in mind. It turned out it was quite easy to start the corporation. And I bid on a few projects, and got one for a high school catwalk—it's a walkway raised up above their theater for lighting and acoustic panels. And it ended up being like 26,000 pounds of steel clipped together...We built it in an old airplane hangar that's been deserted for years—my friend bought it and he has this huge amount of space. And he helped with the project. He has a couple of welders...Money-wise, it didn't come out that well. In fact, I would have done much better working for someone else through the summer, but it's given me fabrication experience which is important for engineers to have...And I learned about bidding a project, and about corporate taxes. In fact, I learned a lot more than I thought I would.

An extension of this line of thought was to incorporate the experience of living and working with a disability into one's career plans. For example, the following two speakers felt that teaching would provide them with professional opportunities to draw upon the special understandings and skills they had gained as people with disabilities:

I think I'll probably be a good teacher...There were actually quite a few of us with disabilities who were math tutors. I think all of us were pretty good, and we got a lot of confidence from the students...I could say, 'This is what I had problems with,' and I could explain how I made sense of it. Once I understand it, I can explain it step by step.

My guess is that there are kids using dope in every high school in the land...Awareness of a problem is a big chunk of presenting somebody with an opportunity to help themselves. And I'll probably be able to spot certain kinds of difficulty faster than the run-of-the-mill teacher...Being in recovery and having moved on and achieved so much, gives me some perspective, some credibility and some sensitivity...You have to be on the right side of the river to be able to tell somebody on the other side how to use the bridge...I think there's a teaching role for everybody—but there may be some very important teaching roles for people who have experienced a disability.

Taking their disability into account in making career plans also involved thinking further ahead than, perhaps, do many new graduates. Students with disabilities are mindful of the need for employment which offers medical insurance fairly quickly, and also disability and retirement pension schemes in the longer-term. As already indicated, six of the undergraduates and four of the graduates had no medical insurance at the time of their interview. Several of the graduates had experienced long delays in securing employment-based medical benefits, and, in one instance, this took three and a half years. To the extent that regular, full-time employment is more difficult for workers with disabilities to secure, so too are medical, disability, and retirement benefits:

So actually, from the time I graduated, there was a three and a half year period where I had no medical insurance at all. It was partly because I couldn't go to any outside sources because I either didn't qualify or it was too expensive. And I was doing a lot of temporary positions—I didn't have a full-time permanent position.

I'm at an age where I've been deprived of the ability to work some place long enough to ever get a retirement pension. I guess that's something I'll have to contend with when the time comes.

Those who projected some deterioration in their condition over time also expressed the need to plan for the later stages of their life.

For over half of the total undergraduate and graduate student sample (N=28; 58.3%), the choice of particular types of work, or of working contexts, was influenced by disability-related considerations. However, 18 of the undergraduates, three of the graduate students (N=21; 42.9% of the total student sample), plus six of the working graduates (including the post-doctoral fellow), were following, planning or intending a return to conventional careers—including some at a high academic or professional level. Two were pursuing careers in law (one in patent law), two in academic science, and two in laboratory science (including a new appointment at Fermi Lab).[28] Four of the eight graduates who were in regular, full-time employment portrayed themselves as progressing along conventional career tracks, with good prospects of further promotion. They included, a quality engineer, an information systems manager, a research and development engineer for a laser printer company and a senior analytic chemist with a Fortune 500 company. The broader career plans of this group of undergradutes included work as mechanical, electrical or construction engineers in the same kinds of company settings as most other engineering graduates. Some described more specific plans: design for a major car company; electrical engineering in a Japanese car company (by a non-Japanese participant who was fluent in Japanese); aeronautics in the aerospace industry; satellite communications design; computer system design; network programming; animated modelling; hazardous waste management; coke refinery inspection; design of

---

[28]Plus the fifth graduate student attending medical school, who was not included in the sample because he was unavailable for a full interview.

equipment for biotechnology research; high school teaching (in mathematics, science and special education); and working towards consultancy or self-employment in structural engineering.

It is notable that 21 of the 27 participants who were planning, or following, traditional careers did not choose their career paths for reasons related to their disabilities, and did not expect their work environments to be adapted to their needs. All of this group, which included all of the four working graduates who were engaged in corporate careers, had hidden disabilities. These four graduates had chosen not to make their employers or their immediate colleagues aware of their disabilities. The majority of the undergraduates with hidden disabilities who were also planning traditional careers expressed the hope that they would be able to avoid such disclosure. The preferences and concerns of all the undergraduates planning traditional career paths were largely focused on the same kinds of issues as SMET undergraduates without disabilities (e.g., career opportunities, salaries, working conditions, job satisfactions, etc.). They foresaw no special difficulties so long as they could "manage" their disability, compensate for its specific limitations or "pass" as "normal." The remaining six undergraduate and graduate students who were planning conventional careers had fairly obvious disabilities which they had found to be socially-supported by faculty and others: three were blind or had low vision, and three had mobility impairments. Expressed in terms of our earlier discussion of differential faculty attitudes toward students with disabilities, they all had "faculty-approved' disabilities. Although five of this six expected to need contextual and technical adaptations in order to do the work they planned, their relatively trouble-free experience of being granted such accommodations throughout their education predisposed them to be confident that this would continue into the work place. However, as only one of these had, as yet, actually tested this assumption, it was not possible to know whether this expectation would be met. Three of the six had chosen academic careers where fewer accommodation issues may arise.

Gaining Work Experience

Although almost all of the mature students had relevant prior work experience to offer a prospective employer, younger students approaching graduation were concerned that they had less work experience in a field related to their major than many non-disabled peers with whom they would soon be competing for employment. The importance of both work experience, and a chance to make contacts for possible future employment through internships or "co-ops" was stressed by all of the participants. All SMET majors need such experiences. However, the need appears to be greater for younger undergraduates with disabilities, because they may have fewer opportunities to gain experience and contacts by other means, and attitudinal barriers to overcome where their disabilities are known to prospective employers. Some undergraduates had found their own part-time jobs in relevant areas of work, and were hoping that these would lead to full-time work after graduation:

> I work here in the microscopy center. It's fascinating work...I don't know how much that's going to help in actually getting a job, but hopefully it will be beneficial.

> I had worked at Metro Waste—which is our waste water treatment plant here—as a chemical technician. And I see this as a possible way of maybe working into a similar science-based job. It's not quite the field I want, but you need that start, and those connections.

> I'm working as a design engineer for a small company. I was hired on to work on a project last September, and I've just stayed there—what I'm doing now is basically what I'll be doing when I graduate.

> Well I'm kinda working my way in. I was hired to work on one project in September, and I'm now continuing to work there on other projects. If the system sells, I'll have a full-time job. However, if it doesn't, they may have to trim back and not hire another person full-time. It's kind of 'fingers crossed.'

> Well, it's not a guaranteed placement, but it's experience...and the jobs just aren't there without experience.

For a number of reasons, however, students with disabilities seemed less likely to get undergraduate work placements them did other students. This is partly because they needed to devote more time to their academic work than do many other students, but it may also reflect hesitation on the part of faculty, advisors or co-op employers to consider them:

And I was supposed to be sent out to Brookhaven National Laboratory in about two weeks. There's a group of like eight of us going. And then something apparently happened to our professor's budget—didn't get as much as they thought. And now I'm the only person not going. And I've been in the study group the longest...And I'm thinking, 'Is it just because I'm disabled that I'm not needed, or because I really don't have the capabilities?'...It sure makes me feel stupid and worthless...And my professor didn't have the guts to tell me herself—she got somebody else to tell me that I couldn't go...Maybe they took me on just to be nice.

All but one of the working graduates reported that internships, or other relevant work experience, undertaken while they were undergraduates had been a critical element in getting their first job after graduation. They described how employers who might otherwise have had reservations about employing recent graduates with disabilities, had offered them jobs straight from school, based on direct experience of their capabilities:

I worked as an industrial assignment student, which helped immensely when I graduated. I was seeing what the working world would be like, and so I had a little more confidence...When I was offered an interview for this job, they gave me a pop engineering test too, and I scored 100 percent. It seemed to amaze them. So I think that, plus the fact that I had that undergraduate experience, made them willing to take a chance on me. (Blind graduate)

I worked for the county as a surveyor, so I had some surveying experience. And then, last year, I had my internship and was able to get some experience of working on the auto-CAD, and also in design worked. All of that really helped.

So when a position came open that needed someone with component-level trouble-shooting abilities, he volunteered me because he knew I'd done this with other components and I fit the bill exactly. So I didn't have to go all through the interviewing process trying to convince anyone that I could do it.

Those graduates who had experienced difficulty in getting their first jobs, described lack of experience as a salient factor in their difficulties:

Most of the jobs that I didn't get was largely because of lack of the right work experience going through college.

It made me hesitant in interviews, not having had internships. And that was probably what restricted me in getting my first job more than anything else. And it affected my confidence level too.

Although many undergraduates with disabilities worked, they often worked in low-skill jobs which did not give them the kinds of professional experience which employers in their field were seeking.

Mentors who use their own networks to help students get internships and make connections for graduates seeking work are important to all students. They are especially important to students with disabilities who have more barriers to employment—both in employers attitudes, in their often more limited job experience and in the scope or context of the work they feel ready to undertake:

> My insurance company wants me to do an internship, so I went to see my advisor just today. He had just gotten a call from a local city looking for a student to help them design an electrical system for the fairgrounds. So he called the guy right away, and I got the job. But I wouldn't have known if I hadn't decided to go and see him today.

> I made some close contacts with some engineering people when I was working in a German bio-tech company—and it was these people that sort of inspired me to come here to get this additional education...Anyway, I've maintained contact with them. They know I'm here and they know what I'm doing, and I think that there's a good chance that, when I'm out, they will approach me.

However, it is often harder for students with disabilities to find mentors, and build such networks. Disability Services offers mentors through their Careers Connection program, however (as noted earlier), relatively few of our participants seemed to be aware of this or to have used the opportunity.

Rather than competing for jobs via the application and interview process, a number of undergraduates and graduates described how they had "worked their way in"—and up—by taking jobs in fields of work, or work contexts, that particularly interested them, and being willing to accept a lower level of pay and responsibility than was appropriate for their level of qualifications or experience in order to demonstrate their abilities first-hand:

> I started as an undergraduate, like 10 years ago, and some time after I graduated they promoted me. I just worked my way up.

> I've been here two years as a student engineer. It took two and a half years to find that. But I came in and gave it a shot at that lower level, and things have gone very well since.

> I answered an ad for a junior scientists' job and I started at $6.00 an hour. This was a considerable step down from what I was earning as a bike mechanic—which is how I had been putting myself through school...When I started here, we were working on the first Keck telescope. And there were some problems with the coatings...Anyway, I decided to take all the information that I had and run it into a database on my computer at home. And I found that parts that had been chipped didn't fail what is called the 'tape test'. So I decided to figure out what was different about the chipped parts—and I found they had been sand-blasted. And so we were

able to work out that there had been a production error in the making of the glass pieces. We straightened that out and went from a 40 percent to about a 78 percent success rate—and by the end of the run were up to 94 percent...Oh, the clients were very happy. And the owners were very happy too. They bought me a computer here and about doubled my salary, and in about a year—most importantly—they let me have free run in the projects I took on.

Given the particular importance of relevant work experience to graduating seniors with disabilities, and their greater difficulty in securing it, departmental or university-wide programs (such as Disability Services' Career Connections program) which seek to meet this need in a systematic manner, and encourage students to take advantage of them, are important in improving the job chances of new graduates with disabilities.

Job Search Issues

Some of the participants expressed concerns about the difficulties of the job market in their fields identical to those expressed by SMET majors without disabilities in our 1994 study:

> I've done some internships and I've interviewed with the co-op program...I really liked the internship—but I've gotta get a little broader experience. But as far as the jobs go—looking at the current market—realistically, I don't think I'll get one.

However, when the local economy or particular sectors within it were in recession, graduates and undergraduates with disabilities felt themselves to be at greater risk of losing their jobs, of difficulty in finding them or of being passed over for promotion. Their discourse on these issues, and their actual career decisions, reflect a high degree of realism about their economic vulnerability and a felt need to protect themselves. For 25 of the participants (i.e, 41.7% of the I.T. sample), entry to higher education was very largely seen as a way to off-set their occupational vulnerability:

> It's all really dependent on the employer—you know—their viewpoint. I had a lot of trouble finding work. In fact, I'm still unemployed. So that's a good indicator of how easy it *wasn't*.

Nine of this group reported career interruptions which were directly related to the onset of their disabilities, and 16 had experienced lay-offs for other reasons. Both they, and some of the younger undergradutes, felt particularly vulnerable in field specialties where job availability was known to be limited and actively avoided them. Participants generally agreed that there were risks in becoming highly

specialized in any direction:

> It's a rotten industry—big fluctuations when you're employed and when you're not. I'd still like to get back into aerospace if I had my druthers, but with my health record, and past experience of them, I deliberately specialized in another direction. It's a lousy field for anyone—especially anyone with a disability—to try and stay in. (Mature undergraduate)

> The defense market took a turn for the worst, and the layoffs were occurring every month and it was a very upsetting situation. I mean, guys in their 40s with families and kids in high school and college...It was a good lesson, I guess. I decided to be a really marketable engineer. You really need the ability to do a bit of everything—it's just too risky to get really specialized. (Mature undergraduate)

> Mechanical is a lot more marketable, so they kind of steered me more toward the mechanical end, and I'm very glad of it today...But I'm still here as a student engineer, and we have an economic problem in my group [at work]. There isn't any growth in the market. If there was more growth, they would bring me in as a full-time engineer, but at the moment they can't afford to make that step. (Graduate)

Some of the undergraduates were actively seeking an additional technical qualification at a lower level

than their degree as a way of improving their chances of employment, or were considering abandoning

or deferring completion of their degree in favor of an apprenticeship style of qualification with greater

perceived work potential:

> It's hard now for engineers to get jobs with so many cut-backs. I think it would be easier coming out with a two-year certificate as a technician—easier to get work than coming out with the degree. I'm working on an electronics program at the technical college—on medical equipment—it's a good area to get into—but it's a more repairing, calibrating, fixing hospital equipment kind of thing. If I can keep up the As, I can get a job with the degree—but you have to be at the top.

> I went back to do an electrician's apprenticeship—and I was one of the first three women to get it—we make up just one percent of the electricians.

> The classes at the St. Paul Tech were affordable and they had on-the-job training with a local chemical company, so I could conceivably get a job some place. It's a good way to hook-up with an employer.

In addition, two working undergraduates who had found congenial work with good prospects had decided

not to return to the university to complete their degrees, at least for the foreseeable future.

As outlined in Chapter One, both the graduates and the mature undergraduates expressed strong concerns about job security. Of the 14 working graduates, five described their work situation as "insecure," two were unemployed, two were working on short-term contracts and one had chosen self-employment (a small, specialized engineering company) following difficulties in finding a congenial work setting. Six of the graduates had experienced difficulties in getting positions appropriate to their qualifications following graduation. It had taken them between one and two-and-a-half years to secure an appropriate full-time job. In the interim: they had accepted lower-level, temporary positions in order to get started; had several less-satisfactory jobs before finding their present position; had experienced lay-offs, or had been relegated from full-time employment to contract status. A seventh graduate—now in law school—had returned to higher education partly because of his concerns about job insecurity in the longer term. One of the unemployed graduates had left his employment following a dispute over under-payment. A second graduate (re-employed by the time of the interviews) had resigned from a job in which the nature and scope of his work was at a lower level than he had initially been offered. Although these difficulties have to be seen in the context of a local economy which was just beginning to emerge from a period of economic recession, the participants generally shared the belief that workers or applicants who had disabilities that were known to employers, were more vulnerable to difficulties in finding and keeping jobs than were people without disabilities. In times of economic recession, they suspected that workers with disabilities were seen as more expendable than other workers, and six of the participants recounted direct experiences of discrimination:

> At first it was a good place to work. They had lots of disabled people, and they didn't care so long as you got the job done. But it started to change when the economy started changing. I watched a disabled friend of mine be railroaded right out the door.

> Our division was bought by a company from California, and their attitude was totally different—just awful. I noticed a lot of other disabled people out there in the parking lot with me when I got laid off. There was one guy who needed a big screen because he couldn't see very well—a wonderful statistician. He was a brilliant man. And I knew darn well that he had managed his disability all his working life. But he was out there in the parking lot with myself and two other people I knew that were disabled. And I thought, 'Well, that's nasty, but what

are we going to do about it?' You can litigate. But then you get a reputation as someone who likes to sue people. And you never work again.

Disclosure issues

Given their generalized perception of economic vulnerability, and their undergraduate experiences of financial difficulty, prejudicial attitudes or of actual discrimination, it is not, perhaps, surprising that many of the participants approached the job application and interview process with anxiety. Approximately one-third (N=17; 35.4%) of the undergraduate and graduate student sample who had hidden or less-obvious disabilities, said that they preferred not to tell a prospective employer about their disabilities. Five of the working graduates who had hidden disabilities and who worked in larger companies (including four in regular full-time employment, and one contracted worker) had not disclosed their disabilities to their employers or colleagues. Three graduates who worked in smaller companies were the only employed graduates who had disclosed otherwise hidden disabilities to their employers and co-workers.

The preference against disclosure at interview was largely based upon the fear that, at a time of limited employment opportunities, it might prejudice a prospective employer against making a job offer which they would otherwise have made:

> I never really thought I would tell an employer I'm disabled. It's pretty uncomfortable. I think they would prefer to hire someone who doesn't have a prior problem. A lot of them don't understand you can work as effectively as another person. But just by indicating you have a disability, you're taking a risk...I mean, I don't have it on my resume—but I've thought about it—just so you don't let it slip...Maybe it's a good idea to put it there and let them see what you've accomplished even though you're dyslexic. It's just hard to know. It's a gamble.

> My thinking is, I would like to tell an employer that I have a disability before they hire me, but I really don't think I would—not until after I get the job. Because even though everyone says that they don't take that into consideration, I'd have to think that they would. And I have a hidden disability. So my thinking is I would keep it hidden unless it's obviously to my benefit to mention it.

The choice not to mention their disability in job applications and interviews was supported by advice against disclosure reported to be given by faculty, advisors, the Institute of Technology Placement Center staff, family and friends:

> The people in the I.T. placement office, I talked to them about it, and they said, 'Hide it.' The head of the placement office, he told me that.

> They tend to advise people not to mention their disability. It's good advice. After the interview, I felt like, if I'd told them I don't know that they would have hired me.

A preference for non-disclosure was particularly strong among those who had—or who were recovering from—disabilities which they and their advisors felt were the most socially-disapproved or misunderstood. These included mental and emotional illnesses, neurological impairments, chemical dependency and learning disabilities. The knowledge that a particular employer would require access to their medical records steered some participants away from their preferred career path towards an option where disclosure of medical records might not be required:

> I've talked about this issue with a lot of people. On the one hand, I'd like to be who I am. On the other, I'm an alcoholic. I'm past feeling ashamed about that. But It's a very misunderstood disease. And most people have no reason to be informed about it.

> I always wanted to get into aerospace, but it would mean taking a job with government regulations. They give you this form to sign that gives them access to your medical records. And if I don't sign it, they're not going to employ me, right?

Participants expected prospective employers to be wary of employing graduates with disabilities partly because of the possibility of injury liability claims. Non-disclosure was not an option where access to the company's medical benefits scheme required information on pre-existing conditions. Students with conditions which they thought would attract the most prejudice in hiring (or refusal of medical coverage), avoided these jobs.

Many of those who expressed a preference against disclosure hoped it would be possible to tell their immediate colleagues (and perhaps their employers) about their disability at some point after employment, when they felt confident that their value as workers had been sufficiently demonstrated:

I probably wouldn't disclose anything about it. Usually, it isn't a problem for me—only in certain circumstances...I'd rather deal with it as necessary—with individual people one-on-one, if it comes up.

When I got hired as a medical assistant, I didn't tell them I was disabled. After I got hired, I was able to talk to some people freely about it. I'm not ashamed of it, so I tell them...Sometimes it helps; sometimes it doesn't. Sometimes they are a little bit more considerate; sometimes they are just expecting you to be a bit slower.

I tell the people I need to tell in order for them to understand how to accommodate me. I find that gives them some ownership in my progress. And most people don't know—my disability is pretty well hidden.

Those whose condition posed potential safety problems in particular work contexts were especially conflicted around this issue. They felt vulnerable to rejection at the interview stage, but had little choice but to disclose their condition to colleagues at an early point following employment:

I decided that, during the interview, I wouldn't address it unless I was asked point blank...Then, once I'd entered the job, I'd tell people. Because there are times when my blood sugar gets low enough for me to pass out. So I thought I'd tell people who work with me, just to make them aware that there might be times when I would get weak, and I just needed somebody to give me a drink, or something to eat that would bring my blood sugar level back up. It's important to tell them what to do.

You can't have that sort of risk in the lab. But I didn't tell my employer. I told the guy that was training me the second day that I was here. And I asked him not to tell anybody. I just told him to watch out for certain changes in my appearance or behavior...If I'm not thinking clearly, my eyes get kind of strange. And if I turned on the lathe and had a seizure, I could fall into it and tear my face off. So I told him, and asked him not to tell. And after I felt comfortable—it was a month or so—and I'd done a few things that made me think I was worthwhile—then I told them about it...I told the boss that I'd already told everyone I work with, and that they were comfortable with it. So, in the end, he decided, 'All right. We'll give it a shot.' But even though everyone had told him I was doing fine, his first reaction when I said the word 'epilepsy,' was 'Oooh, no!' So, on balance, I think my initial decision was right on. It seems like it's the way it has to be—regrettably.

One working undergraduate with a visually-apparent disability was relieved that he had been able to avoid the issue altogether by getting his job through a family and friendship network:

That can be a real leery thing. I was extremely lucky with this job. My brother had graduated in electrical engineering with the vice-president of the company. So when a position that fit my abilities came up, he mentioned me...I didn't have to go through the interviewing process, and trying to convince anyone. They already knew something about my work.

154

Another way of resolving the dilemma of sharing with colleagues was to let them discover the disability

in a natural way, and then find a way to 'normalize' it:

> You find, as an engineer, you have to do a lot of group facilitating. And you have to write on the board, in front of everybody. You have to spell. I hated that in high school—although I've gotten used to it now. Because you find in college that all the other engineers in your class don't know how to spell either. So it's not such a big deal...I notice quite a number of the engineers I work with now have similar problems. So if anyone notices, I say, 'It's not uncommon for engineers to be like that.'

Letting people find out in an unplanned way could back-fire. Colleagues could feel hurt that they had

not been trusted with the information:

> They don't really notice that I'm slower. But now I tell them why, because, one time, I had to stay over an hour late to get the work done. And I explained to my supervisor then that it was taking me that much longer because I'm dyslexic. And she said, 'Why didn't you tell me before?'

They could also be angry and upset at being confronted with an emergency to which they did not know

how to respond:

> So we talked about it the next day. I mean, I went to apologize to him...And he said, 'You should wear a bracelet or something. You could at least wave your arm at me!' (laughing). And I said, 'Yeah. You're right. I really should.' And, after that, I did start to wear a bracelet.

Several participants who recounted such experiences reported that they now disclosed their condition to

colleagues or an employer as a matter of personal responsibility:

> I learned the hard way that, if you don't tell them and your boss does not know, that some work situations are potentially life-threatening. You can both get into a lot of trouble...I wanted to work so badly, I took the first job I could get—in an ecology lab analyzing soil samples—which I thought would be okay. I didn't mention my allergies...I didn't know he was also studying prairie grasses, and that he had some of his old ragweed samples stored above the false ceiling of the lab I was working in. If I had told him, I wouldn't have gotten the job—but I wouldn't have put myself in a situation that could have been deadly, either...When I started getting really sick on the job, he pressed me to say what was wrong. When I told him, he was very upset. He said, 'I could have been responsible for your death, and I wouldn't even have known about it!'...So it's absolutely essential—you have to tell them up front.

Others who said they would prefer to be "up front" about their disability with prospective

employers, felt, on balance, that they would probably not do this, largely because they were afraid of losing a good job by doing so. Four such pragmatic decisions were based on actual experiences of discrimination:

> I wouldn't tell. Because, the people you'd be telling would be the personnel people who have no right to decide on what that means about you. Why disclose to people who don't need to know, and couldn't use the information properly if they did? When they were laying people off in this facility that I worked in, they knew they were eventually going to close. And so people got really ugly with each other toward the end. They all wanted to be the last ones there when the doors closed. And somebody slipped something into my personnel file that shouldn't have been there...So I have real low faith in who gets to see your personal reports and who makes judgments about you. And I think I have based my view on that one experience.

> I don't know yet, because I had a bad experience once. One time, not too long before I got laid off, I had a seizure and the word got back to the boss that something was wrong with me (crying). And I never felt he looked at me quite the same again.

> It's not comfortable at all to declare a disability as part of the application process. There's many things that they can find not to like about you if they don't like the fact that you have a disability. People just have no concept of what epilepsy is. They think that you might foam at the mouth or throw things...At one job interview I told them about it, and they were real friendly and it looked like I was going to get the job. But they didn't give me a second interview—and that was the end of that.

> I guess I'll never know if his finding out had anything to do with his decision to put me on the lay-off list.

Some of those who expressed a preference for openness felt they would try to get a feeling about an employer's attitude before risking disclosure. They expected to be open with some prospective employers, but not others, depending on their assessment of the atmosphere in a particular company:

> It's tough. I play it by ear. If it appears there's some willingness to talk about it, and it won't be prejudicial, then I will tell them...I don't have a hard and fast policy. I would love to be real up front all the time, but it's just not possible with every employer.

> If I'd told them, I don't know if they would have hired me. You know, the way this guy acted. And yet, at some point, you'd have to—if it's going to become an everyday sort of matter.

Some of the working graduates stated that they would never disclose their current (or former) health conditions; some said they were waiting until they felt that they had "proved themselves"; some thought

156

their co-workers might discriminate positively, and preferred to build up their level of confidence by "making it" without collegial assistance:[29]

> It was pride at the time—at getting my new job, and not wanting to let these people down—especially the person who helped me get the job. And you don't want people who are going to be your peers looking down on you. There's a sense of needing to prove yourself right from the start—and especially coming in as someone's friend—that's one barrier already. So you need to get over that barrier, and if I'd exposed myself right away, I thought I'd never get over the disability barrier. So I tried to keep it hidden as long as I could—which wasn't very long—about two months—until I had to write my first report.

> It's just my sense of inferiority— fter all I went through in college—that I have to make it through without any favoritism. So it's not only the fear that they might do something bad that keeps me from telling them. It's the fear that they might do something nice. It sounds strange, I know, but I have to make it on my own abilities—to gain the confidence. Or else I'm going to have even more doubts if I ever do get into grad school.

> And before I said anything, I'd try to prove myself—that I was the right person for the job. And I wouldn't take on a job that I didn't think I could handle. And if I learned right off that I couldn't handle it, I'd get out. So then I'd bring it up in a casual conversation—perhaps a month or so after I'd been doing the job and was confident in it—and make it sound like it's no big deal.

For the approximately two-thirds of the whole sample whose disabilities were either hidden, or not immediately obvious, disclosure was a major consideration in their thinking about post-graduate employment and was discussed in terms of balancing the advantages of accommodation against the possible disadvantages of prejudice or discrimination:

> It's a double-edged sword. There's some preferential hiring on the one hand. On the other, the placement office here advises you not to risk it.

> I don't know that I'll say right off—not with the job market as it is. I don't know what they are going to say about someone like me...I don't know if it's going to be an advantage or a disadvantage to say I have a disability. It's just that I'll be slow in picking things up initially. But once I've got them, it's not going to matter. I know from the past I'll do a good job. I'll probably work circles around most people.

---

[29]In *Talking About Leaving* (1997), Seymour and Hewitt discuss a parallel difficulty and response among students of color who avoid seeking the academic help that they actually need, either from peers or from faculty. Avoiding the risk of stigma that is thought to attach to students who admit to needing help places these students of color at high risk of academic failure and of field switching.

It's weighing the costs versus the benefits. I mean, do I want to put up a sign (laughing) to alarm the whole world, knowing that a lot of people are going to get very alarmed, versus, what are the chances of something happening?

I wouldn't have a problem telling anyone, but I'm not sure that it's a good idea—just worrying that someone might think there was something wrong with the work I do.

The dilemma was particularly evident in cases where employers offered preferential hiring for graduates with disabilities. Students were not entirely sure they could trust such offers:

I haven't disclosed a learning disability to them yet. That will come when I go through my orientation on Monday. I'll have to sign the paperwork, so I'll disclose it then. But I'm not very comfortable with it. This is a very aggressive company—from the type of people that I've met who work there. I'm a little nervous about getting eaten alive. If something were to go wrong, they will have the disability to blame it on...So I'm a little concerned, but I'm going to take them at their word—for whatever that's worth. They say they are an equal opportunity employer. Okay. Let's see if they are...I have another company I can go to if this doesn't work out.

My colleagues and my seniors don't know anything about it. No one does, and I've no intention of telling them. They've got this strong equal opportunity deal—the federal government is big on that. But I'm not going to take chances.

Notwithstanding their inclusion within the law, after their undergraduate experiences with faculty and others, students with one of a number of hidden disabilities wondered whether employers who were openly seeking workers with disabilities would accept their condition as "a real disability":

Plus, the kind of disability most companies are asking for is people in a wheelchair—or blind people. They are asking for physical disabilities...So when you fill in the form, they ask if you have a disability, but they don't have a space to explain what kind. They don't even think about that.

I'm not really disabled in their eyes because I don't have a wheelchair...I'll look into it and see if I can claim disabled status, but I'm not sure what the ramifications are. Is it fraud? Is there a criminal penalty for a false claim? That would be my concern. (Graduate)

I've been trying to figure out if a learning disability qualifies as a disability. Putting it in an application might give me an edge in an interview. But once they bring me in, they may say, 'Hey, you don't have a disability.' And I'd have to say, 'Yes I do. I've just done a very good job of working around it.'

They also expressed concern about the dangers of becoming the company's "token" employee with a disability, and in that situation, doubted they would be treated on their merit:

They said, 'Just be patient. We'll start giving you more demanding work eventually.' But they kept me dinking around in their data department doing all sorts of not too demanding work...Later, they were short of an engineer, so suddenly I'm in my own cubicle being an electrical engineer, but not being paid a salary—they put me on an hourly wage. So I ended up working there for two years, and I did get a good feel for what engineering was like...But when I finally told my boss I was leaving, his jaw dropped. My supervisor took me aside and said he wanted to have lunch with me. And he told me they were grooming me for a spot somewhere in the organization. (Graduate who uses a wheelchair)

Only four undergraduates and three working graduates who felt they had the option of whether or not to disclose their disability expressed a preference for disclosure to all prospective employers and colleagues. Their reasons were partly practical, partly a matter of self-pride. In practical terms, they saw it as necessary to explain their limitations from the outset, so that they did not place themselves or their co-workers in potentially dangerous situations or, by default, find themselves facing work tasks they could not accomplish satisfactorily. The three graduates who had chosen this option were pleased with the results of their decision. They felt relieved to be working in companies and among colleagues who accepted and accommodated them:

Common sense told me that I had to be up front—if someone doesn't know you have a visual problem, they may give you, say blurry copies of a problem set, or a hand-written 10-page memo instructing you to do something. They might put you in front of a computer that's not suitable for you, and say, 'Have this done by tomorrow.' And you would be saying, 'What in the hell have I gotten myself into?'...It was hard at the interview, but it was one of those 'Count to 10 and jump in' situations. I knew right away, 'Damn it. You'd better be up front with everybody, or you're going to get screwed.'...But it turned out they have a wonderful attitude toward disabled people. All they want to know is what can you do. And it's evident with everyone there—there's no discrimination. I love it! It's just wonderful...I was always worried before—even terrified—that someone would find out and I'd be passed over; that I wouldn't be asked to do things—or be fired.

Those who preferred disclosure as a matter of principle were proud of their achievements and felt they had more to offer to an employer by being honest about their current or former health states:

It makes me very proud of what I've done...And when I do share that I have a disability, I tell people that I am proud of it. And that it wasn't handed to me on a silver spoon, you know, that I've worked hard for this. I am proud that I can do so well at this.

At interviews, they sometimes asked, 'What would be one of your biggest accomplishments?' And when I said, 'Overcoming cancer.' I know some of them were a little worried about that...But I think most of them felt that I had done something special by graduating after going through all of that, and I think few of them held it against me.

It's much more acceptable to have a certain number of years of recovery behind you. Someone who's very early in recovery, that's something they don't want to touch...But because they know I've gone all through college dealing with a heavy work load and that I have a lot of years of sobriety, I think they respect that.

Finally, there were six graduate and undergraduate students among those who had disabilities which were likely to be obvious to an interviewer. These participants were less concerned about disclosure than about how to manage social interactions at interviews with minimal awkwardness and embarrassment. They had become adept at explaining how their disabilities did, and did not, impair functioning of different kinds and at explaining their needs:

It's a little awkward because when you go for an interview the people don't know you have a disability, so they stick out their right hand to shake it, and it's kind of awkward...I could stick my arm out first so they can see I have an artificial limb, but I don't know if I should do that because it's the whole shock value thing...So I basically just let go and see what happens. If they ask me, I tell them. If not, I figure they're just not interested. I just basically try to prove that I'm a normal person, and that I'm capable of doing virtually anything...It's more in a second interview that they will ask—they just kind of slip it in. It's usually more of a personal inquiry because they can see it doesn't limit me.

Interviews are harder. Normally I tell them up front that I have a speech problem. And I show them that it doesn't affect the way I interact with other people—that I'm real personable—that I get on with everybody.

I mean, more times than not, employers will be darn accommodating if you let them know what's going on...They can't create an environment that works for you if they don't know your specific needs. The most you can ask of anyone is to be accommodating. But you need to help them out by defining and explaining those needs.

Some of these participants also worried whether they would be able to cope with the work:

I think the closer I got to graduation, my attitude went to hell. Because, subconsciously, I think it scared me to death to think of having to get out in the working world, and starting to go to interviews and telling people that I'm legally blind—you know—'These are my limitations, but I think I can do this job.'...Even assuming you can get the position—which is a one percent proposition—then, you've promised the world to these employers, and you now have to actually know how to do it. And there's another one percent chance that you're going to be able to confront everything successfully. So one percent times one percent, that's a .01 percent chance overall that you're going to be successful. So thinking about whether I could do it scared the hell out of me.

> Because of the surgery, I have some problems with my legs. So I have to do physical therapy. And that takes a lot of energy. So, at some points, I have to take off more time than a weekend and rest...In this society, where everything has to go fast and you have to be productive, there's no time for rest...So I have to find a job that will be part-time—or maybe something I can do by myself.

> I have to know that my job is going to be within the limits of what I can do.

> I might have all the qualifications to do the job, but I wouldn't be able to do it. So I'd simply stay away. Employers don't have to worry about that. It's a self-monitoring thing. It's my problem. I understand my limitations.

Even those with "socially approved" types of disability did not necessarily feel safe from discrimination:

> I've interviewed numerous times, both in engineering and for law jobs. And sometimes I've had the feeling that, you know, I was probably discriminated against because of my eyesight. But it's hard to know. Maybe I wasn't right for them in terms of personality or experience.

They also expressed some concerns about how they would be accepted by co-workers, clients or members of the public in their chosen careers.

It is largely, we feel, because of the dominance of the disclosure dilemma that discussion of job choices and preferences for particular working environments turned rather less than we had anticipated upon issues of accommodation, assistive technology, and adapted work contexts, for the majority of our participants. It is also the product of a sample which reflects the whole spectrum of disabilities actually represented at the Institute of Technology at the time of the interviews.

The Disability Services staff were well aware of disclosure issues and of other anxieties related to making job applications, being interviewed and adapting to new jobs. These issues are directly addressed by those students who take advantage of their Career Connections program. Disability Services has also worked to identify employers who are interested in receiving applications from graduating seniors and graduates with disabilities, and sought effective ways to make these opportunities known to those seeking employment.

In 1994, they began a new on-line computer service, by which students can explore recent job and internship/co-op opportunities submitted to the university by employers who are committed to equal opportunity hiring. Employers can also review the resumés of qualified and interested students or graduates with disabilities. In addition to the convenience of being able to scan current work options, students who make an application for jobs shown on this register know that the employer is expecting students with disabilities to apply and that disclosure is not an issue.[30]

The service was very new at the time of the interviews, and we asked every student if they were aware of it: we found that only a few undergraduates (all of whom were active in the Disabled Students' Cultural Center), and none of the graduates or graduate students, as yet, knew about it. However, by keeping a stack of brochures on the new service to hand during the interviews, we discovered a very high level of interest in and acceptance of this method of bringing job seekers with disabilities into contact with employers who were predisposed accept and accommodate them:

> Yeah, I'll take a look at this. I mean, if there's a company that's saying that they're looking for an engineer that has a disability, then that would make all the difference. I'd obviously be happy to tell them about it.

Searching for a congenial work context

The kinds of working environment which were most often mentioned as optimal by working undergraduates, graduating seniors and recent graduates with disabilities were small companies, or smaller units within larger companies. They were preferred as contexts in which to build experience and self-confidence; were thought more amenable to accommodations for those who needed them; and easier contexts in which to risk disclosure of a disability. None of the graduates who were working for larger companies, or in larger working units within them, had chosen to disclose their disabilities, and only two of the working undergraduates with jobs in such contexts had done so. When the number of immediate colleagues was small and there was personal contact with the employer, the participants felt that the value

---

[30]The same on-line network also offers an extensive data base of job accommodation resources and adaptive technology product listings. As with other Disability Services, its project coordinator also has a disability.

of their work was more likely to be recognized and the danger of job-loss reduced—even if their disability became known:

> In a big place, I was afraid that I couldn't get the right people to notice that I was actually contributing something...There was no one else that could steal my ideas here...When I generated the idea for the Keck telescope, if I had had an immediate supervisor that was not the owner, he might have taken the idea and said, 'Look what my division found.'

> Every time I applied to the big places, I applied without my heart. When I stumbled upon this place, I applied with a little more heart.

> They are a good company, but I don't think I'd like to work there—the department seems so huge. I wouldn't mind, though, if I could work with a small team in a company of 200 or less. That wouldn't be bad.

> I think working in a smaller company with fewer engineers would give me more of a feeling that I'm contributing to the company.

Along with this preference came the hope for a personal style of working relationships, acceptance of a known disability and patience with them as new graduates learning the job:

> I definitely want to work in a place that is really friendly. I don't want to work where there's people just sitting at computers or hacking away at numbers. I've applied to a consulting firm. My job would include going out and talking to clients.

> In the perfect job, everyone would know that I had a disability and they would understand and accept me, but wouldn't be condescending. Just knowing how it was with me, and checking in now and then to see how I was doing—just make sure I understand what they're talking about before they say, 'Do this.'

> I think, what's most important to me is the people that I work with—that they be understanding and kind.

> If I can land a job where I like the people and the community the company is in, I'll probably stay there forever—even if the pay isn't great.

We have also found such preferences (especially for first jobs) to be common among seniors who do not have disabilities, but who are anxious about the transition to work. Like many of their non-disabled peers, graduating seniors with disabilities hoped for interesting work, some control over its nature and direction, support while they learned, opportunities for further training and some flexibility in work schedules:

I have a lot of control over what I want to do—I can develop that system how I see fit. It's a young and lively group that I work with.

I'm pretty independent and flexible in how I work...I don't think I'm going to have a problem...I guess my desire to prove myself worthy—that I have something to contribute—that's going to help me keep this job.

More than anything else, I want a place where I'm not going to get too stressed out by the work—where the work is interesting, I can do it well, and have a little bit of fun with the people around me.

Some of the more problematic work experiences of new graduates and undergraduate interns in larger companies were identical to those which we encountered among similarly-qualified engineers and science graduates who did not have disabilities. They complained of over-long working hours, "hack" work, unreasonable or erratic demands for project completion, low salaries and inadequate supervision or training. In the following examples, the first two descriptions came from participants who had not disclosed their disability; in the last three instances, the employer was aware of the worker's disability:

Their theory was they wanted you to see what it was like in the trenches...They said, 'Just be patient. We'll give you more demanding work eventually.'...They call themselves a 'leading company,' but they are notorious for being tight-wads. They squeeze as much as they can for as little money as possible out of their younger engineers.

He talked about getting 'a visibility profile.' Like, 'Any time you get the chance, to jump in front of an overhead projector while the big shots are around, take it.' That's one of the attitudes that triggered my realization that I didn't particularly like the kind of people I was working with.

I was given an enormous amount of responsibility. I was to design a product solo. No one would give me any help. It was just dumped on me. So I designed the product, found the people to build it for me, got all the prototypes done, and dealt with the code. And I brought it to where they were supposed to give me a raise. And they refused. I'd been working 12-hour days for $8.50 an hour.

He said, 'It's a shitty job'—and he was right. The only good thing about it was the money. I could see it being different if you were working in some sort of small operation where you had our hands directly on something—your own designs—something you had a stake in. But as far as I'm concerned, engineering for a big company is a rotten job.

It was wearing me down, and I realized that if I was going to spend that much time and energy doing anything, it wasn't going to be for another big company.

Although the preference for small, supportive working environments is shared by many students, students with disabilities have a set of extra reasons for their preference. These include: an often greater need for relevant hands-on experience; an opportunity to build self-confidence; a safe place to risk disclosure of their disability and to seek its accommodation; and the chance to make a contribution that is recognized—and, thereby, a better chance of job security. The comparative experience of two working graduates illustrates these points. Working in a context with less than ten other employees had given each of them opportunities they might otherwise have missed. They had worked on a variety of projects; had been included in work on some highly specialized projects; and had worked directly with clients. In one work setting (a chemistry laboratory), the employer and all the workers shared every kind and level of work; in the other (a highly specialized engineering company), the new graduate was encouraged to show his talent for creative thinking and technical problem-solving—and was rewarded for this. Both felt they had received good apprenticeships. The chemist moved on to more specialized work in a larger company, and, thence, into a senior position in a large, well-known company. The engineer remained with his original employer, although with his current business contacts, he knew that he could move elsewhere if he so chose. The chemist had never disclosed his disability, and never expected to seek accommodation. The engineer disclosed his disability at a very early stage. His decision to stay in the small company (despite one very good offer from a larger company at a much higher salary) was related to the ongoing interest of the work itself, and the high level of respect expressed toward him by clients, but also preferred to stay because he was well-accommodated by his employer and co-workers. Both graduates felt they had made the right decisions.

As in the above examples, working graduates whose level of comfort with their work setting required that their employer and colleagues understood the "way their disability worked," were likely to remain in smaller companies or units where definitions of normal work activity are more likely to be extended to include greater variation in work patterns, and where special accomplishments are more likely to be recognized. In these settings, fluctuations in health and their consequences for the work, were also thought to be accommodated with greater tolerance and support:

> A couple of months ago, I solved two problems, neither of which had I realized I was thinking about. One was a gas discharge problem associated with ionization gauges. The second was a problem associated with the furnaces—that had been in the back of the minds of the people working here for 30 years or more. And the answers just came to me suddenly—for both of them. And then I went back into one of my periods of gross stupidity again! (laughing).... They're quite tolerant of me here. Sometimes I don't think particularly well. And if I want to sit at my computer and play games, that's fine with them. Because they know that as soon as I'm back on track, I'll be jumping on the work and getting it done again. And our customers seem to think the situation here is quaint too. At any rate, they seem well pleased with our results.

> Some place where you fit in—there's no feeling like it in the world. I get up in the morning, and I'm going to work and I'm really enjoying it, you know. There's nothing like it. For a person with a disability to go to a job in a place they hate—I guess you have to do it sometimes to put food on the table—but, boy, be looking for somewhere else...My boss—he doesn't care that I'm different. His attitude is, 'This is the job in front of us. This is our team, and our resources. How can you help? How can I help?'...There's days when I can barely walk—I can be in pain from head to toe, but I don't care. I love being there. People notice the changes, and encourage me on bad days. They know there's a disability, and I don't have to hide it or worry about it—which is wonderful.

As these, and a number of other accounts in this section illustrate, particular jobs and job settings are seen as congenial when the kinds of mental, physical and emotional demands that they make "fit" with the constraints, patterning or unpredictable aspects of the disability. One of the most dramatic examples of a good fit was that of an undergraduate who had both immune system deficiencies and severe allergies, and who worked in a clean room:

> For the first time in my life I found out what a clean room is...Standing in front of a clean air shower all night long on a second shift, within two weeks I was off all my medication. I was sprinting from one end of the building to the other 'cause I felt so good. I had no idea I was doing it until the security guard stopped me and told me I couldn't run in the halls. And I had never run in my life—not without severe pain and wheezing. I can't run for a bus without taking my inhaler. When I'm in a clean room, I'm brilliant. When I'm not, I can almost feel my IQ dropping! I feel better at work than I do at home. And it's getting to the point where I can even tolerate short trips to the university.

Flexibility in the work place, no less than in the class room, is key to a sense of well-being in workers with disabilities. Workers who are allowed to have peaks and troughs in their creativity and who are assessed on their productivity overall, expressed contentment with their choice of a work place.

Those participants who considered themselves well-accommodated and supported indicated that this was not serendipitous. A good tone was set by their employer or (in larger companies) by senior management as a matter of company policy. It could also be initiated by a powerful external body:

> They had a really bad attitude about deaf people—the people they were supposed to be working for...And there wasn't one deaf or hard of hearing person in the whole institute. So the National Institutes of Health sponsored this program and brought in six staff interns—and I was one of them. And, in one summer, we got them to completely review all their usual practices with clients. It was very exciting...That was a situation where they were forced to rethink and retrain...The results were really cool. I could care less about the motivations behind the changed behavior—so what if they were just being P.C. at the start? It worked!

> And the owner, she is very accepting of my sometimes odd behavior. If sometimes I'm running around looking confused and doing nothing constructive, it doesn't matter. She takes the view that it'll work itself out. And the others see that it doesn't bother her, so it doesn't bother them.

> It's there in the corporate charter, and in everything that they publish...They make it clear that they want people to be creative and to contribute, and to feel that their contributions are welcome...There are some barriers—mostly because of the attitude of a few people. But it's easier to persuade them because of the prevailing attitude.

As in our discussion of accommodation on campus, the greatest problems of accommodation at work appear to be problems of attitude, not architecture; not how to adapt facilities or equipment, but the willingness to do it.

Self-employment

As noted throughout this study, five of the undergraduates, and one of the graduates, were supporting themselves by self-employment. Another seven of the participants were planning some form of self-employment (i.e., consulting, free-lance work, or starting their own company). Some of the reasons offered for these choices were unrelated to disabilities. These included: the scarcity of employment opportunities in a particular field; building a business on a foundation of prior work experience or a pre-existing business network; flexibility and control over one's pace, hours and work setting; and the satisfactions of shaping one's own career:

> There are no interviews set up for construction engineering at all through I.T. placement. And I'm looking at self-employment once again. And that doesn't scare me so much—I've been doing it most of my working life...Having the sheepskin will just help me set a certain salary level, and people may be more ready to accept my advice.

> I'm just finishing my master's degree and have done a lot of the work for the Ph.D...I was briefly employed in engineering, although now I'm self-employed. I redevelop dilapidated property in south Minneapolis. So I work as a carpenter, electrician, plumber—just doing all the work needed for re-construction—I'm mostly self-taught.

> I still have a great many friends in good positions back in the industry, so going back into consulting is do-able. It's a hard business—evening out the work is tough—but I've done it before, and it's something I really enjoy. And in my own mind at least, I'm an experienced professional with an awful lot of background to offer my clients.

> It's just a perfect mix for me. It's got technology that fascinates me and that I understand. It's got creativity involved and it deals a lot with people—which is fun. The awkward part is the money side of thing—not so hot on that yet—but it will work out.

> And another thing I like, I can drop everything and go for a wheel around the park whenever I want to—I get to set the pace.

As with other SMET students we have encountered, some students with disabilities sought ways to use their education and skills in support of either a strong personal interest and/or a valued social goal:

> I currently own and run a small business that supports me. But I'm also involved with a non-profit organization that makes machinery for the Third World. They've developed a bicycle-powered corn grinder that they've been taking to El Salvador...They need to build several hundred of these, and I'm thinking of a way to work that into my own business...It's also related to my specialty, mechanism design and analysis, and the demand for people with this specialty isn't that high right now. Most people in my special field who go into corporate America end up in some broader area, so this idea touches a number of bases for me.

> I realized the only way I'd be happy was if I did something I had a passion for. And I also decided that I needed to dictate my own hours of work. So after I had dinked around for a year looking for a job that didn't exist, I started my own business...It's in the realm of audio-engineering. I'm what they call a mastering engineer—I'm the last stop before they make the master copy of a compact disk. I make the master disk that gets sent off to the factory to make 10,000 duplicates. And it's all computer—all digital. I have a digital audio work station made by a company out in California, and it's pretty slick. I really enjoy it. And the fruits of my labors are just now coming in.

However, for six of those who were, or who were planning to be, self-employed, their choice had been strongly influenced by considerations raised by their disabilities. Five of this group had reached their decision based on their experience of salaried employment in medium- to large-sized organizations. The difficulties that they had experienced included: experience (or fear) of discrimination in job interviews, or in lay-offs for disability-related reasons; difficulties in travelling to and from work; and absences from work caused by health variations:

> And it was horrible, that routine. Like during the winter, I'd be on the freeway. It would be 6:00 a.m., pitch dark, 20 degrees below zero, and I'd think, 'I don't want to do this. This stinks! What if I have car trouble, and get stuck on the road? It's dangerous.' So I quit work and started my own business.

> I suddenly realized that the working world didn't want me. And I also realized that I didn't need them in order to make money—I know how to do things. I don't need them to give me a job. I can make my own job and earn my own money. It won't be as a mechanical engineer, but in the long-run I'll make more money than a mechanical engineer would earn—and under better working conditions.

> I think working from home suits a lot of disabled people. It's physically comfortable—and with my need for para-transit, and the general difficulty in getting from A to B, it makes a lot of sense...And I never know when I'm going to have a fracture—it's not a big deal to me, but it's hard for employers when you tell them that you're not able to come in for six weeks until this thing heals up.

> Yeah, I really think people pre-judge you. And there's a risk. I think I could easily lose a job because of my disability. Being your own boss gives you more control over your life.

Two of this group, both of whom were active (and founding) members of the Disabled Students' Cultural Center, and one of whom had both mobility and visual impairments, proposed to build home-based services around their knowledge and experience in addressing disability issues:

> My heart is in consulting...I'm just going to work on my own business. I wrote a small business plan which was accepted and, in a month, I'm getting a computer system. I'll be speaking about disability, and doing free-lance writing out of my own home.

> My major is electrical engineering and math, and I'm still very interested in teaching. So I would like to teach software usages—including e-mail—that would help other disabled people get through school. And I'd like to work with some adaptive technology and do some of the programming that's involved with that.

For all of these participants, running a business from a home base had strong appeal, especially for those for whom daily commuting and business travel presented difficulties. Foremost among these were: control over project timetables; taking on as much work or responsibility as they could manage at a particular time; congenial, adapted working conditions; greater variety of work; and dealing with customers directly. They also had some caveats, including the need to draw a line between work and private life, and being careful not to become socially isolated:

> I always thought that, once I had established a client base and a steady flow of work, I'd be able to afford to move to a rented location. But what's happening is I'm getting feedback from my customers that they rather enjoy the home atmosphere.

> It's nice, but you have to watch out. For instance, I don't go near my computer on Sundays, no matter what. And I don't go officially on-line until noon. I turn off and use my answering service. So I can get up and enjoy breakfast, read the paper, whatever.

> For anyone in business, there's the danger of giving it too much of your life—and when it's right there with you every day, that's a concern—and disabled people who live on their own need to be careful not to withdraw into their work too much.

Work Accommodation Issues

The small size of our sample, and the wide array of types of disabilities that it represents, make it impossible to generalize about the degree to which disabilities that are known to employers are accommodated in ways that seem satisfactory to the workers themselves. Three of the graduates, and two of the working undergraduates, expressed fairly unreserved satisfaction with the accommodations they had encountered at work. All five had less-obvious types of disability which they had disclosed; all were happy with this decision; and none required adaptations in work facilities or equipment. Their work accommodation needs were expressed entirely in terms of attitudes and ways of working. It was the meeting of their need for acceptance, tolerance and support which—added to the intrinsic satisfactions of their work—made their working lives enjoyable:

> I know three other disabled people here. They have door openers and elevators to accommodate those needs quite well. And one man who is blind in one eye and partially blind in the other—they have put in a camera that blows up the letters on the screen really large...I think, for

all of us, however, the big thing is attitude—the attitudes you meet here are generally pretty positive.

I think especially in the area that I work, it's mostly a very professional, well-educated group of people who try to accommodate you the best that they can.

What they have done to accommodate me is, well, first, they were very forgiving. That was one nice thing. They also found people in the group willing to help me through the process of learning how to write a better report...So I have three people I normally draw on to get my reports done in a clear format and a logical order. They are all closely involved with what I do anyway, so they can understand what I'm trying to get across.

Beyond these five participants, it is hard to make any clear statements about the extent or adequacy of work accommodation.

Nine of the 11 current and former students who had more serious physical disabilities related to mobility, hearing and sight[31] had not tested the willingness of employers to accommodate them—either in terms of a supportive emotional environment, or by the adaptation of physical facilities and working tools. Three of this group had entered graduate school; one had begun, and a second was planning, a home-based business; one planned to work in a context where all the workers had disabilities; none of the undergraduates had worked or experienced internships. (Two had applied for internships, but both had been turned down.) Thus, those participants who might have told us most about the availability and efficacy of assistive technology and work access provisions were not in the kinds of work settings where they could comment upon these. Although six of this group were planning more conventional careers (including academe), only two of them had experienced work in conventional environments. Both were engineers; one was blind; the other used a wheelchair. Both had chosen to withdraw from these kinds of work for reasons which were not essentially related to accommodations. One had entered law school, largely because he felt it offered a more economically-stable long-term future. The second had opened a home-based business because he disliked the corporate culture and the stresses of car commuting and

---

[31]These included: five participants who used wheelchairs, and other mechanical or electrical aids to mobility; four who were legally-blind; and one deaf student who required an interpreter.

because the opportunity to follow his own interests presented itself. By entering graduate school soon after completing an undergraduate degree, or choosing types of work where they had direct control over their own working environment, seven of this group had, in effect, side-stepped the issue of accommodation within conventional settings. The four non-working undergraduates were, perhaps ironically, among the very few students in this sample who were sufficiently well-funded not to need to work. They had, therefore, neither acquired the kinds of relevant work experience which they were likely to need to secure a job, nor tested the willingness of employers to accommodate them.

Of a second group of eight undergraduates who had somewhat less limiting forms of mobility impairment, six were mature students with prior work experiences and who had acquired disabilities as a result of accident or illness. However, none of them had experienced work in a conventional environment since their impairment. The seventh worked, but had not disclosed his disabilities. The eighth had recently graduated, was about to start his first job as an engineer in a medium-sized, local engineering company and did not feel that he needed assistive technology or any special facilities.

There were, thus, 19 participants (i.e, 29.2% of the whole sample) whose conditions were such that they most closely approximate what many people (including employers) think of when the term "disability" is used. All but one of these participants had disabilities which were fairly apparent, so disclosure was not an issue. We noted earlier in this chapter a preference for conventional careers among those undergraduates and graduate students with physically-limiting disabilities who had been well-accommodated in college. However, the actual career decisions and experiences of this group (including several instances of self-employment) were such that they did not constitute a test of the willingness of employers to accommodate them. It would be interesting to learn whether there is some tendency among those with more seriously-limiting forms of physical disability not to enter forms of work where they will need to negotiate accommodations with employers and colleagues. A study with a more selective focus might clarify this issue.

172

Without such information, the nature of work accommodation problems to which participants with current work experience actually drew our attention, was largely attitudinal and system-related, rather than physical or technical. Indeed, it was precisely because the attitudes of employers and fellow workers were felt to be so critical to their employment and job satisfaction, that the issue of disclosure—rather than that of accommodation—dominated the work-related concerns of the majority of participants. It would be important to get a clearer understanding of which workers with which kinds of disabilities experience what kinds of accommodation, what needs are less-well met, and whether graduates with particular types of disabilities tend not to enter job settings where they will need to negotiate accommodations. It would also be important to learn from a study of employers whether the participants' concerns about disability disclosure are justified and, if so, what the issues for employers are. Both questions go beyond the reach of this small study. However we offer the following observations from two of the graduates with whom we discussed these issues. One was blind; the other had a learning disability. Both were now graduate students, but each had several years of work experience:

> Because we with disabilities are emotionally difficult to deal with, in general, the world doesn't like us. You know, we all pretend that people in wheelchairs and blind people are okay. But I think a lot of people feel vague resentment towards us. And the natural reaction—not intellectual, but emotional—is that we make people uncomfortable. And they would rather ignore us or reject us.

> I think more people than not are very reasonable, and will bend over backwards to help somebody out if they consider them to be disabled...I really believe that people are good at heart, and, given a chance, want to help you. They get a good feeling out of doing something for somebody. But they've also got to weigh that against, you know, the competitive realities of our free enterprise society.

CHAPTER FIVE: OVER-ARCHING ISSUES AND PARTICIPANTS' RECOMMENDATIONS

"Disability" as a "Disadvantage of Time"

Throughout this account, we have sought to distinguish those problems which students with disabilities share with other SMET majors; those which they share, but experience in heightened form; and those which only students with disabilities experience. Because of the particular categories into which we have divided our findings, we have addressed only in a fragmented way one dominant feature of the higher education experience for students with disabilities, namely, issues of time. Coping with time-related problems was a universal feature of the experiences of all of our participants. It distinguishes their difficulties from those of other SMET majors, is a facet of every type of difficulty they encounter, and transcends differences in the problems of students with disabilities of different types. Indeed, given the many types and degrees of medical conditions which are encompassed by the term "disability," one way to understand the commonality of their experience is to see all students with disabilities as students who are "time-disadvantaged."

As we described in Chapter Two, the educational experience of students with disabilities is mediated—both directly and indirectly—by the nature of particular conditions and their treatment. Although participants coped with some very different types of condition-related problems, two-thirds (59.5%) of all of these references involved issues of time. The time issues that participants raised were of five broad types: problems of pace; speed of learning, comprehension and recall; temporal disruptions in mental and physical functioning; time-related educational needs; and time expended in dealing with all types of problems.

Approximately one-third of all time issues which participants raised referenced the slower pace at which all students with disabilities—for an array of different reasons—are constrained to work. Participants described how particular aspects of their disability slowed down the pace at which they could proceed. For example, students with mobility and visual impairments mentioned the extra time they needed to get to and from campus, or from class to class, and how the faculty's choice of particular buildings or rooms eased or exacerbated these difficulties. For students with mobility impairments, and those recovering from illness or injury, fatigue dictated the commitments they could undertake and the pace at which they could tackle them. Across a wide spectrum of different disabilities, participants described how both the regular patterning of their condition, or its medication, as well as periodic set-backs in their health, forced them to miss particular classes, tests or assignment deadlines. They sometimes had to leave school abruptly without completing a particular class, or to be absent from school for whole periods of time; were unable to attend classes or meetings at particular times of day; or found it impossible to proceed through their degree on a full-time basis. Dealing with the trail of "incompletes" created by periods of enforced absence further slowed down their pace. Where the relevant "make-up" classes were not available every semester, this, again lengthened the time they needed to set their academic record straight.

The problems of working at a pace which was slower than that of other students arose partly as a consequence of their disabilities. Problems of pace were also created—as were all time-related difficulties—at the interface of the disability with the expectations of faculty and with the university as a social system. For example, it is because SMET faculty have traditionally made the execution of particular learning tasks to particular standards in particular time-frames the criteria for academic success (as opposed to demonstrations of knowledge and comprehension in other forms) that the slower pace at which students with all types of disabilities must work becomes a critical disadvantage. Similarly, the rules by which the university system deals with class withdrawal and "incompletes" make it more or less difficult to recoup the consequences of time lost in dealing with health problems. The degree to which problems of physical access to facilities are met by the university, those provisions are maintained, and transportation difficulties are resolved, determines the amount of physical energy they can give to their academic commitments, how much fatigue they experience, and, thus, the pace at which they can operate. Managing a disability so as to remain in optimal health becomes more difficult when the heavy demands of a traditional SMET curriculum make it hard to maintain the regimen necessary to preserve the stability of a health condition. Many SMET students complain of "overload," but the difficulties of meeting the medication or nutritional schedule needed to control the symptoms of, for example, diabetes or severe allergies, heighten the effects of work overload. Even casual faculty practices—such as informally extending official class times—increase the time pressures on students whose pace to their next class is, necessarily, slower than that of their peers.

Students with a number of different disabilities, but especially those with learning and other neurological disabilities (i.e., approximately one-half of the participants), explained why they needed more time in order to understand concepts and theories, to commit material to memory or to recall facts and ideas. They described how insights often came in delayed fashion, and the peaks and troughs in their intellectual progress. Because they are not "hard-wired" to learn in the same ways as other students, they must always find alternative ways to absorb and apply class materials, all of which takes longer than working by standard learning methods. As we have illustrated, these times lags may not affect the longer-term outcome in terms of academic achievements and total time to graduation. However their intellectual differentness often has negative short-term consequences when they are under pressure to complete particular learning tasks as quickly as their peers.

Students also described the temporal disruptions to concentration, and to other mental and physical functioning, wrought by medication, treatments, surgery and the experience of pain and discomfort. Temporary disturbances in their own normal, or best, level of functioning were reported by participants across the whole spectrum of disabilities. For some participants (for instance, those with epilepsy, bi-polar disorder, immune deficiencies, asthma, and those in stroke recovery), temporary breaks in concentration, memory and in other mental abilities, were part of the normal, expected pattern of their disability. Knowing these patterns, and learning how to work around them, were the key to optimal everyday functioning. However, these interludes inevitably disrupted the continuity of their academic effort, and set in motion a cycle of lost grades, lost financial aid and further losses of time in recovering from each of these.

Thus, to be a student with any form of disability almost certainly means needing more time than is normally allowed to do almost anything that the university expects of its students. The underlying request, therefore, which is implied by all forms of accommodation requests, is for more time. Accommodation requests are not pleas for exemptions, or a lowering of standards, but for sufficient time to meet the same standards as everyone else. All forms of assistive technology, all improvements in access, all services—whether large-print or taped books, scribes, readers, interpreters—and all test and assignment accommodations are partly, or wholly, means to allow students with disabilities to achieve the same standards as other students, and all address some aspects of time disadvantage.

Test accommodations were by far the commonest form of accommodation request. Because of problems with concentration, pain, fatigue, and the intellectual processing problems which especially characterize leaning disabilities, requests for more time to complete a test were often coupled with requests for a quiet place to work. Special requests, such as larger print test papers, are also time-related: they allow visually-impaired students to work more quickly. Because of past problems with tests for which extra time was not given, students with disabilities often have an even higher degree of anxiety about performing to their own best standard during tests than do many other students. Anxiety that a test accommodation may not be granted or, if granted, may not be honored, increases test pressure on students with disabilities. A request that faculty be flexible about when tests are taken, or in setting the deadline for the submission of assignments, is a further concern to students who have periods of time when they are partly, or wholly, incapacitated by their health condition, or its treatment.

Finally, coping with the difficulties raised by their disabilities also takes time. As already described, successful students with disabilities have taught themselves to manage time more effectively than have many other students. They begin to plan for each class well in advance; requesting syllabuses, class reading materials and assignment schedules from faculty; ordering special materials (e.g., books on tape); arranging auxiliary aids (e.g., scribes, lab partners, interpreters); working out the route to the classroom; finding places to park; and arranging their accommodations.

Dealing with any resistance to the granting of accommodations, with any disputes over financial aid, vocational rehabilitation funds, the resolution of access, transportation, parking and other practical problems, all takes time, slows their pace and consumes precious reserves of energy. It may also limit the time students can spend on social contacts, and contributes to the danger of social isolation.

In Chapter Three, we discussed the apparent difficulties SMET faculty face in trying to distinguish one form of disability from another, in order to decide whether they should allow some relaxation of the moral rules governing progress through their major. It might be useful for faculty who struggle with this dilemma to understand that the central problem of all higher education students with disabilities is, essentially, a disadvantage of time.

Participant Recommendations

We asked all the participants to offer recommendations which they felt would improve the undergraduate experience for students with disabilities, and increase their chances of success both in SMET majors and in the transition to appropriate post-graduate employment. As Table 7 indicates, the participants directed about half (50.9%) of their suggestions to other students with disabilities, and half (46.1%) to the university, SMET departments and faculty, and to state and federal agencies. The issues in this latter category are broadly divided between the system of higher education (25.1%) and learning access issues (21.0%). Some of these recommendations imply changes in public policy and provision;

Table 7. Recommendations related to persistence in undergraduate majors: by number and percent of all recommendations offered by participants with disabilities in the University of Minnesota sample (N=65).

Recommendations	N. of Times Offered	% of All Times Offered
TO OTHER DISABLED STUDENTS	(85)	(50.9)
Practical coping strategies	61	36.5
Developing "survival" attitudes	18	10.8
Strategic choices	6	3.6
TO THE UNIVERSITY, SMET DEPARTMENTS, FACULTY & GOVERNMENT	(77)	(46.1)
Pedagogical change/access to learning & facilities	35	21.0
Attitudes/policy changes	14	8.4
System changes (in financial aid)	11	6.6
Job placement services	9	5.4
Other services/needs	8	4.8
TO ELEMENTARY/HIGH SCHOOLS	(5)	(3.0)
TOTALS	167	100.0

and some address aspects of traditional SMET pedagogy and curriculum. A small number of recommendations (3.0%) were addressed to elementary and high school teachers.

To the university, to SMET departments and faculty, and to state and federal agencies

The participants were generally appreciative of the University of Minnesota's system of support for students with disabilities. Indeed, as we have described, a number of students chose this institution because they regarded its system of accommodation to be well-developed, compared with that of other institutions. There were two major foci to the participants' recommendations to the university. Both have strong bearing on the students' time disadvantages. The first was that the institution clarify, codify and disseminate information detailing its policy and support services for students with disabilities. The second—related to the first—is that the university actively seek ways to improve faculty attitudes, particularly those in SMET disciplines.

As we have indicated, students commonly did not know at the outset what help the university offered, and how its accommodation system worked. In the process of discovering this system, they lost time and money, and experienced unnecessary distress. The suggestion made by many participants that the university compile and disseminate a comprehensive explanation of all aspects of its accommodation and support system illustrates this difficulty. Most participants were clearly unaware of the efforts made by Disability Services to bring their services to the attention of all students with disabilities through letters to freshmen and recently documented students, general newsletters, brochures on particular services and outreach in the student press. As is the case of the Career Connections program, the Disability Services Director expressed disappointment with the low level of uptake of this, and of some other services, for which the students in this sample expressed a need. The problem of reaching a diverse and dispersed student population, many of whom struggle with problems of disclosure and social isolation, would seem to be generic, rather than peculiar to this campus, where a strong and constant effort is made to reach them.

However, what the participants clearly offer to administrators at all institutions wishing to address student informational needs is a check list of the contents they would like to see included in handbooks for students with disabilities. Their content should include: a statement of the institution's accommodations policy; a description of the eligibility and documentation process; explanation of the role of its disability services office; the procedure for requesting accommodations; the source, nature and extent of financial and other forms of help available within the institution (and from other agencies with which the universites interact), and eligibility criteria and application procedures (including timing) for these programs. The needs and services which students wished to see addressed are: financial, academic, health and medical, administrative, library, facilities and equipment access and adaptation, technical adaptation, transportation, academic and career advising, personal counselling, work study, employment, housing, social contact with peers (including student organizations) and how needs specific to students with particular types of disability can be met. Students stressed that this information should be comprehensive, accurate, and kept up to date. Handbooks might also discuss the kinds of problems which students with disabilities commonly encounter and offer practical advice on how to address them. Students with disabilities should be consulted in the compilation of institutional handbooks.

Copies of handbooks should be automatically sent to students immediately following documentation of a disability. Where possible, they should accompany letters of acceptance to an institution. They should also be readily available on a pick-up basis at many locations on campus, and be placed on-line for remote computer access.

Neither were the participants at this institution aware of Disability Services' ongoing, systematic educational outreach in which they explain the law, and the university's policies and procedures to faculty, administrators, and staff in all university departments. Because they encountered university employees who behaved as if they had not received this information, students felt that much of the educational burden fell upon their shoulders. Ironically, they shared the view strongly expressed by the director of Disability Services that no university employee should be able to claim ignorance of the official system. As our interview data indicate, where institutional rules and policies conflict with the strong professional or social norms and values, faculty or staff may be disinclined to acknowledge or follow them. The process of informing and explaining institutional guidelines, clearly, must continue. However, even in an institution where formal provisions for students with disabilities are as well-developed as those at the University of Minnesota, an active program of education and attitude change is indicated. For example, maintenance staff need to understand the consequences for students with mobility or visual impairments when systems intended to improve access are not maintained and operated as intended—when paths or ramps are not cleared of snow, when elevators used by students are locked. Students felt that a system of pro-active management, employee accountability (as well as clear communication of the system rules and the reasons for them) was needed. Students recognized that effectively addressing faculty resistance to reasonable accommodation would also take more than periodic reminders of university policy. They saw it both as an educational and as a management issue, and recommended that deans and chairs take the lead in faculty education. Most participants were not, however, in favor of taking disciplinary action against individual faculty.

The participants were much less certain about how to address their second most serious difficulty—chronic financial problems. They expressed a strong need for clear, comprehensive explanations of all the financial options open to them in a single source document (which was also accessible on-line). This was one of the most important types of information they wished to see included in an institutional handbook. They needed to know all the financial resources accessible from within the institution, plus those available from other private or public agencies, including criteria for eligibility, details of application procedures and deadlines. They also felt that some of the rules by which funds—especially financial aid—are currently awarded (or withheld) need to be amended to take into account the kinds of problems which many students with disabilities unavoidably face: the need to progress more slowly in their degree program than some other students; to take time out; and to attend school part-time. Attention to these difficulties will involve changes in financial aid regulations at state and national levels.

While they sought greater flexibility in the administration of financial aid, they sought less exercise of discretion in the award of public funds by state Vocational Rehabilitation counselors, and a more timely and uniform disbursement of Workmen's Compensation funds. They wished to see eligibility for public funds ear-marked for students with disabilities (for example, state-funded university tuition waivers) extended to include the whole range of disabilities.

A number of the participants pointed out that, although students with disabilities are nationally-recognized as an under-represented group in SMET disciplines and careers, they have not (as have women and students of color) been the focus of special programs of recruitment, retention or financial support. However, they were in general agreement with SMET majors of all ethnicities in the 1994 study, that the best way to meet the needs of under-represented groups would be to address the declining availability of financial aid for all students with limited personal financial resources. Most of the students with disabilities thought they had most to gain by a comprehensive overhaul of the national system of financial aid, rather than extension of affirmative action. However, as indicated above, they wanted changes in the rules for the award of financial aid so they did not work to the exclusion of students with disabilities.

Where the participants sought more targeted action was in the university's system of work study, internships and co-operative work experience. Getting sufficient career-relevant work experience prior to graduation was a common problem that transcended different types of disability. Some students wished to see departments take the initiative in ensuring that all students with disabilities got career-relevant work experiences. Those who were uncertain about an affirmative action approach, thought that departments offering majors leading to particular occupational fields should incorporate work experience packages into their educational program in such a way that no student graduated without relevant hands-on work experience. As already indicated, knowledge and uptake of Disability Services' Career Connections program for all majors was limited and, in the director's view, disappointing.

Among other career-related recommendations, we noted a concern (which was wide-spread across all SMET majors), to make institutional academic advising and career counselling coherent and accessible, and the information which is offered reliable. This need was particularly emphasized by two groups of students with disabilities—those who had limited work experience, and mature students who were in the process of changing their career fields.

Although mentoring is often proposed as one way to engage and support SMET students from under-represented groups, none of the students with disabilities had experienced mentoring programs, including the mentoring program offered by Disability Services. Their need for mentors was largely defined in terms of aiding the transition between their educational experience and the occupational worlds they sought to enter. They needed information about work opportunities, professional introductions and "insider" know-how about working successfully within particular work contexts. Lacking the kind of professional organizations which help to orient and connect women and students of color with particular professions and actual jobs, students with disabilities looked to the Institute of Technology and to their departments to develop mentoring programs focused on work placement and transition.

Those who had experienced Disability Services' Career Connections program mentioned its career preparation provisions (especially resumé writing, interview techniques, and self-presentation) and the new on-line employment location service, as examples of good programs from which more students could benefit. The problem of how to make more students aware of these was unresolved.

Another university service cited by many of the participants as valuable, but in need of expansion, improvement and publicity, was the tutoring service. Students with learning disabilities especially used tutors. They expressed a preference for a departmentally-based system of discipline-specific tutors,[32] with continuity in the tutor-learner relationship over time. They thought that volunteers from their own classes made better tutors than TAs—who had many other duties and concerns. Volunteer tutors had more patience and, in the context of regular meetings over time, were more likely to develop an understanding of how particular learning difficulties worked and were more motivated to seek ways around them.

---

[32]Those students who needed the help of writers for class notes and tests also emphasized the importance of scribes who know the subject material.

184

As we have indicated, students expressed a high degree of satisfaction with Disability Services, especially the continuity of support that they received from particular staff members over time. They especially appreciated the employment of Disability Services staff who also had disabilities, and recommended the number and range of disabilities represented be expanded. There was also support for the expansion of the power, funding, and responsibilities of Disability Services to be the primary resource for students with documented disabilities in finding and negotiating an optimal financial and work study package, and in resolving financial support difficulties with other agencies.

Perhaps the most basic need for all students with disabilities is qualifying for access to institutional services. Securing formal documentation was an insuperable difficulty for those students whose learning disabilities became apparent only after university entry, and who could not afford the cost of the diagnostic testing. Without this, they were locked out of the university system of help. They recommended that the university offer an affordable testing service by sharing facilities and costs with other local educational institutions.

Access to learning

Beyond the improvement of those SMET faculty attitudes and practices relative to accommodation (which transcend departments), participants also made recommendations intended to improve their access to learning and the quality of their learning experiences. The most commonly mentioned recommendations addressing these issues were not essentially related to difficulties raised by disabilities. They were based on the same premise as the main recommendations of SMET majors in our 1994 study, namely, the most important changes needed in class rooms and labs were changes of pedagogy, student assessment practices and curriculum. Along with 74% of the SMET majors in the 1994 study, SMET majors with disabilities recommended a shift toward student-centered learning in which encouragement to achieve, rather than weeding students out, was the primary focus of SMET pedagogy. They advocated: more selectivity in syllabus content; more cohesion in overall curriculum design for each major; better organization and presentation of syllabus materials; a better fit between the objectives and methods of student assignments; and routine distribution of syllabus and assignment schedules prior to class starting dates. Such changes were expected to benefit all students, but to be of particular benefit to students in under-represented groups, including those with disabilities.

Some suggestions involving computer access, which were mentioned as having particular value for students who were unable to come to campus for disability-related reasons, were also thought to have value for many other students. They included: computer registration as an option for all students; programmed learning supplements to classes; on-line descriptions of class content, level, assessment and grading systems, teacher-evaluations, and details of books and other class materials. Greater faculty use of e-mail as a pedagogical tool was also advocated: for example, in setting up student assignments and self-paced tutorials, and for individual teacher-student dialogue. Some classes (mostly at a higher-level or in other departments) offered sets of video-taped lectures which students could check out. Extending this to introductory science and mathematics classes was expected to benefit all students, including those with disabilities.

Another recommendation with wider applications was offered by mature students. Although the university offered classes on evenings or weekends, they were only at lower academic levels. Students with disabilities who worked and had family responsibilities (including several single parents) felt that offering higher level classes only on a day-time, week-day basis presumed that most students come straight from high school, have no family responsibilities and work only at part-time jobs. As the traditional composition of universities—especially state universities—shifts towards a higher age range, they suggested that an increasing proportion of students would (regardless of disability) benefit from an extension of the evening and weekend class system.

Recommendations involving attention to the physical attributes of classrooms had a more specific application to students with disabilities. Students with a wide array of disabilities mentioned the need for good lighting (especially of chalk boards), faculty microphones for all larger teaching rooms, and provision in all teaching rooms of some flexible (rather than entirely fixed) seating and writing surfaces.

Finally, there was a small number of requests for assistive technologies which students did not know were already available at the five Twin Cities university sites. They included several computer adaptations: closed-circuit magnification devices; voice-activated computers; and screen enlargement programs. This, again, raises the generic difficulty of how to ensure that students with disabilities know what their institution provides. For those whose disabilities were known in high school or at community college, some training in how the higher education system for students with disabilities works and how best to use it, would be appropriate. It would avoid the losses of time, money, and energy reported by students who had discovered institutional resources later than was useful to them.

Elementary and high school issues

Although some participants raised educational problems that they had experienced prior to university entry, to have systematically explored them with all participants would have taken us well beyond the scope of this study. However, we were made aware of two types of problems which deserve study in their own right. Students who had attended schools for children with visual or hearing impairments described a lack of rigor in their pre-college preparation in basic subjects. These students were obliged to improve their basic knowledge in a community college before they could undertake college science and mathematics. They highlighted the need for college-track preparation at par with other high schools at schools catering to students with specific disabilities.

Some of the students with hidden disabilities (especially learning disabilities and hearing impairment) had attended public schools which did not know how to cater to students with their type of disability. They described serious problems with teachers who did not understand the clinical basis of their learning problems, and did not accept their disabilities as the cause of poor performances in particular learning tasks. They reported long-lasting emotional and behavioral problems (including truancy) caused by lack of awareness or understanding by teachers. For example, being pulled out of regular classes to attend remedial classes was a common, humiliating experience which exposed their disability to peer stigma.[33] These experiences had ongoing consequences for the self-esteem and attitudes of those who described them. They recommended a national effort to raise the knowledge level of teachers about the academic, emotional and behavioral difficulties of school children with disabilities, and to provide education system support for their teachers and parents.

Advice to other students with disabilities

The recommendations which our participants offered to other students with disabilities who might follow them into SMET majors at the Institute of Technology fell into three categories: making strategic choices about where to undertake their higher education; practical advice on how to cope with problems they were likely to encounter; and descriptions of attitudes which would help others to survive, as they had done.

Their most basic advice was to think twice before assuming that the university or the Institute of Technology is the best place for students with disabilities to undertake preparation for work in science-based, technical fields. Their caveat was based partly on the difficulties they had experienced (or which they expected) in finding relevant post-graduate work and with job insecurity. It was also based on the difficulties they had experienced with SMET faculty in getting the accommodations they needed. Finally, it reflected their financial struggles in completing their degrees. They advised other students to consider vocational or community college education, which would be less expensive, take less time to complete and offer more certain results—particularly if it was geared towards specific work placements.

For those who decided to enroll in the Institute of Technology, the most often repeated piece of advice was that students identify themselves straight away to Disability Services, document their disability

---

[33]By contrast, several students with learning disabilities credited their teachers with correctly identifying the nature of their learning difficulties, getting specific diagnosis and appropriate help.

and draw upon the good counsel and practical know-how of the Disability Services staff at every stage in their education. They also advised that newcomers find out everything the university has to offer, not just those services intended for students with disabilities. Some of the facilities they cited as valuable were: the student health center; the recreation center; classes on study methods; and all workshops or seminars on careers and job searching. They stressed the importance of taking active steps to protect one's health against the stresses of undergraduate life and, to this end, using student health center programs (for example, their workshops on good nutrition on a student budget) and the support groups run by Disability Services. To students who were uncertain about their condition or its diagnosis, they advised seeking medical diagnosis and assistance at an early stage, as all forms of on-campus support depended on medical certification of their disability.

They counselled their successors to expect academic problems as a normal part of undertaking SMET majors and to seek the help of faculty or TAs as soon as academic difficulties arose. Some participants thought a good way to approach this was to make oneself known to teachers early in a new class and, through regular use of office hours, build credibility as an interested and hard-working student. This would stand them in good stead when they needed academic help—or for those occasions when they had to ask for accommodation. They advocated straight-forward explanations of their disability, and how it could limit their classroom (or other) functioning, and what accommodations they needed on a regular or occasional basis. We noted, however, that this advice was most often given by students who had 'approved' forms of disability and had less experience of faculty resistance to granting their accommodation requests. However, given the unfriendly reception which almost all other participants had experienced from particular SMET faculty, it is remarkable that they too saw it as essential to be active in seeking out faculty—even though they knew that any student with a disability could expect rebuffs. Not being afraid to go and talk to faculty and to TAs at the first sign of academic difficulty was one of a number of pieces of advice which matched the advice commonly offered by SMET majors without disabilities in the 1994 study.

Notwithstanding their difficulties with peer study groups, those who were comfortable with disclosure strongly advocated seeking out peers with whom they could work on a regular basis in what one graduate described as "mutually parasitic relationships." Even those for whom fear of disclosure had been a barrier to seeking help from class peers, felt that all undergraduates must expect periods of frustration and low self-confidence and times when they would need the encouragement and practical help of others who understood what they were going through. They had sought to meet this need in a variety of ways—through the DSCC, room-mates, family and friends. There was clear agreement that the worst thing SMET undergraduates—especially those with disabilities—could do was to try to get through the degree on their own. To support the point, they told stories of their own follies in this regard.

There was, as described above, less certainty about how to deal with the financial difficulties to which they saw students with disabilities to be especially prone. They advocated being organized well in advance of college entry and searching out and applying for every possible source of financial assistance. However, they warned that it would take great persistence to get money from the financial aid system, and that prospective undergraduates should be prepared for frustrations and refusals. At times when students with disabilities felt able to take on a full load of classes, they advocated getting sufficient financial aid to pay for this rather than going to school part-time and trying to pay (via their own employment) as they went along. To do this, might involve a shift of attitude toward seeing oneself as worthy of help, and the funder as making a good investment.

They advocated changes in attitudes which they had seen in themselves at an earlier stage and which they had found to be detrimental to persistence. Important among these was overcoming a learned reluctance to ask for help, especially for "anything special." They encouraged their successors to be bolder about asking for what they needed, to ask early and to be persistent. They also admonished them

190

to plan ahead for all accommodations, adapted equipment, materials, or facilities that they would need, and to remind faculty of arrangements they had agreed to, and the dates on which accommodation materials (e.g. test papers, assignment schedules, book lists, etc.) would be needed. Being well organized was universally agreed to be critical to success. Good organization included good planning, good time management and realism about how much they could undertake. Being realistic included keeping the number of classes at a level they could handle without risk to health, setting sensible deadlines and giving oneself plenty of time to complete work. It also involved being prepared to devote more time to homework than other students.

Their advice often echoed that given to all aspiring SMET majors by students in the 1994 study: for example, never taking information from any single source within the university on trust, but always checking it with several other sources, including other administrative staff and peers. This was thought especially important with respect to information given by academic advisors—whether faculty or otherwise. (We encountered many students in this, and in the 1994, study who had lost time, money and opportunities by not checking information given by advisors on the availability of particular classes in subsequent semesters or quarters.)

The participants also offered those who followed them advice on building and maintaining self-esteem and confidence. This too included a strong thread of realism. They should anticipate the experience of difficulties, including unfairness and some discrimination, both in academic and working contexts which were largely unprepared to receive them. They should disregard messages that underplay the difficulties which students and workers with disabilities face. However, they should not take discouraging attitudes and behavior personally. They advocated not wasting energy on "proving" that they are the same as everyone else, and making one's differentness an asset wherever possible. Some advice offered by students with more obvious disabilities was not to hold back from doing something out of fear of stigmatizing behavior from other people. This was reinforced by the most often repeated advice of all—to have faith that what your aspirations are, indeed, achievable and not to be dissuaded or side-tracked from them by people who do not believe that you can succeed.

Some Implications of this Study

If readers who have bourn with us this far will return to page eight of Chapter One, they will be reminded of the findings from Mary Litsheim's (1993) focus group study conducted with 25 undergraduates with disabilities from all types of majors on the Minnesota and St. Paul campuses. With the benefit of a larger sample specifically targeting current and former SMET majors, and intensive individual interviews, we have confirmed and augmented her findings, and offered some explanations for what both studies have found. We have also clarified the relative importance of the issues participants raised. This concurrence is encouraging in a number of ways. All qualitative researchers seek validation for their findings—both from independent sources within their data set, and from comparable work. These two studies validate a shared set of conclusions about the sources and nature of the problems experienced by students with disabilities.

One of the many striking features of our findings is that the problems which we have identified, and the extent to which they are experienced, were found among students at a university which has (both by national comparison, and in the view of the students themselves) made substantial efforts to develop appropriate policies for the accommodation of students with disabilities. If students at the University of Minnesota experience such difficulties, one is obliged to ask, What may be the situation in the majority of institutions which have done less, or nothing at all, to support students with disabilities? The relative simplicity of the methods by which Litsheim was able to identify some of the larger issues, and the strength and clarity with which the issues have emerged in the present study, should encourage the leaders of institutions, schools or departments who are concerned to understand the situation at their institution to begin similar conversations with their own undergraduate and graduate students with disabilities.

It is important for those seeking to improve the higher education chances of this group of students, and wondering where to place their emphasis, to have clear directions from the students themselves about what they need the most. The most important implications for action raised by our findings are that, in order for the potential of students with disabilities to be fully realized, and the risk of losing good students minimized, priority should now be given to changing SMET faculty attitudes and to improving the financial situation of students with disabilities. In terms of cost-effectiveness, improving faculty attitudes—especially towards the granting of "time" accommodations—will increase the chances of success for more students with disabilities of all kinds than will a dominant, or exclusive, focus on adaptations of faculties, equipment and campus layout. The latter are, of course, critical for access to higher education for an important sub-set of the disabled student community. However, concentration on access and on assistive technology, while neglecting to encourage faculty to consider what "reasonable accommodation" means for the majority of their students with disabilities is, we conclude, to pursue un unbalanced agenda. Paradoxically, a focus upon changing architecture and equipment rather than attitudes also serves to reinforce common faculty stereotypes about who "the disabled" actually are. In this conclusion, we echo and re-emphasize the concludsion reached by the NSF's (1990b) Task Force on Persons with Disabilities: "Negative attitudes are the single most significant barrier faced by students with disabilities at all levels of education...and in careers in science, engineering and science education" (NSF, 1990, p. viii).

Evidence from this study also supports and reinforces the movement for reform in undergraduate science teaching which is already underway. Different facets of traditional SMET faculty practices have negative consequences for the persistence of particular groups who are now recognized as "under-represented" in SMET majors. Aside from resistance to accommodation requests, common pedagogical practices which place students with disabilities at serious disadvantage are: inadequate advance planning and organization of class syllabuses, reading materials and test schedules; and insufficient attention to the structure, sequencing and presentation of materials in the classroom. Students who are already time-disadvantaged are obliged to spend more time compensating for flaws in pedagogical organization and technique. Students with disabilities are also disproportionately disadvantaged by the difficulties they experience in evoking mentoring response from many SMET faculty. They are not, of course, alone in these needs. However, as many of the participants in this, and the 1994 study, made clear, although improvements in pedagogy will benefit all SMET majors, they will have a disproportionately beneficial effect on students in under-represented groups.

In foregoing chapters, we have explored some of the reasons why it is difficult for the university to ensure that its policy works as intended. A broad, partial explanation would be that some of the remedies for the difficulties which students report cannot be addressed by the university without outside help. Making appropriate revisions in financial aid provisions requires changes in public policy. Universities could undoubtedly influence such changes, but cannot, unilaterally, make them. Similarly, the attitudes of SMET faculty reflect long-standing professional mores and practices which are nationally and internationally embraced, and which are hard (though perhaps not impossible) to change on a single campus or in a single department. As the students pointed out, there is currently no national movement which parallels that for students of color and for women of all ethnicities to recruit and retain students with disabilities in the sciences, or to support their placement in relevant employment. There is, as yet, no debate in science, mathematics and engineering journals or at disciplinary and professional conferences about why and how to accommodate students with disabilities. Without such a discourse, individual SMET faculty have no professional imperative to reconsider their customary responses to those students with disabilities whom they meet one at a time. Thanks to the efforts of the disabilities rights movement and the publicity surrounding implementation of the Americans with Disabilities Act, there has, in recent years, been greater public awareness of some disabilities rights issues. However, public attention has mostly been focused on problems of physical access, and this may have reinforced SMET faculty stereotypes about which conditions are (and are not) "real" disabilities, and what sorts of accommodation they feel it is morally legitimate to concede.

Throughout this account, we have compared findings from this study with those of our seven-institution study of students who either leave SMET majors for non-SMET majors, or persist in them. The confluence in findings between the two studies is more than just "interesting." From an early stage in our interviews and analysis, we were struck by the degree to which the nature of the difficulties which students with disabilities experience with SMET faculty, and the strength of faculty resistance—especially to time-related accommodations—which students with "non-approved" disabilities routinely encounter, support and compliment the findings of our earlier, more comprehensive, study. One of the fundamental findings from the 1994 study was that, whether SMET majors switch or persist, they experience (in comparable numbers) the same kinds of problems with aspects of SMET pedagogy, curriculum and student assessment practices. We also found that the nature of these problems was shaped less by the essential character of SMET disciplines than by long-standing traditions about appropriate ways to teach them. Because particular requests for accommodations are determined by the nature of disabilities themselves, students are inadvertently obliged to challenge some of the pedagogical rules which SMET faculty see as necessary for the protection of high academic standards. By their requests—and their persistence in making them—students with disabilities "stress-test" the limits of these pedagogical boundaries and, in doing so, expose and clarify the nature of these boundaries. We, thus, found in the accounts of students with disabilities strong confirmation of the essentially moral character of the criteria for academic progress in SMET majors which had emerged in the accounts of switchers and persisters in our earlier study.

Whether faculty pedagogy and student assessment practices actually function to ensure that only the "best" students proceed to higher level work is open to serious doubt. We found that the 40 to 60 percent "wastage" rate which SMET majors consistently sustain in the first two years included (at all seven types of institution) many able students—including some very able students—as well as those whom faculty intend to discourage through the weed-out process. These losses include young, white men, as well as disproportionate numbers of students of color and women of all ethnicities (many of whom leave with higher academic performances than the men who remain). The reasons for this lie in the structure and culture of SMET teaching, not in the inherent difficulty of these disciplines. What distinguishes the survivors from those who leave is their development of particular attitudes and strategies, receipt of appropriate forms of help at critical periods in the early stages of the major and a strong interest in their discipline, and in the careers to which they aspire.[34] Throughout this study, we have found that students with disabilities, as a group, have much in common with other SMET majors who persist to graduation: only the most able and determined enter college where they choose majors largely on the basis of interest, and demonstrate an organized, well-disciplined approach to their work, a focus on learning over grades, and a learned ability to survive adversity. On the other hand, by the nature of the educational problems and needs which their disabilities dictate, they are forced into conflict with the formal and informal system rules which govern progress in their majors. There is, thus, a constant tension between personal characteristics favoring persistence and success, and the cultural and structural barriers to academic progress and financial survival which characterize their educational experience. Thus, even in an institution which offers good support, students with disabilities simultaneously demonstrate a high potential for success, and a high risk of being lost.

We found contradiction of a number of stereotypes about students with disabilities in our study. These include illustration of Henderson's (1992) finding (from her analysis of CIRP data), that freshmen with disabilities are more likely than other freshmen to aspire to graduate school. As our sample profile also indicates, SMET departments are likely to encounter students both with serious physical impairments

---

[34]Summaries of our 1994 findings can be found in two recent articles: *American Journal of Physics, 63(3)*: 199-202; *Journal of College Science Teaching, 24(6)*: 392-400.

and with learning disabilities among their graduate students. They may also discover that these students have career plans which are as conventional and ambitious as those of graduate students without disabilities. That no thought appears to have been given to the financial needs of graduate students with disabilities is also perhaps because no one expected to find them in graduate school.

Our findings also call into question a number of stereotypes about students with learning disabilities. We found no evidence to support the faculty argument that students with learning disabilities should not be accommodated because they are unlikely to encounter accommodations in the working environment and must, therefore, learn to manage without them. As we have illustrated, graduates with learning disabilities were among the most academically and professionally successful of our participants. They largely tended to follow conventional academic or professional career paths and, because they overwhelmingly preferred not to disclose their disabilities to employers, were found to be operating successfully in unaccommodated work settings. Given that SMET majors are likely to attract a higher proportion of freshmen with learning disabilities, and given the good academic and career potential demonstrated by them in this study, it would seem foolish for SMET departments to risk losing this group of students by refusing their "time accommodation" requests—particularly on the basis of a spurious argument.

The small size of our graduate sample makes generalization inappropriate. However, we have documented some trends which suggest some need to refocus efforts to promote successful careers in science-based work by graduates with disabilities. First, if graduates with hidden disabilities—and a strong preference for non-disclosure—tend to pursue conventional careers in unaccommodated settings, they need more "co-op" and internship programs, career mentoring and job introduction systems (similar to those at the University of Minnesota) which bring graduates with disabilities together with those employers most ready to welcome them. Encouraging more employers to declare themselves to job applicants as supportive of workers with disabilities and promoting attitude change favoring acceptance and accommodation among employers, would help a large number of graduates for whom discrimination in hiring and promotion and job insecurity are their most pervasive concerns.

Second, the discovery that graduates with disabilities (including some with severe physical limitations) may opt for to establish their own businesses, rather than seeking accommodated employment, points to the value of organizing programs of practical support for students starting such businesses. Of those participants who had begun or were planning their own businesses, only one had received any practical or financial help from an organizational source: one student who was setting up a consultancy had been given an adapted computer system by a society which supports blind students. As the accounts we have quoted make clear, none of the self-employed participants had received any training in the essentials of business practice and were learning these skill as they went along. Addressing the need for business capital and business skills would seem a useful addition to campus programs for students with disabilities who are considering self-employment.

Finally, as we have illustrated throughout our account, "disability" encompasses a wide spectrum of conditions and condition-related needs. Many of these needs are not met because our stereotypical expectations about which conditions are more likely to define "students with disabilities" draws us into policies and attitudes of helping some groups to the neglect of others. This mis-perception also perpetuates our attempts to draw moral lines between those who have a legitimate claim upon us and those who are excluded from our help and concern. Historically, we have, in effect, ignored or discouraged the largest proportion of students with disabilities.

Though students with disabilities are often included among those groups who are "under-represented" in SMET majors and the occupations for which they prepare students, under-representation is not the strongest argument for attempting to remedy our disattention to students with all types of disabilities. In reconsidering who are the students and workers with disabilities in these fields, and how best to increase their access to independent life-styles, we exercise an enlightened self-interest: it is not to our benefit to continue to risk the loss from science, mathematics and engineering of so able and highly-motivated a group of people.

Appendix

The following list of issues were explored with both undergraduates and graduates (as appropriate). Additional issues were explored as they arose.

Educational Choices.

Why did the participants choose this institution, these majors, to do a degree at all?

What influenced their choices?

Who has encouraged or discouraged them in their aspirations?

What is the role of work experience, work options/the local economy, career aspirations in their choices?

What are their sources of motivation? What helps them to persist?

Have they experienced pressures to opt for a lower level of education than that of which they are capable? What are the sources of any such pressures?

What is their experience of two-year institutions? What do the have to offer to students with disabilities, compared with the university?

Have they had any periods out of school? Why?

How long will it/did it take them to graduate? Will they graduate?

Educational Needs.

Finances

How do students with disabilities meet the costs of higher education and their living expenses?

What resources are available to them?

How do they learn about them?

How adequate is the help they receive?

In what ways are the higher education expenses of students with disabilities greater than those without disabilities?

Access

Do access and communication barriers exist (to educational facilities, libraries, labs, and work sites, etc.)?

What unresolved problems of access do students encounter?

How do problems of access contribute to the difficulties of students (and workers) overall?

Time

People with disabilities may need more time than others to complete degrees or research projects, write-up or publish research findings. Explore all facets of "time" issues.

Assistive technologies

How available are practical aids needed by students and employees with disabilities?

What would make study or working easier or more effective?

Who helps?

How well do university provisions work?

Medical/therapeutic help

Do students/workers with disabilities get the medical help they need? If not, explore why not.

What is the contribution of doctors/therapists to educational access/persistence?

Difficulties arising from disability

What limitations on their capacity to undertake a degree in SMET majors arise from the nature of their condition(s), and its treatment/medication?

How do they deal with these?

What help do they need?

Do they get it?

From whom/how?

Gaining experience

Do students with disabilities get sufficient opportunity to gain hands-on experience relevant to their disciplines or careers?

What other needs exist?

Explore.

Services and Accommodation.

What on-campus and off-campus services are students aware of?

What services do they use?

How well do these services work?

What needs do they meet (and not meet)?

How coherent are they as a system?

Disability Services.

How, and how well, does the university's system work?

How well organized are they?

What do students like/not like about it?

What are its strengths and limitations?

How well does the university accommodation system work?

What are the most common types of accommodation requested?

Are all types of disability treated equally?

What suggestions for improvement do they offer?

Educational Experiences.

Generally

What are their sources of satisfaction and dissatisfaction with their university education?

What has helped or hindered their educational progress and persistence towards their goals?

Faculty

How do SMET and non-SMET faculty respond to students' requests for accommodations?

Do students with disabilities experience the same kinds of problems as all/most SMET majors? What do they share?

What role do the pedagogical and student assessment practices of faculty play for students with disabilities in the quality of their educational access?

Do traditional 'weedout' practices have the disproportionately negative impact on students with disabilities which they have for women and minorities (Seymour & Hewitt, 1994)?

What problems are distinctive to students with disabilities?

What role do the norms, values, and professional priorities or practices of SMET and non-SMET faculty play in the students' educational experiences?

What do faculty know about the university's provision for students with disabilities?

Do they support/comply with university policy?

How difficult or easy is the students' task of preparing a new professor, classroom, or lab to accommodate them? How do students do this?

Attitudes

Explore the extent to which negative attitudes and stereotypes (on campus or in work contexts) reduce access to classes, research experiences, internships, jobs, or promotion opportunities.

Disclosure

Is disclosure an issue—on campus, at work, or in the search for employment?

Which people, with which types of disabilities, are most concerned about disclosure?

What advantages and disadvantages are there in either disclosure or non-disclosure?

Stigma

Do negative stereotypes limit their self-view or aspirations?

Are there differences by type of disability?

Gate-keepers

Are gate-keeping attitudes and practices evident/significant?

Do parents, teachers, faculty, advisors, agency staff, etc., discourage entry to university education or science-based careers, or seek to shield them from possible failure?

Peer groups

What is the role of peers (with and without disabilities) to SMET undergraduates and graduates?

Do disclosure issues, or isolation, limit possibilities of peer group interaction?

Are there other limitations to using peer groups?

Role models

Role models of successful working engineers and scientists with disabilities are lacking or invisible. How, and how much, does this shape their aspirations?

Nurturing and mentoring

Who nurtures or mentors students or workers with disabilities?

How are these linkages made?

What is the nature of these relationships?

How important or effective are they?

Double or triple jeopardy

Women, or members of ethnic minority groups, who also have disabilities, face two or three layers of difficulties. Which issue predominates?

Career Choice and Placement.

Generally

How did they approach career choice or career change?

How did consideration of their own conditions shape their choices?

Why did they chose a particular career path or field?

What kinds of work in what work contexts do they prefer?

Have these preferences changed? Why?

What help do/did they get with job placement?

What work experiences have they had, in what contexts?

What do they now do, in what setting?

How did they arrive at their present type of work?

How satisfied are they with the work that they find?

How well are their disabilities accommodated by employers and colleagues?

What adjustments have they made in order to make their work setting agreeable?

Salaries, status, and career structures

Do graduates with disabilities find parity in their pay, conditions of service, and opportunities for promotion/career development with colleagues without disabilities?

Misperceptions about disability

What misperceptions about the nature of disability do students and workers encounter?

Negative attitudes in the work place

Are prejudices and discriminatory attitudes and behaviors encountered?

What form(s) do they take?

How serious are they?

Are disabled workers more vulnerable to lay-off, failure to promote, etc.?

Compliance with the Americans with Disabilities Act.

How well do the university, employers, other agencies significant to students and workers with disabilities, comply with the obligation to provide reasonable accommodation?

What difference does the legal sanctioning of reasonable accommodations make to the quality of their experiences in higher education, work, and everyday living?

Recommendations.

What do participants recommend—to the university, disability services, to other public or private agencies, to faculty, to employees or work colleagues, or to others with disabilities?

Bibliography

American Association for the Advancement of Science. 1989. *Project 2061: Science for all Americans*. Washington, D.C.: AAAS.

American Association for the Advancement of Science. 1991. *Barrier-Free in Brief (Booklet Series) Laboratories and Classrooms in Science & Engineering, Workshops and Conferences for Scientists and Engineers, Access in Word and Deed*. Washington, D.C.: AAAS.

American Association for the Advancement of Science. 1978, 1986, 1995. *Resource Directory of Scientists and Engineers with Disabilities*. Washington, D.C.: AAAS.

Anonymous. 1981. Guide to teaching chemistry to the handicapped. *Chemical Engineering News* 59 (26): 23.

Arnold, K.D. 1987. Values and vocations: The career aspirations of academically-gifted females in the first five years after high school. Paper presented to the annual meeting of the American Educational Research Association, Washington, D.C.

Astin, Alexander W. 1985. *Achieving Educational Excellence: A Critical Assessment of Priorities in Higher Education*. San Francisco: Josey-Bass.

Astin, Alexander W., et. al. 1988. *The American Freshman: National Norms for Fall 1988*. UCLA: Higher Education Research Institute.

Astin, Alexander W., Green, K.C., & W.S. Korn. 1987. *The American Freshman: Twenty Year Trends*. UCLA: Higher Education Research Institute.

Baughman, J., Jr., & D. Zollman. 1977. Physics labs for the blind. *Science Teacher* 15: 339-342.

Becker, Howard S. 1963. *Outsiders: Studies in the Sociology of Deviance*. New York: Free Press.

Bennefield, Robert L., & John M. McNeil. 1989. *Labor Force Status and Other Characteristics of Persons with a Work Disability: 1981 to 1988*. Washington, D.C.: Bureau of the Census.

Boyer, Ernest L. 1990. *Campus Life: In Search of Community*. Princeton University: The Carnegie Foundation for the Advancement of Teaching.

Bureau of the Census. 1986. *Disability, Functional Limitation, and Health Insurance Coverage: 1984/1985*. Washington, D.C.: Bureau of the Census.

Cicourel, A. 1970. Basic and normative rules in the negotiation of status and role. In *Recent Sociology, No. 2*, ed. H.P. Dreitzel. New York: Macmillan.

Clayton, Julie. 1992. Can They do Science? *New Scientists* 135 (1837): 31-34.

Davies, Daniel K. 1992. *Understanding Disability in the Computing Profession: Survey Conducted for the Association for Computing Machinery.* Colorado Springs, CO: Meeting the Challenge Inc.

Davies, Daniel K. & Randy W. Dipner. 1992. A.C.M. membership survey of disability and disability issues. *Communications of the A.C.M.* 35 (5): 91-93.

Davis, Fred. 1961. Deviance disavowal: the management of strained interaction by the visibly handicapped. *Social Problems* 9: 120-132.

Department of Education. 1992. *Disability Statistics Abstract* Number 4. Washington, D.C.: National Institute on Disability and Rehabilitation Research.

Eichenberger, R. 1977. Teaching Science to the Blind Student. *Science Teacher* 41: 53-54.

Ellis, R.A. 1992. Access to engineering: measuring participation of persons with disabilities. *Engineering Manpower Bulletin* 121. Washington, D.C.: E.M.C. & A.A.E.S.

Fern, Edward F. 1983. Focus groups: a review of some contradictory evidence, implications, and suggestions for future work. *Advances in Consumer Research* 10: 121-126.

Ficke, Robert C. 1989. *Digest of Data on Persons with Disabilities.* Washington, D.C.: National Institute on Disability and Rehabilitation Research.

Freidson, Eliot. 1966. Disability as social deviance. In *Sociology and Rehabilitation,* ed. M. Sussman. Washington, D.C.: The American Sociological Association.

Goffman Erving. 1963. *Stigma: Notes on the Management of Spoiled Identity.* Englewood Cliffs, NJ: Prentice-Hall.

Green, Kenneth C. 1989a. A Profile of Undergraduates in the Sciences. *Scientific American* (September/October): 475-480.

Green, Kenneth C. 1989b. Keynote Address: A Profile of Undergraduates in the Sciences. In *An Exploration of the Nature and Quality of Undergraduate Education in Science, Mathematics and Engineering.* National Advisory Group, Sigma Xi, the Scientific Research Society. Racine, WI: Report of the Wingspread Conference.

Henderson, Cathy. 1992. *College Freshmen with Disabilities: A Statistical Profile.* Washington, D.C.: American Council on Education/HEATH Resource Center.

Hewitt, Nancy M., & Elaine Seymour. 1991. *Factors Contributing to High Attrition Rates Among Science, Mathematics, and Engineering Undergraduate Majors: Preliminary Report to the Alfred P. Sloan Foundation.* Boulder, CO: The University of Colorado.

Hewitt, Nancy M., & Elaine Seymour. 1992. A Long, Discouraging Climb. *Prism: Journal of the American Society for Engineering Education* (February): 24-28.

Hippolitus, Paul. 1987. *College Freshmen with Disabilities: Preparing for Employment*. President's Committee on Employment of the Handicapped and Higher Education, and HEATH Resource Center, Washington, D.C.

Hughes, Everett C. 1975. Dilemmas and contradictions of status. *American Journal of Sociology* 50: 353-359.

International Center for the Disabled. 1986. *Bringing Disabled Americans into the Mainstream*. New York: Louis Harris & Associates.

Jones, Chris. 1992. Putting Ability First. *Prism: Journal of the American Society for Engineering Education* (February): 34-35.

Kimball, M.M. 1989. A new perspective of women's math achievement. *Psychological Bulletin* 105 (2): 198-214.

Kraus, Lewis E., & Susan Stoddard. 1989. *Chartbook on Disability in the United States: An Info-Use Report*. Washington, D.C.: U.S. National Institute on Disability and Rehabilitation Research.

LaPlante, Mitchell P. 1988. *Data on Disability from the National Health Interview Survey, 1988*. Hyattsville, MD: National Center for Health Statistics.

LaPlante, Mitchell P. 1993. *Disability Statistics Report: State Estimates of Disability in America*. National Institute for Disability and Rehabilitation, Washington, D.C.: U.S. Department of Education, Office of Special Education and Rehabilitative Services.

Lemert, Edwin. 1975. Social pathology. In *Theories of Deviance*, ed. Stuart H. Traub and Craig B. Little. Itasca, IL: Peacock.

Litsheim, Mary E. 1993. Reflecting disabled perspectives in the University of Minnesota. Ph.D diss., University of Minnesota.

Levy, Sidney J. 1979. Focus group interviewing. In *Focus Group Interviews: A Reader*, ed. James B. Higginbotham and Keith Cox. Chicago: American Marketing Association.

Lollar, Cynthia. 1991. Access to engineering: new project for students and faculty with disabilities. *Science* 251 (4996): 952.

Lucky, Luretha F. 1989. Boosting science careers for the physically handicapped student. *Florida Scientist* 52 (3): 145-153.

Matyas, Marsha L., & Shirley M. Malcolm (eds.). 1991. *Investing in Human Potential: Science & Engineering at the Crossroads*. Washington, D.C.: American Association for the Advancement of Science.

McNeil, John M. 1993. *Americans with Disabilities, 1991-1992*. U.S. Bureau of the Census, Current Population Report, Washington, D.C.

National Academy of Sciences. 1987. *Nurturing Science and Engineering Talent: A Discussion Paper*. The Government-Industry Research Roundtable. Washington, D.C.: N.A.S.

National Center for Education Statistics. 1987. *Profile of Handicapped Students in Post-Secondary Education, 1987: National Post-secondary Student Aid Study*. Washington, D.C.: U.S. Department of Education, Office of Educational Research and Improvement.

National Council on the Handicapped. 1988. *On the Threshold of Independence*. Washington, D.C.: N.C.H.

National Science Foundation. 1986. *Undergraduate Science, Mathematics and Engineering Education*. N.S.B. Task Committee on Undergraduate Science and Engineering Education. Washington, D.C.: NSF.

National Science Foundation. 1989a. *Report on the N.S.F. Disciplinary Workshops on Undergraduate Education*. Washington, D.C.: NSF.

National Science Foundation. 1989b. *Report on the National Science Foundation Workshop on Science, Engineering and Mathematics Education in Two-Year Colleges*. Directorate for Science and Engineering Education, Division of Undergraduate Science, Engineering and Mathematics Education. Washington, D.C.: NSF.

National Science Foundation. 1990a. *The State of Academic Science and Engineering*. Directorate for Science, Technology and International Affairs, Division of Policy Research and Analysis. Washington, D.C.: NSF.

National Science Foundation. 1990b. *Report on the N.S.F. Task Force on Persons with Disabilities*. Washington, D.C.: NSF.

National Science Foundation. 1990c. *Women and Minorities in Science and Engineering*. Washington, D.C.: NSF.

Oakes, J. 1990. Opportunities, achievement and choice: women and minority students in science and mathematics. *Review of Educational Research* 16: 153-222.

Office of Special Education and Rehabilitative Services. 1989. *Eleventh Annual Report to Congress on the Implementation of the Education of the Handicapped Act*. Washington, D.C.: U.S. Department of Education.

Office of Technology Assessment. 1989. *Higher Education for Science and Engineering: A Background Paper*. Washington, D.C.: U.S. GPO.

Public Law 101-336. 1990. Americans with Disabilities Act.

Seidel, John V., Kjolseth, Rolf J., & Elaine Seymour. 1988. The Ethnograph: a Program for the Computer Assisted Analysis of Text-Based Data. Littleton, CO: Qualis Research Associates.

Seymour, Elaine & Nancy M. Hewitt. 1997. *Talking About Leaving: Why Undergraduates Leave the Sciences.* Boulder, CO: Westview Press.

Seymour, Elaine & Nancy M. Hewitt. 1994. *Talking about Leaving: Factors Contributing to High Attrition Rates Among Science, Mathematics, and Engineering Undergraduate Majors: Final Report to the Alfred P. Sloan Foundation on an Ethnographic Inquiry at Seven Institutions.* Boulder, CO: The University of Colorado.

Spradley, J.P. 1979. *The Ethnographic Interview.* New York: Holt, Rinehart & Winston.

Strenta, C., Elliott, R., Matier, M., Scott, J., & R. Adair. 1993. *Choosing and Leaving Science in Highly Selective Institutions: General Factors and the Question of Gender.* Report to the Alfred P. Sloan Foundation.

U.S. Government. 1989. *Changing America: The New Face of Science and Engineering.* Final Report, the Task Force on Women, Minorities, and the Handicapped in Science and Technology. Washington, D.C.: GPO.

Vetter, Betty M. 1988. Demographics of the engineering student pipeline. *Engineering Education* 78: 735-740.

Vetter, Betty M., & Eleanor L. Babco. 1989. *Measuring National Needs for Scientists to the Year 2000: Report of a Workshop.* Washington, D.C.: Commission on Professionals in Science and Technology.

Ware, N.C., & D. Dill. 1986. Persistence in science among mathematically able male and female college students with pre-college plans for a scientific major. Paper presented at the annual meeting of the American Educational Research Association.

Weisgerber, Robert A. 1991. *The Challenged Scientists: Disabilities and the Triumph of Excellence.* New York: Praeger.